Fine Feathers and Other Stories

FINE FEATHERS
AND OTHER STORIES

FINE FEATHERS

AND OTHER STORIES

E. F. BENSON

Selected and Introduced by
Jack Adrian

Oxford   New York
OXFORD UNIVERSITY PRESS
1994

Oxford University Press, Walton Street, Oxford OX2 6DP

Oxford New York Toronto
Delhi Bombay Calcutta Madras Karachi
Kuala Lumpur Singapore Hong Kong Tokyo
Nairobi Dar es Salaam Cape Town
Melbourne Auckland Madrid

and associated companies in
Berlin Ibadan

Oxford is a trade mark of Oxford University Press

Introduction and Selection of Stories © Jack Adrian 1994

British Library Cataloguing in Publication Data
Data available

Library of Congress Cataloging in Publication Data
Benson, E. F. (Edward Frederick), 1867–1940.
Fine feathers / E. F. Benson ; selected and introduced by
Jack Adrian.
p.   cm.
I. Adrian, Jack.   II. Title.
PR6003.E66F56   1994   823'.912—dc20   93-38186
ISBN 0-19-212325-4

1 3 5 7 9 10 8 6 4 2

Typeset by Graphicraft Typesetters Ltd
Printed in Great Britain
on acid-free paper by
Bookcraft (Bath) Ltd
Midsomer Norton, Avon

ACKNOWLEDGEMENTS

Most of the stories in this collection have been tracked down in the Stack of the Bodleian Library, Oxford, or its out-station at Nuneham Courtney. I am thus immensely in debt, as ever, to the staff of that excellent and civilized institution, in particular: Richard Bell, Head of Reader Services, and his deputy Alison Northover; Christine Mason and Rosemary McCarthy; and John Slatter, guardian of the air-conditioned book-sheds at Nuneham.

I should also like to acknowledge, with gratitude, the following: Bob Adey; Richard Dalby and David Rowlands; Barry Pike, who originally lent me his copy of the scarce limited edition of 'The Male Impersonator'; Philip Scowcroft, from whom I gained the vital information that 'plasmon' (as featured in the short story 'The Simple Life') was a 'soluble proteinaceous extract of milk', said to 'build up the tissues', from which all kinds of nutritious and (doubtless) flavoursome substances could be made, including chocolate, biscuits, cocoa, and even oats; Allan Downend, who very kindly let me have a copy of the story 'James Sutherland, Ltd.' from the E. F. Benson Society archive; Bill Lofts, who, as usual, laboured long and hard on my behalf in the British Library; Marc Bridle, Archivist of the magazine *New Statesman/Society*, Christopher Sheppard, curator of the Brotherton Collection at Leeds University, and, particularly, Beth Inglis, Assistant Librarian (Manuscripts) at Sussex University, for her help in the matter of E. F. Benson's papers; Noel Lloyd and, especially, Geoffrey Palmer, whose letters are always a delight and whose opinions are often enjoyably trenchant; and Tony and Cynthia Reavell, for their always generous and unsparing aid and encouragement and, particularly, for alerting me to E. F. Benson's book-that-never-was.

There are currently two societies devoted to the life and works of E. F. Benson: the Tilling Society (Organizers: Cynthia and Tony Reavell), the Martello Bookshop, 26 High Street, Rye, East Sussex TN31 7JJ; and the E. F. Benson Society (Secretary: Allan Downend), 88 Tollington Park, London N4 3RA.

In addition, Hermitage Books, of 4c Church Street, Harleston, Norfolk IP20 9BB, is in the process of reprinting in severely limited editions rare stories and articles by E. F. Benson, many of which have never before been published in bookform.

CONTENTS

INTRODUCTION

LIKE Byron before him, Lytton Strachey and Rafael Sabatini after, E. F. Benson 'awoke one morning and found himself famous'—or at any rate returned to England in the summer of 1893 from an archaeological dig in Greece to find that his first novel *Dodo*, just published by Methuen, was an entirely unexpected, and phenomenal, success. It was being bought in its thousands by readers eager to crack what they were convinced was a scandalous *roman à clef* featuring society hostess Margot Tennant (later Lady Oxford) as the vivacious, electric, and extravagantly nonsensical heroine Dodo.

The book's first edition sold out in its month of publication (May), a second came out in June, three more were called for in July, and by November it was already well into its eleventh. And in that same month of November 1893, the fledgeling firm of Osgood, McIlvaine, which had dramatically launched itself only two years earlier with a similar *succès de scandale*, Thomas Hardy's *Tess of the D'Urbervilles*, issued a volume of short stories by Benson, *Six Common Things*, in their 'Short Stories by British Authors' series. Benson was just 26. Clearly a glorious literary future beckoned.

Thereafter, however—at least during the remaining half-dozen years of the century—his fortunes were distinctly mixed. His second novel *The Rubicon*, published less than a year after *Dodo*, was savaged by the critics ('quite without distinction . . . a mistake which will take both time and labour to redeem' and 'an absolute failure, the writing forced and uneasy, the character-drawing . . . crude and . . . unwholesome' were by no means the most bludgeoning of remarks directed at it). His third novel *The Judgement Books* was issued in 1895 by Osgood, McIlvaine after appearing in a severely truncated form in two issues of the glossy society weekly *The Graphic*. It sank without trace, as did, not too long after, its publisher (in fact the firm had been ailing since 1892 when one of its two American founders and its driving force, J. R. Osgood, had died at the relatively early age, for a Victorian publisher, of 55).

Benson's fourth novel *Limitations* was published by A. D. Innes in 1896. Innes, too, was a newly established house, eager to cash in on the wealth of young literary talent then burgeoning. An early bestseller (at least three editions in its first year of publication) had been John Collis Snaith's historical yarn *Mistress Dorothy Marvin*, a breathless combination of Stevenson and Stanley Weyman. Weyman himself (then the most bankable 'costume' novelist of the day) had appeared with his romance of the Thirty Years War *My Lady Rotha*. Other Innes discoveries and captures were the journalists Fred T. Jane (much later, creator of the naval and military reference lists) and Francis Gribble, Basil Thomson (quondam Prime Minister of Tonga, later governor of Dartmoor Prison and Wormwood Scrubs, head of Scotland Yard and MI6, and arguably inventor of the 'police procedural' novel in crime fiction), Max Pemberton, Frank Barrett, Fred M. White (his first book *The Robe of Lucifer*, which heralded a long career as a prolific and successful melodramatist), Eden Phillpotts, and A. E. W. Mason, whose historical novel *Lawrence Clavering* was an immense success, the hit of the 1897 season, both in critical and sales terms. Innes (an erstwhile *belle-lettre*ist and critic, whose own study of Browning, Tennyson, Matthew Arnold, Wordsworth, and Elizabeth Barrett had been much praised) also had strong history and biography lists, a flourishing line in travel memoirs, and a short handful of new society comedies by another priceless commercial asset, Anthony Hope.

Limitations—an artist rejects lofty aspirations to create high-paying marketable trash, a theme which clearly obsessed Benson since he utilized it again and again throughout his career, from *Limitations* itself to *Travail of Gold* nearly forty years later—garnered respectable reviews ('His range is much wider than it was; his character-drawing has gained in depth, delicacy and precision', *Daily Telegraph*) and doubtless Innes would have published more by him, had the firm not crashed too. Mildly disastrous as this might have been for Benson (not to mention Innes), the firm's dissolution proved to be a boon in disguise. Its assets were taken over by Ward, Lock, a middle-of-the-road and middle-class publisher with the safest monthly fiction magazine on the bookstalls, the *Windsor Magazine*, whose editor Arthur Hutchinson later eagerly purchased Benson's short fiction on a

gratifyingly regular basis. Even so, having obtained the copyright to *Limitations* (and keeping it in print well into the 1920s,
although almost certainly without paying a penny in royalties—
at any rate judging by other authors' bitter experiences), Ward,
Lock showed no interest in acquiring original novels by Benson.

A single volume was published by Putnam, in 1897, *The Babe,
B.A.*, a youthful *jeu* which was promoted as a novel but was in
fact a series of only tenuously connected sketches celebrating
(though fictionally) the madcap undergraduate escapades of one
of Benson's friends at Cambridge.

Following *The Babe* it was back to Methuen—a full four years
after the publication of *The Rubicon*. This is unusual. In publishing it is an invariable that when a house has what it, and the
reading public, perceives to be a hot property it clings to it with
a ticklike tenacity. *Dodo* was a sensational success. It must surely
have been the case that Methuen tied this blazing young comet
of an author to a contract for future books. *The Rubicon* was
the first of these; why, then, was Benson allowed to stray to
other houses for three books before Methuen issued his long
(over 170,000 words) historical novel dealing with the 1820 Greek
War of Independence *The Vintage* (1898) and its equally prolix
sequel *The Capsina* (1899)?

There is strong circumstantial evidence that Methuen rapidly
cooled towards Benson, despite the huge commercial success of
Dodo—which must after all have earned its advance many times
over from 1893 right through to the 1930s, when Allen Lane
issued it as one of the very early Penguin titles.

Amongst Methuen's announcements of new books for the
Spring of 1895—Kipling's *Ballads*, Henley's influential anthol-
ogy *English Lyrics*, Gilbert Parker's latest costume drama *The
Trail of the Sword*, the first mainstream edition of Anthony
Hope's maiden novel *A Man of Mark* (which Hope had in-
trepidly issued at his own expense in 1890 at the fearsome cost
of £50, gaining only a miserable £13 in royalties)—was *Lady
Massington's Resurrection and Other Stories* by Benson. Prolific
even at this early stage in his career, Benson, in eighteen months,
could certainly have accumulated enough tales to fill a six-shilling
volume. During 1893 and 1894 his stories appeared in *Longman's
Magazine*, *Pall Mall*, *The English Illustrated Magazine*, and *The
Sketch*, amongst other periodicals. Moreover, the title-story 'Lady

Massington's Resurrection' was not only one over which he had taken great pains in the writing, but a story, as Brian Masters has shown in his recent *Life of E. F. Benson* (1991), that mattered a great deal to him since it demonstrated his then firmly held belief that Good can conquer Evil through self-sacrifice (this view changed as he got older). Yet the book, though announced, never appeared.

It may be argued that Algernon Methuen wanted rid of Benson as early as 1894, after the débâcle of *The Rubicon*. Given that that was probably one of the most excoriated novels of the 1890s (another reviewer deemed the book 'the worst-written, falsest and emptiest . . . of the decade'), Methuen may well have decided to wash his hands of Benson while the going—or at any rate sales of *Dodo*—was still good, convinced perhaps that Benson was strictly a one-book man. It is thus hardly surprising that *Lady Massington's Resurrection* never saw the light of day, a volume of short stories—especially those by an author who looked as though he might turn out a distinct liability so far as sales went—being notoriously difficult to shift, particularly to a circulating-library readership still used to the two- and three-decker novel of 150,000 words or more.

As far as *The Vintage* and *The Capsina* went, Methuen almost certainly sanctioned publication of these himself, since they were historical novels and he had a known weakness for the genre—perhaps influenced by the fact that then, and thanks to Stanley Weyman's roaring bestseller *Under the Red Robe* which Methuen himself had published in 1894, the historical novel might almost have been considered a licence to print money. Doubtless Methuen came to regret this generous U-turn, since the Greek War of Independence, as a setting for the kind of derring-do indulged in by Weyman, S. R. Crockett, Henry Seton Merriman, and the rest of the leading costume-drama authors, fell far short of Paris during the Terror or on St Bartholomew's Eve, say, or Geneva during the 'long night' of the Escalade in 1606, or Nuremburg before Wallenstein's murder, or the Scottish Highlands after Culloden. And despite *The Vintage* having been pre-sold to *The Graphic* as a serial for a sum that would doubtless have offset Methuen's initial advance, it is perfectly plain that it and its sequel *The Capsina* fell far short of their projected sales targets. This may be inferred from an interview Benson gave to the literary tuft-hunter Raymond Blathwayt in 1896 in which the Greek saga is referred to as 'a trilogy'. Whether the third volume (which would have featured 'a brief appearance of Lord Byron') was ever written, it was certainly never published, due, one can only assume, to fairly wretched sales of the first two volumes.

There are two critical points to be made regarding Benson's early career. First, although the publication and subsequent success of *Dodo* opened far more doors to him than would otherwise have been the case (even as a son of the Archbishop of Canterbury he would not necessarily have been guaranteed entry into the kinds of circles—artistic and High Society—which clearly fascinated him, and about which he wanted to write), his first decade as an author was by no means the extended triumph that a glance at his list of published works would seem to suggest. And second, from the very start of his writing life the short story was immensely important to him. (Perhaps three points, the third being that he had absolutely no natural talent for the historical yarn.)

Even while writing *Dodo* he was penning short fiction: the stories that were later collected by Osgood, McIlvaine as *Six Common Things* (published in America as *A Double Overture* with the addition of a single story). These may originally have appeared in the periodicals of the day; on the other hand (as none has yet been located), the stories were more likely to have been written for book publication only. Once *Dodo* had burst upon the literary world, however, the editors of the monthlies were happy to open their pages to Benson, and he, reciprocally, was happy, indeed eager, to oblige them.

Benson used his short stories for a variety of purposes. Sometimes they were templates for later novels. Scenes, characters, and incidents in a number of his 'Amy Bondham' stories (written originally for *The Tatler*, later the *Windsor Magazine*) were then infiltrated into his celebrated 'Mapp and Lucia' saga. On the other hand, he could also impudently boil down an immense novel into its component parts. His 120,000-word novel *The Challoners* (1904) was later reduced to a mere 6,000 words and printed in the *Daily Mail* in December 1905, as the short story 'Two Generations'. Again, 'The Exposure of Pamela' (included here) contains a good deal of the meat of Benson's revenge-filled novel *Alan* (1924).

Benson always strenuously denied using real people and real situations in his fiction, yet it is clear that events that happened to him, and people he met, were quite often recycled to comic or tragic effect in his novels and stories. 'Dodo', for instance, was Margot Tennant and yet not Margot Tennant, in that Benson started work on the story of the society girl who was (as Margot Tennant herself much later encapsulated the character) 'a pretentious donkey with the heart and brains of a linnet' long before he met her. But he finished it after he had been introduced to her and had visited her, and as she admitted in her autobiography, his description of Dodo's sitting-room was as near a description of her own as makes no difference. The truth was Benson drew freely on Margot Tennant's character and idiosyncracies (of which there were many), never thinking that his book would sell more than a few hundred copies to Mudie's Circulating Library.

Margot Tennant was certainly cross about Benson's pilferings from her store of character-tics (her letters and peer-group evidence show this) but she appears not to have exacted any kind of retribution. Others were not so tolerant of Benson's larks. In 1901 he wrote a series of amusing quasi-detective stories for *The Onlooker*, a glossy weekly aimed at the upper echelons of society. One of the stories featured a Mr and Mrs Arthur Lewis, Mrs Lewis having pronounced kleptomaniacal tendencies and a habit, when on country-house weekends, of pinching other guests' jewellery while her husband kept *cave*. Readers were alerted that something was up the next week when a notice suddenly appeared emphasizing that all the characters' names in Benson's stories were 'entirely fictitious'. That this was not enough—was by no manner of means enough—was clear the week after when a long editorial 'Apology' (in bold caps) was printed: 'We very much regret ... Mr and Mrs Arthur Lewis, of West Cromwell Road ... extreme pain and annoyance ... We beg to state most positively ... purely imaginary ... we wish most publicly to express our regret and apology ... offensive ... unwarrantable ...' There is the hint that rather more than mere words on a page was demanded, and later acceded to.

Whether this was a case of the whimsical use of acquaintances' names that went badly wrong, or a piece of mild revenge on Benson's part that got out of hand, or simply a genuine mistake, it is hard to dismiss the notion that on occasion stories or novels were used to settle ancient scores. When Henry James, a family friend, was sent the raw manuscript of *Dodo*, his response by letter was by no means as helpful as one suspects Benson thought it ought to have been. That this rankled for years is evident from *Alan*, which was published over three decades after James's typically tortuous though damning verdict, nearly a decade after his death. James, in the character of the failing, middle-aged novelist Alan Graham, is comprehensively savaged. Alan, pompous, patronizing, as prolix and obfuscatory in his speech as in his books—in this, precisely like James—is the Old God, the once famous novelist whose star is on the wane. The Young God is represented by his much younger cousin Timothy (in essence Benson himself, as he saw himself), an aspiring writer. On one level the portrait of Alan/James is hilarious, Benson capturing James's agonized circumlocutions in a style that goes beyond mere parody into brilliant pastiche; on another level it verges on the heartless: there is a good deal of relish in Benson's descriptions of Alan's final stroke and subsequent speechlessness and helplessness. But prior to this, in a crucial scene, Alan loftily dismisses Timothy's writings utilizing a telling—and verbatim—passage from that thirty-years'-old letter.

Alan is a fascinating, but in the end bad, novel: fascinating as a glimpse into Benson's complicated psyche, bad because his manifest dislike of his target (however close he was supposed to have been to James in real life, and however many friendly, indeed gushing, letters he may have written to the older novelist) produces a complete breakdown of the critical faculty, causing him to lose sight of his plot which, banal as it might be (young blood versus old blood), could still have been used as a vehicle for explicating the creative process.

He could also seem distressingly insensitive. In *The Challoners* there is a searing portrait, in the dogmatic and cold Reverend Sidney Challoner, of his own father, the Archbishop of Canterbury. Many of his personal idiosyncracies are displayed; several scenes in the novel echo real life as recalled by Benson much later in his various volumes of memoirs. The EFB-character (to an extent) is the brilliant Martin Challoner who is continuously at odds with his hopelessly intolerant father. At the end of the book there is a measure of reconciliation as Martin dies in his father's arms—just as in real life Benson's eldest brother, also

Martin, also brilliant, dies virtually in his father's arms, or at any rate watched, as his life ebbed away, by both the Archbishop and his wife. *The Challoners* was published in 1904, less than a decade after Archbishop Benson's own death. Benson's mother, however, was still very much alive and read all of her sons' work assiduously. Happily she never read the horror novel *Across the Stream* (1919) in which Benson again used his dead brother's name, this time for a revenant possessed by a Satanic entity.

Other 'pilferings from nature' were lighter, more affectionate in tone. It is not too difficult to see something of Benson's close friend and sometime collaborator (mainly on sports books) Eustace Miles, a eupeptic positivist, go-getter, and health fanatic, in the character of Henry Attwood, concocter of the universal nostrum in 'M.O.M.', or the bustling and ingenious eponymous hero of 'James Sutherland, Ltd.' (both stories included here). Miles turns up in other guises, in other stories and novels, as does his wife Hallie, although portraits of her are perhaps not so kindly. A short, dumpy woman with a voice that her nieces recalled as 'quacking', she fits the description of any number of the more irritating and grotesque of squaddies from the ranks of Benson's monstrous regiment.

As a short-story writer Benson was fortunate enough to be living at a time when quality monthly periodicals (all more or less indebted to George Newnes's enormously successful *Strand Magazine*) occupied an expanding niche in the publishing market. Too, the very start of his career (the early 1890s) co-incided with a significant change in editorial policy in the oversized glossy weeklies which, up until then, had only run half-yearly, or even yearly, serials featuring vast slabs of print and very few pictures to break them up. The market-leaders—and rivals—here were *The Graphic* and *The Illustrated London News*, both of which were essentially weekly news-magazines reporting and illustrating (with line-drawings and 'cuts') the great events of Empire, only peripherally taking in the rest of the world. The revolution in print technology of the 1890s, which enabled the printing of photographs rather than 'cuts', trans-formed both papers and paved the way for a host of imitators, though all now more biased towards leisure, fashion, and 'the Season' than hard news: *The Sketch*, *The Sphere*, *Black And White*,

The Bystander, The King, The Tatler, The Onlooker, The World And His Wife.

Similarly, glossy women's weeklies such as *The Lady's Pictorial, The Gentlewoman,* and *The Queen,* which had previously printed not much more than 'Court gossip' and page after page of fashion pictures, now began to feature strong fiction: *The Queen* in particular, its literary editor scorning 'women's interests' and 'domestic' fiction and instead snapping up the latest novels and stories of the younger literary lions. Conan Doyle, Anthony Hope, and Stanley Weyman all wrote for *The Queen,* as did Arthur Morrison (his much admired novel of nineteenth-century witch-finding in Essex *Cunning Murrell* first appeared as a serial), Arnold Bennett, H. G. Wells, Flora Annie Steel (her great Highlands novel *Red Rowans*), Jerome K. Jerome, E. Nesbit, Rider Haggard, Beatrice Harraden, Somerset Maugham, H. B. Marriott Watson and, of course, Benson, who published a number of stories in the magazine as well as (a record for any author) five of his novels, including (perhaps oddly) the strongly homoerotic *The Angel of Pain* (1906; serialized the previous year).

The glossies were immensely useful to a skilled writer such as Benson, who could easily tailor his talents to their requirements. Although eager for short fiction, six thousand words or more was rarely for them. Three thousand words was a good length; fifteen hundred to two thousand perfect, especially during and after the Great War when space was at a premium. Many writers found the short-short inhibiting; Benson never. Apart from the salient (to a thorough professional such as Benson) fact that the Society weeklies paid more per thousand words than the all-fiction monthlies, he was a miniaturist by inclination, if not nature; in the 1920s in particular a deft assembler of amusing and ironic trifles. Even the majority of his full-length novels are little more than a succession of unintegrated incidents, often ending on a downbeat, at times an outright absurdity.

In so many of his early novels and stories especially major plot problems are shuffled aside and forgotten about after a convenient climactic death; either that or the remarkably sudden onset of a crippling or debilitating desease brings all the warring factions together. Another trick he utilized was the power of prayer to solve difficulties. While this may have been forgivable at a time when such was, if not the norm in real life, at least acceptable in fictional terms, it still leaves the modern reader with the uneasy feeling that the author has merely adapted the oldest plot-device of all: 'with one bound Jack was free.'

Still: other times, other mores—this was clearly what editors of the time welcomed or Benson would never have contributed so prolifically to so many of the monthly magazines of the day (*Windsor Magazine, Pearson's, London, The Storyteller, Cassell's, Hutchinson's,* and many others) or the illustrated weeklies (*The Graphic, The Onlooker, The Illustrated London News, The Bystander, Black And White,* and so on). After the war he wrote subtly crafted short-short ghost stories for *Eve* and then found a niche for himself for a time in *The Tatler,* usefully just as he was beginning to hone his best barbs for the loose novel-cycle celebrating the superb and farcical doings of Miss Mapp and Mrs Lucas (the peerless Lucia).

Of the thirty-one stories in this present collection only two have appeared in mainstream hardback-form before. Another two have been printed in small-edition booklets by Hermitage Books of Norfolk.

The stories represent all periods of Benson's long career, the earliest from 1894, the most recent 1931. The range, as ever, is wide. There are astringent stories, frothy comedies, ironic and deflatory small sagas, two strange tales of the kind at which Benson was so adept, as well as an amusing weird squib, 'Atmospherics', which stars Benson himself undergoing a mildly unsettling experience in his beloved Rye. Dodo returns (for probably her final appearance) and, although now in what might be termed her Do-dotage, imperiously quells an upstart *arriviste.* Also returning, in 'Fine Feathers', is the redoubtable Mrs Ames, arguably Benson's first fully fledged and mature comic creation. And Miss Mapp too suffers a ghastly retribution in 'The Male Impersonator'. Originally written as a Limited Edition booklet in 1929, then forty years later bundled away at the back of a library reprint, 'The Male Impersonator' at last finds a place in a Benson collection.

JACK ADRIAN

THE FURTHER
DIVERSIONS OF
AMY BONDHAM

The Lovers

A GREAT many people in London had been following with ecstatic interest during the course of this season the amazing career of Amy Bondham, and about the middle of June it was generally felt that she had attained her social zenith. Never had meteor flashed so resplendently; she streaked her way across the floors of heaven, burning ever brighter, and though she had only made her humble rising a couple of years before, she now knew everybody, and so far from going everywhere, she brilliantly refused a quantity of invitations which a year before would have filled her with rapture. The climax came when she said she really could not be bothered to go to the Duchess of Middlesex's dance.

'Dear Queenie Middlesex is such a bore,' she said, 'and like gravitates to like. I am sure that all the heaviness in London will be there in their tiaras.'

Of course, ill-natured folk laughed and said that Amy had not been asked, but they were quite wrong. There was the card of invitation on the chimney-piece of her sitting-room, and it certainly testified that both she and her husband had been bidden. She kept it there for several weeks after the date, so that the malicious and ill-founded rumours might be refuted.

It was generally felt, however, that her raging energies would not permit her to rest; the only question was to what fresh summit of distinction and notoriety she would climb. But to nobody was this conundrum of greater interest than to Amy herself, as she drove back one afternoon from the Divorce Court, where she had listened to the odious and unsuccessful attempt of Lord Knightsbridge to be rid of his wife.

He was a cantankerous old miser married to a young, popular, and pretty woman, and the verdict was hailed with loud applause, which the President made no effort to suppress, and Amy found herself violently envying Alice Knightsbridge. She fell into a train of concentrated thought as her Rolls-Royce purred round the Park for her to get a breath of air after the stuffy hours, and enjoy the beauties of nature and art as seen in the waters of the Serpentine and the Albert Memorial.

She was aware that Alice Knightsbridge was a tremendous object of interest. It was all very nice to go to parties and dinners and concerts, but it was one thing just to be there, and a vastly different one to know that everybody else was excited to know that you were there. Alice was like that; though she was not prettier or wittier or more charming than many others, it was thrilling and delightful to see her, and to see who was with her. . . .

A light dawned for Amy as she sped along the north side of the Serpentine. Was she so interesting because it was supposed that at least four men were violently in love with her? Really this seemed a possible explanation, for the world always adored lovers.

Amy herself was the soul of fidelity, propriety, and domestic affection, and would have shrunk in horror from the idea of being in love with anyone but her husband, the round, red, cherished Christopher. She would have thought it equally shocking to find that any man regarded her with feelings other than those of chaste and respectful admiration for her intellectual and social qualities; and yet it seemed to confer a sort of cachet on a woman that she should have the reputation of exciting something more than this in manly breasts. She was even aware that, repugnant to her as all illicit affection was, she understood how interesting other people thought it. The names of famous enchantresses occurred to her; she mused over Cleopatra and Diane de Poictiers.

Could not something be done, she wondered, which, while her moral integrity remained totally unimpaired, might confer on her this distinction? She must give the impression of being devoted to some nice respectable man besides her Christopher, and for that it was necessary to think of some nice respectable man who would covet the position of being her chivalrous knight, her Galahad. And then the dawn which had streaked her horizon as she drove by the Serpentine suddenly burst into day.

'Stephen!' she said aloud. 'It shall be Stephen. He's dining with us tonight. How lucky!'

She could not have made a more fortunate choice. Stephen Merriall was an old and chatty acquaintance, whom she used constantly to ask to dinner at the last moment to fill up the place of someone who had disappointed her. She had, in fact, used him so often in this way that by now he was getting quite a nice circle of friends, and was climbing away up this difficult monkey-puzzle tree of social success with an ardour that the arduousness of it only whetted. He was a large, bald, middle-aged bachelor, very celibate in disposition and of an unrivalled snobbishness, and he ate the crumbs that fell from Amy's table with an insatiable appetite.

Tonight she hailed him with a gratifying enthusiasm.

'My dear, too lovely of you to have been disengaged for once,' she said, 'and to have come to the rescue of my little party. You know everybody here, of course. Ruby and Jeannie and Pearl; go and shake hands with them and then come back to me. No, I shall not let you go yet; you must dine with us again on Thursday.... You shan't talk to your friends until you promise me that!'

He put a smooth fat forefinger to his forehead.

'I believe I can,' he said. 'Yes, Thursday; lunch, tea-party ... I can. But you must come to my tea-party first. Just a few friends.'

It was the turn of her forefinger now.

'Ah, any day but Thursday,' she said. 'But let me think a moment. Yes. I'll come just for half an hour. I can't resist it. But don't ask me what I've thrown over, and don't tell anyone I am coming, or I may get in a terrible row.'

Now Stephen had also been a thrilled auditor in the Divorce Court that day, and, with the proverbial parallelism in the working of great minds, had thought to himself what a cachet it gives a man to be supposed to be the hopeless or even hopeful adorer of some prominent woman. He had the same horror of intimate relations with anybody as Amy had, not for any moral reasons, but because he was naturally like an elderly spinster who preferred tea and conversation to passion. But if the gods had sworn to grant him any boon for the mere asking, he would (since he was very well off) have instantly chosen the reputation of being an irresistible fellow. He did not desire to overcome any sort of resistance; to be considered irresistible was sufficient for his needs.

And of all the safe adventures in this sphere of madness and badness the credit of being the impassioned friend of immaculate Amy was perhaps the securest and most notorious.... For some reason, as it abundantly appeared during the two hectic weeks which followed, she seemed to welcome and encourage his compromising behaviour.

She had an ardent compromiser, one who brought enthusiasm to the accomplishment of her innocuous designs. The two were never apart; they sat side by side in the dripping rain at Wimbledon; they attended charitable balls if there were no uncharitable balls to appear at; they arrived at lunch-parties together, and together departed from dinners, and soon, very soon (so quickly spreads the spilt Stygian ink of scandal), Stephen, hurrying home to the cup of hot milk which he always drank before he got into bed, told over, like the beads of a rosary, the interested glances of which he and Amy had been the target. She on her side was no less satisfied; secure in innocence, she plucked the secret fruits of forbidden orchards. And then a very terrible thing happened, which cured them both, as by a surgical operation, of attaining this species of distinction.

The famous Mrs Simeon Cobb was forcibly feeding London this year. She had taken a great house in Grosvenor Street (having been convinced that St James's Palace was really not to be let), and two castles in the country, which she filled with guests alternately for weekend parties. Amy and her husband were asked to one of these, but on the appointed Saturday Christopher was mowed down by an attack of influenza.

Mrs Cobb thereupon asked that famous last-minute guest, Stephen Merriall, to take his place, and as the castle was full from keep to donjon, he was put in the large dressing-room next Amy Bondham which had been allocated to Christopher. These two rooms had naturally a door of communication between them, but Amy's maid had locked it from her side, and Stephen had bolted it from the other. They had neither of them (up till a certain fatal moment) the slightest idea who was the neighbour of each. By an oversight the card outside Stephen's door had not been changed, and still bore the inscription, 'Mr Bondham'.

Amy had spent a wonderful evening when the time came for the women of the party to go to bed. She and Stephen had, with the harmonious intuition of great duettists, pointedly avoided each other, so that no one could have any more doubts about their secret and mutual devotion. It had all been quite brilliant, and as she went upstairs she arranged to go into Adèle Dover's room for a goodnight talk in which she proposed to avoid mentioning Stephen's name altogether in order to confirm this pleasant impression.

Adèle's room was in the same Elizabethan corridor as hers, but some way further down, and Amy went first into her own room, where she assumed a marvellous pink wrapper and noiseless slippers of lamb's wool. She carried with her a glass of hot water to sip during their conversation, but she could not remain long, as she had to write a quantity of invitations for a small concert she was giving in a week's time, and there would be no leisure, with the castle so full of distinguished folk, to do this tomorrow.

As she glided along the polished oak boards to Adèle's room she heard men's voices and men's steps ascending the staircase at the end of the corridor, and just saw the light gleaming on the top of Stephen's head as it appeared above the balustrade. At that sight she made the greater speed, for it would be dreadful to think that he had seen her in a wrapper and slippers. That would be a tongue-tying and embarrassing consciousness when they met tomorrow.

The talk lengthened itself a little, but time pressed, and about twenty minutes later Amy slipped forth again into the now silent corridor, glided along it, and after passing four or five doors, came to that which she supposed was her own. The light in the corridor was rather dim, but her gimlet eyes could easily read the word 'Bondham' on the card tacked up there. She softly turned the handle, and blinking a little in the bright light, which she must have forgotten to switch off, she found herself confronted by a tall, bald figure clad in glowing honey-coloured pyjamas. He was at the moment lifting one of his legs to get into bed. She opened her mouth very wide in the shock of this awful surprise and shut it again. It would never do to scream.

'How dare you?' she hissed out.

He bounced off the bed again on the far side, like an india-rubber ball, violently trembling.

'Get out of my room at once,' he whispered. 'How dare *you*, if it comes to that?'

Her eyes made one sweep over the room like a searchlight in an aeroplane raid, and she saw her mistake, and knew that she was the raider. She gave forth a strangled bronchial noise, like that of escaping gas, and with infinite precautions closed his door, leaving herself outside it. On the instant she heard it locked and bolted from within.

Then her geographical sense returned, and next moment, shaking in every limb, she was back in the heavenly security of her own apartment. Her mouth was dry and her hot water finished, and she drank eagerly out of her bedroom bottle.

Stephen, with his heart thumping against his ribs, dashed to his dressing-table as soon as he had secured the door and took a double dose of bromide. But for hours he did not get properly to sleep; at the most he dozed in a drugged, uneasy manner, starting up in panic at the tapping of his blind that stirred in the night-breeze, and fancying that he heard the click of his door-handle.

And when Amy's maid came in next morning to call her mistress, she found her asleep in an armchair with her writing-pad on her lap and a snow-drift of letters on the floor by her.

She woke with a start. 'Oh, thank heaven!' she said. 'It is day!'

'Complete Rest'

CRUEL... that was the only epithet for it.

That little paragraph in *The Times* quite stunned poor Amy Bondham for a moment, and she took up the paper again in the desperate hope that she had misread the date. But there was no doubt about it: the Countess of Rye was giving a small dance on 13 July, the very evening out of all days in the year, and the very year out of all the uncountable centuries, for which Mrs Bondham had just sent out the cards for her own very small dance: 'Dancing—Brazilian orchestra,' in the bottom left-hand corner.

Then, an ironically little way further down the same columns, was her own announcement, and irrevocably by yesterday evening's post there had gone forth her invitation to the brightest and best of her numerous friends. It would be exactly they who would be bidden to Lady Rye's small dance, and courageous and optimistic as Amy Bondham was, she did not seek to cheer herself by the thought that they would prefer, even when the Brazilian orchestra beckoned them, to go to Thurloe Square on the night that Rye House opened the glass doors of its ballroom.

Amy at once perceived that only those would come to her who had not been bidden by Lady Rye, and they were precisely the people concerning whom she did not care whether they came or not. Even they might throw her over at the last minute if subsequently they received a belated invitation from the other hostess, for Lady Rye's parties had a habit of beginning small and ending large: she was disconcertingly capable of issuing a second batch of invitations.

Even in these first ghastly moments, Amy showed the goodness of her heart in acquitting Lady Rye of any sinister intention. She had, of course, included dear Peggy Rye in the list of her own guests (writing her a little special note instead of the more formal card), and no doubt she would today herself receive a corresponding invitation, which she would be unable to accept owing to her own exercise of hospitality.

That was a bitter morsel, too, for though she had met Peggy Rye a dozen times, she had never yet been asked to the house; she did not therefore, at present, actually address this lady as Peggy, but she always thought of her as Peggy, and spoke of her as Peggy to those of her friends who were not aware how casual the acquaintance was. But Lady Rye would certainly be Peggy to her before long, and it was wise to get used to the syllables. Lady Rye, on the other hand, was more fortunate; she had received several invitations from Thurloe Square, of which she had hitherto been unable to avail herself.

Amy whistled into the speaking-tube which communicated with her husband's sitting-room, and her pleasant, playful Christopher came in. He had a quantity of little pet names for her. When she was writing at her table behind the screen he would put his head over it, standing on tiptoe, for he was a short man, and say, 'Bo-peep'. Today she was sitting, with the fatal *Times* in her hand, on an embroidered puff-ball by the window, and so he hailed her as 'Mistress Muffet'.

'Oh, it's too dreadful, dear,' she said. 'Peggy Rye has fixed on the thirteenth for her dance, and what am I to do?'

Christopher had a firm-rooted pride and confidence in his wonderful wife, touching to behold. He basked in the success of her social efforts, and indeed her achievements in the past two months of the season fully justified him.

'Do, Mistress Muffet?' he said. 'Why, show them all that you can give a better dance than anyone else. Bless you, they'll all come to your house. I've never known you beaten yet.'

'But supposing they don't?' asked Amy. 'Supposing only those come whom Peggy has not asked? It would be better not to have a dance at all than that only the nobodies come. The Brazilian orchestra, too. I meant it to be the wind-up of the season. Nobody's giving anything after the thirteenth. Besides, I should so love to go to her dance. Advise me, dear.'

Christopher always felt as if he was suddenly asked to drive the horses of the sun when Amy asked him for advice on social questions. His usual course was to lay the reins on the back of those fiery steeds, and let them go where they wished.

'Well, I should just wait a day or two,' he said. 'You'll be able to make up your mind better then. You will get replies from your guests, and you'll see what's likely to happen. Don't do anything in a hurry. And you needn't answer Lady Rye's invitation at once.'

There was certainly no need of that, because the invitation had not yet arrived, and so there was neither need nor, indeed, the possibility of an immediate answer. She got up from the tuffet.

'Well, I won't sit and think about it any more,' she said. 'I've got enough to do today to occupy me. There's some private view this morning, and people are coming to lunch, and then I'm going to Ranelagh, and we're dining at Lady Galton's, and there's music at Adèle Dover's. But I'm uneasy.'

The uneasiness was aggravated at lunch, where Adèle Dover had information about Peggy's ball.

'Too sad your having fixed that night as well, Amy,' she said, 'but I promised Peggy before I got your invitation. She got it all up in a minute, or rather in two hours, for she glued herself to the telephone, and asked every soul in London, which is her idea of a small dance—apparently the entire Royal Family and all the diplomatic corps.'

'Ah, it will be too wonderful,' cried Amy bravely. 'It's maddening not being able to go. Peggy—Lady Rye'—she remembered that Adèle was an intimate friend—'should really have told me. We shall spoil each other's party.'

This was quite in the grand style, and evoked response. 'I'm coming to you,' said Magdalen Cheetham, who had not been asked elsewhere, and Edgar Woolwright expressed the same intention. The rest of them carefully abstained from comment.

A couple of days revealed the full extent of the disaster. It was quite as devastating as poor Amy had anticipated, and the fifty, all told, who accepted were precisely those whose presence she did not in the least desire. Meantime, no invitation had come for her from Lady Rye, and the details that leaked out concerning the splendour of that function, mistakenly called small, were hard to bear. The only bright spot was that apparently Lady Rye had tried to get the Brazilian orchestra, but had failed, owing to its being already engaged. Of course, it would be wonderfully chic to have the Brazilian orchestra for a tiny little party consisting entirely of people who did not matter, but where, apart from the workhouse, did that lead to?

Amy was always at her best when faced with difficulties. She did not, Christopher being extremely well-off, mind the expense. What she revolted from was the giving of a party to useless mediocrities who had originally been intended merely to fill up obscure and vacant corners like banks of ferns, and from a sandwichy bar observe the great at their sit-down supper. It was a wanton extravagance (and she hated extravagance though she liked judicious expenditure) to have the Brazilian orchestra for such as these, and she sent Christopher round to see how the land lay with that exotic band.

With Brazilian hardness (like the nuts) the *chef d'orchestre* intimated that, unless another engagement for that night turned up, he would demand his full fees whether he played or not. He was willing, however, to ring up Rye House and say that, his engagement having fallen through, he could play for Lady Rye if she still desired it. Christopher then returned to Thurloe Square, with the gratifying intelligence that they were quit of the Brazilian orchestra . . .

Amy examined her engagement book. The season was dying fast; it would have just one strychnine injection, so to speak, on the night of the thirteenth, but otherwise there was nothing of any supreme importance, and she had not been asked to attend that flicker of vitality. Meantime, she was faced, in a couple of days from now, with this dance of her own, which, when she glanced at the list of her expected guests, filled her with horror. To give a dance on that night and to those would be to proclaim herself a pariah, and the thought gave her an inspiration of genius . . .

Next morning there appeared in that fatal column of *The Times* which had announced the previous disaster a paragraph stating that Mrs Christopher Bondham had been ordered a week's complete rest, and that she had retired to her country house at Harlow. No letters would be forwarded.

That she had retired to her country house at Harlow was true, that she certainly was in need of rest was true also, for she had never felt more limp and lifeless. But amazingly and splendidly false was the intimation that no letters would be forwarded. Never, probably, in the postal history of Harlow were so many redirected envelopes delivered at one house.

These is always a certain satisfaction to be obtained from the knowledge that you have made the best of a bad job, and that conviction sweetened to her the undesired leisure of these days. She worked in her garden, she played croquet with Christopher when he had finished writing short notes of regret to the fifty discarded guests, and she read with stoical firmness the police regulations for the traffic in Park Lane on the night of the thirteenth. She learned also that there were to be two bands—the Brazilian and another—the ballroom was to be a bower of red roses, and the list of the guests who were to dine at the house (at two round tables) made her feel positively ill. Then, since madness lay somewhere in this direction, she threw the odious journals from her.

Now, on that same morning, Lady Rye, who, immersed in these worldly affairs, had not looked at the papers, and was therefore unaware of Amy's indisposition, had occasion to see the *chef d'orchestre* of the Brazilian musicians and interview him about his melodies. She learned from him, quite accidentally, that he had originally been engaged to play for Signora Bondham that night, whom she vaguely remembered as having asked her to dinner on several occasions. Thus Amy's name lingered in her head when she went from the Brazilian to see her secretary with a further list of a couple of dozen more invitations which she wished to be sent out. She added Mr and Mrs Bondham's names to these, for if there was not such a man there would be no harm done, and if there was he might like to come. The joyful envelope was delivered that night at Thurloe Square, and sent on to Harlow by the first post next morning.

That night when the evening delivery came in, Amy and her husband had just finished dinner, and were sitting down to the domestic excitement of a game of picquet. As he dealt she opened a few of her letters, but since nothing that happened in far-away London during the next few days could possibly be of urgent importance, left the rest unread till their game was over. When she had successfully rubiconed Christopher, she toyed with the remainder, and then, leaping to her feet, gave a shrill, jubilant exclamation at that which met her eyes in the last of them.

'What time is it?' she panted.

Christopher was in the ecstasy of a yawn. He finished it before replying.

'"Bed, bed, said sleepy head,"' he quoted. 'Half-past ten, fairy mine.'

'Peggy has asked us both to her party tonight,' she said. 'Oh, the dear thing! Ring the bell and order the motor at once, and I'll telephone to Thurloe Square to say we shall sleep there. We shall be up in town in an hour, half-past eleven, then I must dress. We shall be at Peggy's by midnight. The papers said they were to sup there.'

'What a Cinderella!' said Christopher, to whom her excitement was beginning to communicate itself. 'But what about your week's complete rest?'

'I can't help that. Besides, there won't be a soul at Peggy's who was coming to my dance.'

Already she was at the telephone.

Such friends of hers who had seen the notice in the papers of the rest that had been ordered her, and met her that night, were delighted to see what good even that curtailed retirement had done her. She had never been so full of vitality and enjoyment. Arriving precisely as the royal party left the ballroom to go down to supper, Amy anchored herself most advantageously close to the door through which they must pass, and made curtsey after curtsey as if on springs that trembled slightly, between her bobbings, with the stress of her emotion.

And since her presence there at all was so wholly inconsistent with the orders of her physicians, she made no attempt whatever to explain it away. She was there; that was enough for her, so surely it was enough for anybody else. . . .

After all, Christopher, who knew her best, had said that she had never been beaten yet.

The Five Foolish Virgins

AMY BONDHAM had an Athenian mind and an anxious expression; her Athenian mind prompted her to go in pursuit of any new thing, and her anxious expression was due to the perennial fear that while she was pursuing one new thing, another new thing would usurp the attention of the lively and intelligent world in which she so strenuously lived, and that when she produced her musician or artist or poet, whom she had successfully captured, she might find that nobody any longer took the slightest interest in him.

But she had done pretty well hitherto. Romowski, the pianist, about whom three years ago musical London went crazy, had certainly been heard at her house very soon after his escape from a Bolshevist prison, and her portrait, a dazzling canvas of orange and blue blobs, was one of the first executed in this country by that amazing charlatan, Tony Kettnerkopf. If her artist or author or pianist failed to make good, she ever so gently dropped him, for in her busy life there was naturally no time for the struggling or the unimportant.

She had acquired a very considerable *flair* in, so to speak, 'spotting winners'. This was derived not from any particular knowledge of the art—music, or drama, or painting—in which the winners were running, nor from any power of appreciation with regard to their productions. Music, in fact, she rather disliked, and she seldom entered the door of the theatre unless the popularity of a piece was such that it was a matter of difficulty to get tickets. Her *flair* was due to her untiring attention to what people were talking about, and if within a short space of time she heard the name of some new artist in music or drama or fiction frequently mentioned, she set to work at once to get him to come and dine with her.

There were disappointments, of course; the new lion might prove to be no true lion at all—but such failures were soon forgotten. On the other hand, the successes were of imperishable memory, for she kept them alive herself.

'I hear Romowski, dear Siegfried Romowski, is giving two recitals next month,' she would say. 'Siegfried wrote to me a few weeks ago saying he wasn't sure if he would be able to get here before his American tour, but he can just do it. Of course you must come and meet him, Blanchie; we will have a little dinner for him; something *intimé*, you know. That is what he likes best. Mine was the first house in which he was heard in London. What an evening it was! There were only eight of us, and he played to us till midnight. I always say that you can have no idea what Siegfried is unless you have heard him like that. He always insists on my going to his recitals, and sends me half-a-dozen tickets, and, of course, he is marvellous anywhere. But you must hear him quietly, with just a few friends round him to know what he is capable of.'

Somehow Amy did not look back on that brilliant little speech with much satisfaction, for the very next day Blanche Goulder had found her in the queue at the box-office at Queen's Hall waiting her turn to get tickets for Romowski's first recital, and Amy's explanation that Siegfried, dear Siegfried, had sent her six but that she wanted more roused a faint grin on Blanche's face, which she did not quite like the look of.

Amy had spent a few weeks on the Riviera at Christmas, had lingered in Paris on her way home, and had now returned sun-burnt and shingled for the spring manoeuvres in London. It had struck her in Paris that the world of light and leading was taking an unusual interest in the drama, and she found that impression confirmed at the tea-tables of Mayfair. The interest here was at present only embryonic, but her matchless *flair* told her that the wind blew from that direction, and therefore she had better get to work. She paid no attention, of course, to popular successes in the theatre or to dramatists of well-known repute, for their names were known already, and there was nothing Athenian about them. But she joined the Stage Society and the New Players, and other institutions which brought to light unrecognized talent, and after sitting through a good deal of rather pornographic stuff, found herself listening one night to a very melancholy little piece called *The Sexton's Wife*.

It was only a one-act affair, and it seemed to her a dismal and uninteresting performance, but she was aware of a tenseness in the audience, and at the end of it the author, Henry Garroby, was called for and tumultuously applauded. In a moment her swift mind was made up, and she surged into the foyer, where naturally she met many friends, among whom was Blanche Goulder.

'But marvellous, dear Blanchie, too marvellous, wasn't it? Tell me, who is Henry Garroby? I never heard of him, but you know everybody. I always say, "If you want to know about anyone, ask Blanchie!"'

Blanche was perfectly capable of malice. The *intimé* dinner, with Romowski to play till midnight, had not come off, or at any rate she had not been bidden to it. She could keep people in her pocket too if it came to that.

'Oh, he's a great friend of mine,' she said; 'such a dear.'

'But do bring him to my house,' said Amy. 'Come and dine——'

She closed her eyes a moment, visualizing her engagement book.

'Come and dine on Thursday,' she said. 'Or if that won't suit you, on Saturday, and ask him to excuse all formality on the score of my intense admiration for his work.'

The faint smile played round Blanchie's mouth.

'I didn't care about this play of his much,' she said. 'He read it me, of course, in manuscript. Nothing happened; it just left off.'

'Oh, but that's so like life,' said Amy enthusiastically. 'I haven't seen anything so vivid and true for years. Thursday then, shall it be, or Saturday? Just a few people, quite *intimé*.'

'I'm afraid I'm engaged both nights,' said Blanche stonily. 'Such a pity! Some other night; some time . . . Ah, there's the bell; we must go in again!'

A little thing like that, of course, had no discouraging effect whatever on Amy; indeed, it rather confirmed her purpose. She was much too busy to be vindictive, like poor Blanchie, and an enquiry at the box-office, with the explanation that she had somehow mislaid Mr Garroby's address, easily procured it for her. That very evening she wrote him a charming little note expressive of her admiration of his play, and hoping—'our mutual friend, Blanchie Goulder, encourages me to hope,' was the way she worded it—that he would drop in for a cup of tea next day, or lunch the day after. Her hospitable promptitude was rewarded, and he dropped into lunch on the day after.

The acquaintance ripened rapidly. Amy showered invitations upon him, and asked the brightest and best of her world to meet him, and in the splendour of her magnanimity allowed even the jealous Blanchie to come in after dinner one night to hear him read *The Sexton's Wife* to a small select audience. That was a great success, and he began to be talked about as the coming dramatist who would redeem the theatre of its inane flippancies and absurdities, and produce serious and sterling work.

For himself, he was a very serious young man, already quite convinced of his own transcendent gifts, and completely devoid, as Zola says the man of genius always is, of a sense of humour. The absence of this, no doubt, was the cause of the one contretemps in his growing friendship with Amy, for one day when they were alone, talking about him, he began to make love to her.

In a few well-chosen words she convinced him that she had neither the time nor the inclination for that sort of thing, and extended to him her full forgiveness on condition that he would never do such a thing again. He readily consented, for he had only done so from a mistaken idea that it was expected of him. After that the friendship flowered without blight or canker.

It soon began to be known (Amy took care of that) that he was at work on another one-act play which would revolutionize the whole present trend of dramatic art. She made the original announcement herself to a carefully chosen luncheon-party.

'Dear Harry!' she said. 'I haven't seen Harry for days. Nobody has, in fact. He has absolutely isolated himself down in the country till he has finished his play. Yes, Blanchie, I do know where he is, but I'm under the most solemn vow not to reveal it. However, I got a telegram from him this morning, and he expects to be up here again at the end of the week.'

'And what about the play?' asked Blanchie.

'Marvellous; too marvellous! I've only seen bits of it, but such bits. I'm thankful that I am alive when such work is appearing. I have told him that it's long for a one-act play; it will last for an hour and a half, but it is impossible to make two acts of it or shorten it.'

Blanchie was quite humble now on the subject of Henry

Garroby. Amy had won, and she only wanted to be allowed to follow in her victorious wake.

'Dear Amy,' she said, 'what's the title? What is it about? Can you tell us?'

Amy gave a final stir to the coffee she was brewing in an explosive glass machine.

'Yes, there's no reason why I shouldn't,' she said, 'because all of you, if you're good, will be asked here next week to hear him read it. It is called *The Five Foolish Virgins*, and it's about them, the ones in the parable. The scene is an Eastern street, and the play opens with the marriage procession into the house, and the door is shut. Then, one by one, the Five Foolish Virgins who have gone to get oil for their lamps arrive, and knock on the door. The one who arrives first soliloquizes, the second joins her, the third, the fourth, the fifth, until there is a quintet of the most wonderful and piercing pathos.'

'And what happens then?' asked Blanchie breathlessly.

'They go to sleep; one after the other goes to sleep. The quintet diminishes to a quartet, and down to a soliloquy. Nothing happens; only from inside you hear the sounds of dancing and song. The agony of it is almost too poignant, and yet I don't know. It's too harrowing for words, and yet such a noble harrowing. Ah, what an opera it would make, if there was anyone capable of handling it! Beethoven might possibly have done it, but no one else.'

Amy devoted the week that followed to working up the excitement about *The Five Foolish Virgins*, and by way of keeping the recital thoroughly *intimé* asked some two hundred guests, which was about double the number that her drawing-room could, even uncomfortably, hold.

She cleared every stick of furniture out of it, and planted the floor thickly with rows of little gilt chairs; at the end stood the reading-desk for the dramatist. There was scarcely a refusal among all those who were bidden, and the only cloud in these auspicious heavens was that at the last moment an extraordinarily desirable invitation came for her to dine with the Prime Minister. That she could not do, as she had a dinner-party of her own to precede the reading.

But it might be possible, she thought, to slip away from her own house, after the Five Foolish Virgins had begun to chatter, show herself (which was the great point) for half an hour at Downing Street, return before the Virgins had talked things out, and enjoy the triumph of having launched them.

Her guests streamed in about ten o'clock on the great evening. Many came before that hour, and some took up commanding positions in the hall where they could see the arrivals; others settled themselves in the gilt chairs close to the reader's desk. By a quarter past ten the drawing-room was absolutely full, and the door so choked with those unable to penetrate beyond it that Mr Garroby had the greatest difficulty in getting in at all.

Murmurs, as from a swarm of angry bees, went up from those who could not wedge themselves in, and without waiting to receive the more belated arrivals, Amy let herself out of her back-door, where her motorcar was waiting, and sped off to Downing Street. The evening party which was to follow the dinner there had already begun, and she flitted about with great activity for half-an-hour, so that as many people as possible might know she had been there, and returned to her own house.

She could not understand at first what was happening, for the doorway so lately besieged by incomers was now, although the reading could not have been in progress more than an hour, blocked by those who were going away. Motors were rolling up to the door, taxis were being sought for, and it flashed through her mind that perhaps Harry had fallen dead in the middle of his recital. That would have been very painful, but wonderfully exciting.

She met Blanche in the hall, already equipped for departure.

'My dear, what's happening?' she said. 'Is it over?'

Blanche's faint grin quivered on her mouth.

'Oh no, not nearly, I believe,' she said. 'In fact, I think that's why everyone is going away. They can't stand any more Virgins. Goodnight, darling. Delicious evening.'

Amy found no difficulty in obtaining entrance to her drawing-room. A few people occupied the rows of gilt chairs, and Garroby's voice echoed through the room.

'*Fourth Foolish Virgin.*—Sister, the night is far spent, and the chill of morning is in the air. Sleep, like a fell opiate, invades my limbs, and presses on my eyelids. I can no more. (*Sleeps.*)'

'*Fifth Foolish Virgin.*—My lamp flickers in the night wind. The sound of music and song from within comes drowsily to me. I am very weary; I did not know there was such weariness in the world. Is it the shadow of death that is falling on me? . . .'

The soliloquy went interminably on, and a few more people stole out of the room. Finally, the Fifth Foolish Virgin slept, and the reader's voice ceased. He surveyed the empty rows of gilt chairs with a somewhat acid expression.

'But marvellous, too marvellous, Harry,' said the indomitable Amy. 'What a wonderful evening. I shall never forget it.'

That seemed highly probable. . . .

About a fortnight later the unexpected, as usual, occurred. 'The New Players' gave a performance of *The Five Foolish Virgins*, and the entire press, as well as the audience, hailed it as a masterpiece. Amy, with the bitterness of her party in her mind, did not go to it, but that made no difference. A glance at the papers next morning was enough for her, and Mr Garroby for the first time since the evening party was bidden to dinner again to meet a dozen enthusiastic Garrobites. She had purposely told him that dinner would be at 8.30, and had asked the rest of her guests for a quarter past.

He arrived, therefore, when the rest were assembled, and she ran across the room to greet him.

'It was too wonderful, Harry,' she said. 'I told you it would be. And to think that it was here that you first read it. How proud I am of that! You know everybody, I expect. Anyhow, everybody knows you. . . .'

CROOK
STORIES

My Friend the Murderer

NOONDAY, and a temperature of 102° in the shade; out-side, a driving storm of fine white dust, through which the houses on the other side of the square peer out vague and in-termittent; above, a colourless sky in which the sun hangs like colourless metal plate. Along the edge of the pavement the delicate-leaved pepper-trees are shrivelling before this fury from the furnace-mouthed south, which strips off their fern-like stalks of foliage, and drives them up against the house walls in unresting little eddies. The streets are empty but for cabs sheltering under the north wall of the café at the corner, and a bootblack lying asleep on the doorstep. Though it is so hot, he has wisely wrapped his head up in his coat, to shield his eyes and mouth from the dust.

The errand that took me out this morning in the teeth of this horrible sirocco, which, when it blows in Athens during June, is like the blast from the nether pit, has been a visit to the prison, in order to see Yanni, an old friend of mine, who is to be tried tomorrow on the charge of killing a Greek soldier, and for living for the last year the life of a brigand and an outlaw. On this second count there are no specific charges, but the first count is quite true. I saw him do it myself. It happened in this wise:

Rather more than a year ago I had been travelling in North Greece; the scenery was enchanting, and the weather execrable. Consequently one day, the first half of which I had spent in a leaky khan at the village of Lidoriki, watching the rain fall as it knows how to fall in the south, in closely ruled perpendicular lines, I abandoned the thoughts of going further, and taking advantage of a slight cessation at noonday went down that after-noon to Elatiná, a little fishing village on the north coast of the Corinthian gulf, where one could get a steamer back to Athens. Next day the weather cleared, and from rim to rim the sky was one incredible blue.

A couple of dozen clean white houses stand along the road which runs by the beach, bordered on each side by a row of yellow-flowering mimosa trees, now in full bloom. At short intervals there are built out over the water little wood loggias, the roofs of which are made of oleanders, plucked in their full luxuriance of leaf and flower, and renewed every two days. A wooden balustrade runs round three sides of these loggias, and the roof is supported by four or six big beams of olive wood. Leaning and looking seawards, you see rippling at your feet the clear green water of the gulf, turning blue in the further distance, and on the opposite coast the great giants of the Peloponnese, Cyllene and Helmos, the former the cradle of Hermes, the latter the fountain-head of the Styx, still standing swathed in the bygone winter's snow. Vineyards and olive woods spread up over the plain and lower hillsides behind, and a little to the left of the town, a swift vigorous stream joins the sea; its course you can trace for a mile or two across the plain, by the pink flush of the oleanders which line its banks.

The road from inland intersects this row of houses, and the corner house on the left used to belong to Yanni. At that time Yanni was about twenty years old, six foot three high and good to look upon. He was an Albanian by birth, a Greek by education, and by profession a butcher, a fisherman, an agriculturist, and the owner of a café. He had also built his own house, and he sang Albanian songs very tunefully.

Yanni had a spare room in this house which he had built, with a balcony facing the sea, and this room he consented to let to me until the arrival of my steamer, which was expected vaguely in two or three days, for the sum of three drachmas a day. He also supplied me with meat, fish, and coffee at the current prices.

There were quartered in this village four Greek soldiers, whose duty it was to perform the office of policemen, to put their foot down on all incipient riots, to discourage too great animation in the discussion of political affairs, and above all to see that commodities like meat were sold at tariff prices. They were hot, untidy little men, and Yanni despised them.

As a good man of business, he tried to get the highest possible price for his goods, and collisions between him and them were not infrequent. But since I was his lodger, he made no such exactions in my case, and the little soldier who inspected the bill which Yanni sent in to me, at the end of my first day there, declared himself satisfied.

By about nine o'clock in the evening the professions of butcher, agriculturist, and owner of a café became sinecures, and Yanni went a-fishing. He would come out of his house clothed only in a rough tunic which reached to about half way up his thighs, with a bag full of resin and a small wicker fishing-creel slung round his neck; in one hand a three-pronged spear for catching the fish, and in the other a big iron pan full of burning resin. With those he would wade into water about two feet deep, and moving slowly and gently along speared the fish as they lay open-mouthed and goggle-eyed staring at the light which he held some eighteen inches above the surface of the water.

It was a scene which Rembrandt could have painted, and would have loved to paint. The flaming resin showed in highlight the rippling surface of the sea below the flare, the upper part of Yanni's bared arms, his stained discoloured tunic and the rich brown of his legs, strong and straight above the water, distorted and waving below the surface. Now and then as he turned his head the light would strike the side of his face, the edge of his black crisp curls, or bring out into prominence the strong line of his jaw. At intervals he would raise his right arm, and with a splendid motion full of precision and force plunge his spear into the sea, bringing up on the end of it sometimes a red mullet, sometimes a flat flapping sole, or a young cuttle-fish, all arms and eyes. Behind in shadow stood the black hulls and heavy masts of fishing vessels, and in the furthest distance, more guessed at than seen, rose the great hills on the other side of the gulf. Now and then his pan of resin would want refilling and he stood still a moment, drying his hand on his tunic before adding more to it from the bag round his neck.

Then with a sudden splutter and flare the light shot up again and Yanni with his dry hand would get a cigarette from his pocket, and drawing back his lips from the flames, showing his row of strong white teeth, bent over the flare to get a light, his face illumined vividly, ruddy brown against the surrounding gloom.

The price of fish had long been a standing cause for a quarrel between the little Greek soldiers and Yanni, but it had ended in a complete victory for Yanni. He was master of the art of longshore fishing, which none of the other villagers could make pay, and which was the only means whereby they could get fish, for the owners of fishing vessels were under a contract to sell their catch for the Corinth market, and thus the village was dependent for its fish on private enterprise.

The little soldiers had tried to coerce Yanni into selling his fish at the Corinth market rate, which he steadily and persistently refused to do. He would sell them at such rate as he thought good, or not at all. The quarrel had come to a head about a fortnight ago, when Yanni being short of cash had demanded famine prices for his evening's catch.

He stood there in his tunic, the sea-water dripping from him, with his resin flare in one hand, and his fishing-creel in the other, perfectly good-tempered, but absolutely firm, demanding three-pence apiece for his mullets, and twopence-halfpenny for his soles. This was about fifty per cent in advance of his usual rates, but he explained quite candidly that he wanted money.

The little Greek soldiers argued and threatened, and when they threatened Yanni smiled sweetly and patted the head of the tallest of them in a fraternal manner.

Now it so happened that the brother and sister-in-law of the mayor were coming to stay with him next day, and it was necessary to have fish at all costs to save the honour of the mayoralty. But Yanni was perfectly firm, and announced his intention of eating all the fish himself if there were no buyers; and the mayor, wisely reflecting that he was quite capable of the feat, gave in, and paid Yanni what he asked.

The surrender of the mayor naturally took away the moral support of the little Greek soldiers, and Yanni was victorious. He bore them no grudge, and when the sale was over, treated them to a mastic each.

Sometimes one or other of the villagers would borrow Yanni's second spear, and try to emulate his deeds. One night I remember one of the soldiers came in as Yanni and I were drinking coffee after dinner, and he was preparing to go fishing, to ask for the loan of his spare weapon. Yanni grinned and said:

'My little man, you will only catch your own toes,' but he gave him what he wanted, and said that if he would wait a minute he would come too. So after drinking another cup of coffee Yanni pulled off his trousers and coat, kicked off his boots, and watched the little soldier rolling up his trousers to the knee with an indulgent smile. Then the two set off together, the soldier stumbling painfully over the boulders on the beach, and picking his way delicately among the sharp stones, and at the sight thereof Yanni's mouth was filled with rude, loud laughter.

They fished to the left of the village and I wandered along the beach watching them. The stream which joins the sea here has cut for itself a deep passage round a ledge of rock, and as we approached this I suddenly saw Yanni making violent signs to me to look.

The incautious little soldier was going first, elated at having captured a cuttle-fish and forgetting the deep hole. I could see Yanni's huge shoulders shaking with laughter as he approached it, and in another moment with a howl of dismay the soldier disappeared. Yanni pranced out into deeper water along the edge of the hole, and as the little soldier was swept down the current, speared him adroitly in the slack of his trousers, drew him in, and lifted him on his feet.

He fished on by himself for half an hour or so after this, for the other was wet and sad, and then coming to land sat down by me on the beach and examined his haul.

'Fish are cheap tonight,' he explained, 'because, you see, you pay me three drachmas a day for the room, and get your provisions from me. Six mullet, and four soles, two cuttle-fish. Would you like cuttle-fish tomorrow at breakfast?'

'No, thanks.'

'Don't you eat cuttle-fish in England?' he enquired.

'No; but we use that brown stuff which you throw away for paint.'

Yanni wrung out the bottom of his tunic which had got wet in the rescue of the Greek soldier, and lit a cigarette at his flare.

'Tomorrow some travellers come here,' he said, 'and they will want meat. I must kill a lamb tonight. These travellers are usually fools, and meat will be rather dear tomorrow. What do a few drachmas extra mean to them?'

'You'll have a row with the soldiers,' I observed.

'I suppose I shall, but I don't mind. Of course, if you want some lamb you may have it at the usual price.'

The travellers arrived next day, with a cook from Athens, who came in due course to Yanni to buy meat. Yanni charged twopence in the pound more than he ought to have charged, but the cook paid it, and was just walking out of the shop with his purchases when one of the soldiers came in and stopped him.

'How much did you pay for that?' he asked.

'Two drachmas a pound.'

The soldier turned to Yanni.

'You swindling lout,' he said, 'you'll go to prison for this.'

'Get out,' said Yanni smiling. 'Have a mastic?'

This was bribery.

'You son of a pig,' said the other. 'I wouldn't drink your filthy mastic. It's half water, and you would charge me for it.'

This was a direct insult, a slight on Yanni's hospitality, and he began to get angry.

'Go to the devil,' he said, 'or to the dunghill you were born on.'

Then this misguided little Greek reached up and hit Yanni on the face, and in another moment Yanni's great arm had come swinging down, and his clenched fist had struck the soldier full on the temple. He fell with a broken clatter on the floor, striking the edge of the table with his head. At that moment a second soldier came in, and Yanni, grasping the situation, knocked him down, and fled.

In another moment the whole place was astir. The two remaining soldiers got their rifles and went in pursuit of Yanni, who, however, had got a good quarter of a mile start, and the village doctor came bustling in to attend to the other victims. The second soldier was none the worse, but only very angry, and he soon went off after the others. The one who had struck Yanni, however, was unconscious. He died that evening.

Yanni, fearing the worst, had struck straight up a gorge towards the mountains. From behind the village I could see him running up the bare hillside, and about four hundred yards behind him ran the foremost soldier. They passed up, and up, and I saw the two other soldiers overtake the first, and all three stopped for a moment. Then they unslung their rifles, and kneeling down, deliberately fired at Yanni. In all, eight shots were fired, without effect, and then, their ammunition being exhausted, they continued the pursuit.

Half the village were standing with me, watching the pursuit of Yanni, but public sympathy, wavering before, went round entirely to him when those shots were fired. He was a hunted thing, unarmed, and pursued by armed men, and that divine human sympathy which every hour gives the lie direct to a hundred cynical proverbs which label it anything but divine, at once enlisted itself on the side of the defenceless.

Later in the evening, three sorry figures limped back to the village, torn and bedraggled. One of them had a dirty handkerchief bound round his face, and the arm of the third was in an extemporized sling. They were received with derisive laughter by the unsympathetic village, which had quite recovered from the shock of the fourth soldier's death, and was disposed to canonize Yanni there and then.

Later on, the story of their mischance leaked out, and the derisive laughter was redoubled. Yanni, it appeared, had drawn the right conclusion from the cessation of shots, and knowing that they had no more ammunition, sat down on the top of a high rock and parleyed with them. He wished to know, first of all, what had happened to the man who had hit him in the face, was he dead or alive? That the soldiers could not tell him, and Yanni, with his irrepressible hopefulness, opined that he was alive, but had a very sore head. He then wished to know what the devil they meant by shooting at him, and, getting no answer to this enquiry, threw a stone at the attacking force, which, being sent with much precision of aim, hit No. 1, who was not looking, in the face. Yanni laughed rudely, and advised him to go home.

This exasperated the military, and they again started in pursuit, and Yanni took them a healthy run up the side of Elatos. When they stopped for sheer want of breath, he stopped too, and being still grieved because they had tried to shoot him, he threw some more stones at them. But they were on the look-out for stones, and none of these took effect; so Yanni strolled on, leaving them in the rear.

They then held a council of war, which evolved a very subtle plan. No. 1 was bleeding considerably, but fired by the heat of personal prowess, he proposed that he should take off the bandage which Yanni had seen him tie over his injured eye, and with No. 2 go in pursuit. No. 3 was to make a detour, and try to reach the top of the pass by which Yanni must get over the mountain before him and cut him off. In the meantime, the others would pursue him but leisurely, in order to give No. 3 time, and the fugitive, seeing two uninjured men pursuing him, would conclude that No. 1 had decided to go home, acting according to his advice, and would not expect the stratagem. It was beginning to get dark, and at a couple of hundred yards distance he would not be able to distinguish faces, and the bandage alone would identify No. 1, for they were all little men.

The first part of the stratagem succeeded beautifully. No. 3 gained the top of the pass, and saw Yanni making straight for it at a quiet trot, pursued at a respectable distance by the two others. He had nothing to do but to hide behind a tree, grasp his rifle by the muzzle, and be ready to bring the butt down on Yanni's head. But at this point the stratagem broke down.

Yanni, whose keenness of vision had been sharpened by much catching of fish in the dark, saw the end of a rifle-butt projecting from a tree ahead of him, and reflecting, with admirable commonsense, that rifle-butts did not grow on pine-trees, concluded that there was also a little soldier behind that tree. So he ran on up the path until he came close to the tree, and then, dodging quickly off the path to the left, hit No. 3 so sharp a blow on the arm that was preparing to bring down the rifle-butt on his own head that No. 3 dropped, and exclaimed that his arm was broken, which it was not.

But Yanni had had enough of guerilla warfare. His sense of humour had been sufficiently tickled by the thought that he had hit in the eye one of those soldiers who had been firing at him with rifle-bullets, and perhaps broken the arm of another, and his instinct of self-preservation asserted itself. So he struck off the path into the mountains, and personally, I did not see him again for twelve months.

Just a year after this, I was camping out, for archaeological purposes, at a place on the Corinthian Gulf called Aegosthena. At that time there were only two or three houses there, none of which seemed to be lived in. But for several days in succession I had seen some twenty sheep feeding on the plain, apparently without a shepherd, and I began to wonder whether what I had heard at Athens was true, and that there were brigands in the neighbourhood.

One night, I was sitting on the warm sea-scented beach after dinner, listening to the gentle ripple of the waves, and thinking, oddly enough, of the evenings I had spent at Elatiná watching Yanni fishing, when I saw, some half mile to the left, a light moving slowly along on the edge of the sea. Once it nearly died out, and then suddenly sprung into flame again, and with a scarcely formulated guess in my mind as to who it was, I walked along the shore in its direction. It was moving slowly away from me, but quite suddenly, when I was within about two hundred yards of it, it stopped, and then, with a hiss, was quenched in the water, and, in the silence that followed, I heard stealthy steps plashing through the water towards the shore. Then my guess suddenly became a conviction, and calling out 'Yanni, is fish cheap tonight?' I sat down and waited.

For a moment there was silence, then the sound of steps along the shingle, and after a pause I heard my own name called cautiously out of the darkness.

'Yes, it is I,' I said, 'and alone.'

The steps renewed themselves in double time, and in a moment I was aware of a great man close by me, who sat down by my side, and took my two hands in his.

'Praise the blessed Virgin! it is you,' he said, 'and I—I have not seen a face I know for a year.'

And the great giant burst out crying, and somehow or other, with the arm of a murderer, outlaw, and perhaps brigand, round my neck, I was nigh to crying too.

My servant had gone up to the village that evening, after dinner, to buy meat and wine, and as it was a six hours' journey there and back, he would not be in again till early morning. So Yanni and I went back to my tent and sat there talking. He had not yet had supper, so I relit the little iron charcoal stove, and he cooked his fish.

'I am lodging in your house tonight,' he said, 'see, shall I pay you three drachmas? You know I am very glad to see you; when one has not seen a friend for a year it is a good sight. I have grown too, have I not?'

He got up and stretched himself after his meal, and for a moment I really thought his head would go through the top of my tent, and, standing on a chair, I measured him against the pole. He was just over six-foot-six.

'Yes, you have grown,' I said, 'and your tunic is getting too short. Take a cigarette, and tell me what has happened to you.'

He lay down on the floor of the tent, and suddenly burst out laughing.

'The little soldiers knelt down on the hillside and fired at me eight times,' he said. 'Why couldn't they come and fight me like men? How I would have knocked their heads together! Were they very tired when they got home?'

'Very tired, and two of them very sick,' I said.

Yanni looked thoughtful.

'It is a good thing to live out of doors,' he said, 'to sleep under the sky, and awake under the sky. That is what I did until winter came, and since the winter has passed. I have a little hut up in the mountains over there on Helicon, and I have now twenty sheep.'

'How did you get them?' I asked.

'I took six from Elatiná,' he said. 'Only two nights after I had killed that fool of a soldier—he must have been a weak man to die so easily—I went back to my house and carried them off, two by two. On the other side of Helicon they do not know me, though I think they take me for a brigand, but I sell them good meat, and, as they are wise, they ask no questions.'

'Then do you live quite alone?'

'Yes. For a month or perhaps more I joined some other men who used to live like me, but they were devils, and I left them. One night they made a descent on a wretched little starving village, and they killed two men, and used the women worse than that. It was in the winter, and we were half starving. I had not gone with them, but when I saw them coming back, with blood on their hands, bringing with them the women they had taken, I went off that night, and I have not seen them since. They have gone north I think. And they have offered a reward to any one who takes me.'

'Yes, and the papers say you were taken once!'

Yanni laughed softly to himself.

'It is quite true. I was taken at Varsovini, over by Misolonghi, many miles from here. Shall I tell you about it?'

'Do.'

'It was about three months ago. I had begun to be afraid they knew me here, so I sold off all my sheep, and went away over towards Misolonghi, to this village Varsovini, quite a small place. It was just the time of year when they hoe the vines, and I got plenty of work. I lived with a widow woman who had got one

son about eight years old. Well, one evening as it was the end
of the hoeing, and I had been paid for my work, and as there
would be no work next day, I got very drunk. I was sitting
in the café with two or three other men, and I fell asleep.
When I woke I saw that another man had come in, and I heard
him say, "Yes, that is he; we will send to Misolonghi tomorrow."
Little Stavro the widow's son was there, and was listening to
them. So I pretended not to have heard, and I drank another
glass of wine and went off home with Stavro. I meant to wait
till the house was quiet, and then slip off; but I had hardly
lain down for two minutes, when Stavro came in with a bit
of cord in his hands. He said to me, "Are you Yanni, who
killed the soldier?" and I, of course, said "Yes". So he came up
to me and says, "We are very poor, and there is a reward
for taking you. I shall tie your hands and take you to the mayor."
I burst out laughing, being very drunk, you understand, and
said, "Come along then." So he tied my hands behind my back,
and led me off to the mayor's house, a little house I could have
put on my back, mayor and all. The mayor had heard that I
had been recognized, and was just sending off to Misolonghi
when Stavro and I came in. "Here's the brigand Yanni," says
Stavro, "I have captured him." "That is true," said I, "pay the little
chap his reward, and let him get to bed." So they paid him his
500 drachmas then and there, and Stavro said goodbye to me and
went home.

'The mayor was whispering to another man. "He is very
drunk," he said, "we will shut him in the stable, and the soldiers
will be here long before he is sober." That suited me very well,
because when I am drunk I am very strong, and there was a big
wooden beam in the middle of the stable, as I knew, supporting
the roof. So they led me off into the stable, and locked the door,
and I heard the mayor say, "I will wait here with a gun, and you
must ride to Misolonghi as quick as you can."

'There was a small window in the side opposite the door, and
the moonlight came through. The walls of the stable were not
more than six feet high, and I could not stand upright. But I
could see the big beam quite plainly, and when all was quiet
again I put my arms round it, and pulled; the whole thing came
down together, and with it the top of the wall in which was the
door by which the mayor was sitting, and this fell outwards on

the top of the mayor. I heard his gun go off, and he screamed for help. So I vaulted over the remains of the wall, and pulled him out of the rubbish and wished him goodbye.

'As I passed Stavro's home, I could hear the little chap crying inside, so as I had plenty of time I went in to see what had happened. Stavro was crying because he had given me up, but when he saw me he cheered up, and thought of the drachmas. I walked all that night, and all the next night, sleeping in the mountains during the day, and since then I have lived here. I bought some sheep with the money I earned at Varsovini, and they have done well; I have twenty now.' Yanni paused a moment, pulled aside the tent flap, and looked out.

'I hear a mule bell coming down the hillside,' he said, 'and look, it is light in the east! Your servant is coming back and I must go. Do you stay here long?'

'About another fortnight.'

'That is good. I shall see you again many times. I will come whenever it is safe, if you will sit out upon the shore where you sat tonight. And you must come and see my hut on the mountain. I will take you there tomorrow evening. It has been very good to see you, for you are a friend.'

And after the manner of the Greeks to their friends, he kissed me on the cheek, and went off silently into the darkness.

But evening after evening passed, and I waited in vain for Yanni. Some rumour of his whereabouts, I suppose, had got abroad, and he had changed his quarters. And when my week was finished, I went back to Athens without seeing him.

Three weeks passed, and yesterday I saw in the papers the news of his capture. Some overpowering desire, I imagine, of seeing his own people again had come over him, and he was taken at Elatiná. Warned by previous experience of Yanni's little ways, as soon as it was known that he had been seen, they sent off to Salona for twenty soldiers, and surrounded him as he was sleeping quietly in the vineyard at the back of his house. He made no resistance, and was brought to Athens the next day. He will be tried tomorrow.

I was allowed to talk to Yanni for about twenty minutes. His chief desire was to have some cigarettes, for he had no money on him when he was captured, and except for the occasional kindness of his jailer was smokeless. That need, however, I was able to supply, and we sat side by side on his plank bed, and he talked quite cheerfully and unconcernedly.

'They certainly will not execute me,' he said, 'because I have never committed a murder before, but I suppose I shall have two or three years in prison. That will be very dull.'

He looked out through the narrow grating of his cell. 'This is an abominable day,' he said; 'it is all dust and hot wind, and there are bad smells: it is not like the pinewoods. Did you wait for me on the beach at Aegosthena after that last night I saw you?'

'Yes, Yanni. I waited every night,' I said.

Yanni flushed and smiled.

'I thought you would,' he said, 'and I knew you would come to see me here. But it was not my fault that I did not come. I heard next day that they knew I was near Velia, and were look-ing for me, so I had to go away. And after wandering about for three weeks I felt I must see Elatiná again. I was so happy at getting back there, that the second night, instead of going up to the mountains, I slept in the vineyard behind my house—do you remember it—and I awoke to find those little soldiers standing round me. They were wiser this time; they sent twenty.'

He grinned.

'Do you remember the little soldier who fell into the deep hole by the stream? The little devil! I saved his life that night, for he could swim like a lump of lead, and next day he tried to shoot me.'

About ten minutes after I left Yanni, the lawyer who is going to defend him tomorrow came to see him, with the result that while I was still seated at lunch, a hot bald-headed man rushed into the room, and asked me if it was true that I had seen the murder committed. For Yanni's unsupported assertion that the soldier had struck him first was of course valueless in a law court, whereas if an independent witness could testify to it the case would assume a wholly different character. Why this had not struck either Yanni or me before I cannot imagine, and I cursed us as idiots and blessed the bald-headed lawyer as Solomon.

Next day the case came on. There was nothing whatever to show that Yanni had been guilty of lawless acts during his year of outlawry; indeed, the only thing known about him during that time was that he had rescued the mayor of Varsovini from beneath a wall of fallen masonry. It was moreover found that he had been repeatedly shot at by three soldiers, that the evening before the murder he had rescued one of these from a watery grave; and that the murder itself had been unpremeditated and committed under great provocation, Yanni, the immense Yanni, odd as it appeared, having received the first blow.

But for the sake of example, and partly in order to discourage home rule in the price of meat, he was sentenced to six months' imprisonment, which, as he has since assured me, was not at all intolerable. And the bald-headed lawyer, perspiring profusely, shook me warmly by the hand, as Yanni, smiling kindly to his warder, was led off to the cells.

'You are in luck to have saved such a man,' he said. 'A dozen like him could take Constantinople.'

And I felt inclined to agree with him.

Professor Burnaby's Discovery

T HE Hotel Pi-netem at El Nefer on the Nile was, in the year 1919, having a very bad season. Though Luxor, only a few hours away to the north, was crowded with tourists, and Assouan, about the same distance southward, was crammed, the ebbing and flowing tide of visitors swept disdainfully by El Nefer, or, at the most, some driblets of it had lunch there, made a brief excursion to the small, corroded temple built by King Pi-netem (that obscure monarch of the twenty-first Egyptian dynasty) and took train or boat again for more popular winter resorts.

The hotel, owned and admirably run by an Englishman and his wife, seemed to attract nobody; its spacious, comfortable rooms remained mournfully empty; none wandered among the palms and rose-trees of its shady garden, or played lawn tennis on its *en-tout-cas* courts, or strolled down the mimosa avenue which led to the river to see the miracle of sunset on the Nile, and even the donkey-boys scarcely troubled to bring their brisk bedizened little animals up to the gate of the hotel, for there were never any tourists to hire them. The most animated of the activities took place when the post-boat stopped at the creaking moored quay on the river, for then (while a few visitors made their visit to the temple) there would be chaffering over the scarabs and blue beads of itinerant vendors.

But even so there was not much demand for objects dating from that rather insignificant dynasty. It was not a period of high artistic workmanship; the scarabs were coarsely cut and of poor glaze, the beads and the ushapti figures were dull and lustreless. Occasionally a mummied hand or a few yards of the linen wrappings of the dead were put on sale, but the lamentable growth of superstition caused these gruesome relics to be shunned rather than sought after.

But now and then among this tawdry rubbish, which, though genuinely of the twenty-first dynasty, was of clumsy and ill-fashioned workmanship, there would appear some very notable little piece, a royal scarab perhaps, bearing the name of King Pi-netem or one of his successors, a sphinx-statuette of limestone with a well-cut inscription, or a piece of faience of lustrous and transparent blue, and if there was some Egyptologist on the boat, he would probably purchase such a little gem at a fairly moderate price, and account himself lucky.

In fact, the art of the twenty-first dynasty was beginning, about this time, to interest and puzzle archaeologists. Its remains, like the temple of Pi-netem and the rough-hewn tombs in the limestone cliff which here ran parallel with the Nile for a mile or two above the cultivated land, were, of course, clumsy work, and yet every now and then something was bought on the quay at El Nefer which rivalled the beautiful handicraft of the eighteenth dynasty. These few and exquisite pieces were always offered for sale by one man only, the dragoman of the Hotel Pi-netem, a reticent and handsome fellow much valued by the proprietor. One such relic, a wooden box, inlaid with ebony and ivory and bearing the cartouche of Pi-netem, had been purchased here by a Cairo dealer, and had been subsequently acquired by the British Museum.

Christopher Heaton, the proprietor of the hotel, had gone to Bloomsbury, when he was last in London, and inspected it with a good deal of professional pride. The official in charge had amiably pointed out to him the beauty of the workmanship, and told him how exultant the famous Professor Burnaby was over its acquisition.

But when he went on to say how much that treasure had cost the Museum, annoyance mingled itself with the pride on Christopher's good-humoured face, and he determined to bring something of the same epoch to England next year in his own hands, and sell it to the Museum himself, thus eliminating the scandalous profits of middlemen.

On this hot radiant afternoon in early February, Christopher and his wife were seated on the balcony in the annexe of the hotel, where they occupied the top floor, which was pleasantly secluded. Norah Heaton's face, usually very placid and Madonna-like, was a little troubled; a soft perpendicular wrinkle was ruled between her fine black eyebrows, and her mouth drooped with a touch of melancholy. They had been going into the question of their finances, and the subject was not a cheerful one.

'It's terrible, Chris,' she said. 'We've both put every penny we had into the hotel, and now we're faced with this. What it comes to is that, if the hotel doesn't begin to pay next season, we're broke.'

'Yes, darling, to bits,' said Christopher.

She got up and began slowly moving up and down the balcony.

'I can't understand why it doesn't take on,' she said. 'It is better equipped than any hotel between here and Cairo. Lawn tennis, swimming-bath, excellent food, reasonable charges. Yet when Luxor is turning people away, even the overflow doesn't come here. What does it lack?'

He considered this a moment.

'Temples and tombs,' he said at length. 'Temples and tombs have made Egypt from the tourist point of view, just as the Blue Grotto has made Capri. Rameses the Great, who oppressed the Israelites, he's really the patron saint of the Nile.'

'Well, dear, we've got a temple,' said she, 'and plenty of tombs.'

'Yes, but it's a measly temple, and it's too near the hotel. People want an expedition; they don't want a temple at the end of the garden. Besides, Pi-netem is no good; he doesn't hitch on to anybody people know about like Rameses. Tourists are getting frightfully archaeological. As for the tombs, they're just a set of holes in the rock.'

She looked at him sideways.

'Archaeologists are beginning to take an interest in Pi-netem,' she said. 'There's a box of his, you know, at the British Museum.'

He laughed.

'Yes, and there'll be an extraordinarily fine lapis lazuli scarab of his wife's before long,' he said. 'Let's get to work, Norah.'

They went into the room out of which the balcony opened. It was large and littered with antique objects, which under skilful and patient manipulation were, so to speak, the quarry which supplied the materials for their industry. On the table near the window, for instance, was a charming little seated statuette of Sekhet, the lion-headed goddess, on which just now Norah was busily engaged, outlining on the back of the seat an inscription which showed that it was dedicated to the goddess by Ranaka, royal daughter of Pi-netem. In a corner lay a mummy-case with the embalmed body of a woman inside it, which Christopher had lately purchased at Assiout. The hieroglyphics with which it was covered were largely effaced, and at present he had not thought out any destiny for it. Elsewhere were pieces of ivory and ebony inlay, and fragments of ancient boxes; out of such, with infinite pains, the famous Pi-netem box in the British Museum had been constructed. There were bags of beads, rows of blue faience ushapti figures (the glaze of which could be melted off and reapplied to rarer pieces), strings of scarabs, a litter, in fact, of material, coarse and rough for the most part, like the antiques proffered to tourists on the post-boats, but capable of being fashioned into finer things. . . .

Just now Christopher was at work on what promised to be his *chef d'œuvre*. The material on which he was engaged was a beautiful scarab of lapis lazuli, originally uninscribed, but now being engraved by him with the name of Heut-taui in cartouche.

She was the wife of Pi-netem, and no scarab of hers was at present known to exist. The creation of a unique object, therefore, was worth (and indeed demanded) unusual care, for it would have to pass the scrutiny of the most erudite judges. By the greatest good luck he possessed a gold setting, decorated with minute inlaid lotuses, which exactly filled it; and when finished it would be a worthy companion of the box of ebony and ivory with her husband's name in ivory on it. Christopher was not only an able Egyptologist, but a wonderful workman: without doubt under his care and diamond-pointed graver a worthy memorial, though in miniature, of the obscure Queen would emerge.

The two worked on with the fervour of true lovers of their craft till the sun was wheeling westwards, and then set out for a walk.

It was close and sultry today, the south wind threatened to develop into a *khamseen*, that hot and furious blast from the furnace of the desert, and passing through the belt of cultivated land, where the sugar-canes and the maize were already ripening, they mounted the steep limestone cliff, to catch any breath of coolness which might be found on the higher ground. Here lay the long rows of tombs roughly cut in the soft rock, all long since despoiled and probably not worth the trouble of the pillagers, for they were not the sumptuous resting-places of kings and nobles, where glorious loot might be expected to reward the industry of the sacrilegious.

To the native mind the place was of ill-omen; afrits of the friskiest sort were liable to spring on any who wandered after sunset here, and none but the most incautious would venture here alone even at broad noon. But native superstitions had no hold over Christopher and his wife, and though sunset was imminent they still pursued their way till they had come to the end of this cliff which ran parallel with the river and then turned eastward towards the desert. Their walk, if they went in this direction, usually ended here, but this evening they strolled on along the track which was cut high up on the side of the rock. The moon had already risen, and flooded the face of it with the wan light which contrasted strangely with the brilliant pink afterglow of the sunset.

'If only the tales of the afrits were true,' said Christopher, 'that would be an attraction. People would flock to the hotel, and come out at sunset to see the ghosts. The Psychical Research Society . . . hallo, what's that?'

'Oh, my dear, is it an afrit?' said Norah. 'Show me.'

'No, but look at the face of the cliff ahead,' said he. 'There's another tomb there, all by itself. I never knew that.'

The moonlight, striking sideways on the rock, certainly made a sharp black shadow, as from an aperture into the solid wall of it.

'Let's go and have a look,' said he. 'If there is one, there may be more not yet discovered. Fancy finding a new tomb unrifled. That would bring the visitors!'

But their scrutiny led to no such discovery; there was just this one tomb, all by itself, and the cliff on both sides of it showed no sign that other tombs had been made there. Opposite it the track ended abruptly in a wall of rock. The tomb had been entered, and in front of the door of it lay the slab of rock with which it had once been closed. The interior was in deep darkness, except where a shaft of moonlight lay white and narrow on the floor; but it was clear that here was a much more august sepulchre than the row of meagre burying-places which faced the river.

'Odd that it should be alone and apart from all the others,' said Christopher. 'Why is it so far from all the rest?'

'Oh, Christopher, could it have been a king's tomb?' she asked.

'I don't see how it's possible. They were all buried in the Valley of the Tombs of the Kings. Perhaps it wasn't an Egyptian burial at all, but that of some foreigner. That might account for its being so far away from the others. Only a guess, of course.'

'And the guess is that it was a person of some importance,' said she. 'We must certainly come back with candles tomorrow and explore it.'

The afterglow was fading fast, but in the moonshine they easily found their way back along the narrow track cut in the face of the cliff.

'And what's this track for?' asked Christopher suddenly. 'It leads only to that tomb.'

She had no answer for this, pursuing her own train of thought.

'It's in the manner of an Egyptian tomb,' she said, 'but it's an ingenious idea of yours to guess that it's a foreign burial. Some great trader, do you think, who possibly died up here? There was a good deal of foreign trade in the twenty-first dynasty. King Solomon bought war-chariots in Egypt, you know.'

'Of course. One of his wives, too, was an Egyptian princess. Daughter of Paseb-khanu, wasn't she?'

'Sister probably. Could it be a Jewish burial, do you think? Some ambassador of Solomon's who came to fetch the princess and died here?'

He laughed.

'We're getting on rather fast,' he said. 'Why not say at once that it's the tomb of the Queen of Sheba, who on her return from visiting Solomon went home through Egypt and died and was buried at El Nefer?'

He stopped suddenly, and his voice trembled with excitement.

'Indeed, why not say it?' he said. 'And why not substantiate the statement?'

'What do you mean?' she said.

She saw what he meant before he could answer.

'Oh, Christopher!' she cried. 'You mean that next year the tomb we have seen today will be rediscovered, with the slab in place, and that inside will be found . . .'

'Quick! Let's get home,' said he. 'We must sit down and think; think till our heads burst. It's colossal! Discovery of the tomb of the Queen of Sheba! Empty hotel, do you imagine? I've a great mind to begin building an extra wing at once. There'll be enough to do without that, though. But first we must think, Norah; think terribly and furiously.'

The moon was low to its setting when at length he rose from his chair on the balcony outside the workshop in the annexe, where they had talked through the hours of the night.

'When once we have put back into place the slab that closes the tomb,' he said, 'we shall have nothing more to do with what is within. We must not even incur the breath of suspicion which might attach to us if we discovered the tomb. Somebody else must discover it.'

'Who?' asked she.

'Some eminent Egyptologist, the more eminent the better, whom we shall get to stop a night or two here. We'll take him for a walk, that's all. Professor Burnaby, for instance, who bought the Pi-netem box, and who is digging at Assouan. Not one atom of credit shall we get for it.'

She laughed.

'Or of discredit,' she said.

'Yes, plenty of that, for having been so long at El Nefer and not having found it already!'

'But how are we to get the—the things there?' she asked.

'It will be a long job, and a nocturnal one. But luckily not a native will go near the place at night. And before we get the things there, we've got to provide the things. We've got masses of material of the right dynasty, though of course they are not enough. We've got to provide the grounds for the identification. And before we do that we've got to examine the tomb to see if it will do; and before we do that we've got to go to bed, Norah. As for credit, our credit will be at the bank. Good Lord, fancy having the hotel full all winter and far into the spring!'

They spent a couple of hours at the tomb next morning, after which they sat and talked all day and far into the night. Not one touch of the graver did the lapis lazuli scarab of Heut-taui receive; not one stroke of the chisel chinked on the outlined inscription on the back of the Sekhet statue. Often there were long silences as they puzzled over some difficult points; often again, when their course stretched out serene and clear, suggestions poured out swift and pellucid. There were frequent excursions into the workshop, with inspection of its stores, and the female mummy in its battered case came in for much attention. Long they sat reviewing all that they had planned, and at length wearily, but with eyes bright with imagination, Norah got up.

'That's enough to begin on, Christopher,' she said. 'And it's quite clear that we shall have to stop out here all the summer. It's a race against time, for all must be ready by November. Can we do it all, I wonder, in nine months?'

'Got to,' said Christopher.

Midway through November the first paragraph concerning an interesting discovery at a small place on the Nile, little frequented by tourists, appeared in the English press. The great Egyptologist, Professor Burnaby, who, it might be remembered, had secured for the British Museum a unique box inlaid with ivory and ebony, and bearing in cartouche the name of Pi-netem, that little known king of the twenty-first dynasty, had stopped at El Nefer, from which place this box undoubtedly came, in the hopes of coming across more objects that dated from that obscure and interesting epoch when, under King Solomon, the kingdom of Palestine reached the zenith of its prosperity.

He had not been disappointed, for he had procured from the proprietor of the hotel there an exceedingly fine lapis lazuli scarab of Heut-taui, Pi-netem's wife. Subsequently he had visited the tombs which are hewn in the limestone rock above the cultivated land, and had followed a road cut in the cliff which most unaccountably came to an abrupt end. Wondering what could be the reason of this track which led nowhere, he examined the face of the cliff at its termination, and came upon his discovery. There was a tomb there cut in the rock, far away from all the other burials.

He went straight back to the hotel, and got Mr Christopher Heaton, the proprietor, to procure some native labour, and they removed the slab which closed the entrance to the tomb, and found themselves in a chamber which was clearly the ante-room of the tomb itself. Robbers unfortunately had previously entered, for the floor of the chamber was littered with the results of their ransacking, and he conjectured that having found the tomb they had partly pillaged it, and had replaced the entrance slab, meaning perhaps to come back and continue their looting. Certain indications showed that the robbery was probably a recent one, and it was likely that the famous box of Pi-netem in the British Museum and his wife's scarab were obtained here.

It was impossible at present to give any detailed account of what the robbers had spared, but sufficient had been seen already to show that the discovery was of great importance, and might, indeed, prove to be of unique and surpassing interest. On this point it would be premature to say more, but it might be stated that the tomb was that of some foreign and not Egyptian dignitary.

In the far wall of the chamber that had been entered there was a sealed stone slab which would probably prove to be the door into the tomb-chamber itself. That, too, had been penetrated by the pillagers, for there was a hole cut in it large enough to admit a man. But for the present it was impossible to enter it, for a quantity of funerary objects were scattered about in front of it, and it was necessary first to remove these with the utmost care in order to avoid further damage to them. Professor Burnaby had with Mr Christopher Heaton, the proprietor of the hotel in El Nefer, slept and watched alternately in the ante-chamber pending the arrival of the official guard from Cairo which had been telegraphed for.

These preliminary announcements roused a good deal of interest, but no one was prepared for what followed.

On the morning of the twenty-fifth of November every English and Egyptian paper contained under huge headlines the amazing news of the discovery of the tomb of the Queen of Sheba at El Nefer on the Upper Nile. The statement, quite a short one, sent to a press agency was signed by Professor Burnaby, and caused an outburst of feverish excitement to the public. Within a few hours a couple of aeroplanes had started from London for the scene of the discovery, containing special correspondents from the leading English papers, and an eminent travel agency had telegraphed to the proprietor of the Hotel Pinetem offering him a colossal rent for the lease of his hotel during the ensuing winter season.

A decided negative was returned to this, for already shoals of telegrams were arriving for Christopher Heaton, bespeaking rooms for intending visitors, and he preferred to reap all the profits himself, instead of sharing them with a tourist agency. And the whole world eagerly waited for the news which would convey the grounds of Professor Burnaby's amazing identification.

A few cautious journals refused to commit themselves, and

even hinted that the whole thing was a prodigious hoax, but with the arrival next day of further details, they, too, chartered an aeroplane and whirled their correspondents out to the scene.

Professor Burnaby's second telegram occupied two entire columns in the principal page of all the papers; everything else—politics, the state of Ireland, Carpentier's last fight, the railway strike, the cantankerousness of Germany—found place where it could; not another subject but this held the smallest attraction for anyone. . . .

In the outer chamber of the tomb, to which allusion has been made before, Professor Burnaby had found objects which adumbrated the great discovery, but he had been unwilling to publish any hint of these until the matter was placed beyond doubt. From the first the isolated position of the tomb indicated that it was the burial, not of an Egyptian, but of some foreigner; it faced south-east to begin with, instead of facing the Nile, and its marked severance from the rest of the cemetery which dated from the twenty-first dynasty pointed to the same conclusion. It was, moreover, clear that its occupant was a personage of the highest rank and importance, for a road had been cut along half a mile of limestone cliff, to lead to this sepulchre and nowhere else, for it stopped abruptly when the entrance to it was reached. Furthermore, on the slab which closed the tomb was found the official seal of the State necropolis, and this was only used on undoubtedly royal tombs.

A mass of broken and scattered objects strewed the floor of this first chamber. Many of them were of the twenty-first dynasty; there was a seated Sekhet statue (lion-headed), bearing the cartouche of Ranaka, daughter of Pi-netem; a bundle of ebony walking-sticks so fresh that they might have been made yesterday, with the cartouche of Heut-taui; a wooden chair with the cartouche of King Paseb-khanu, whose daughter (or possibly sister) was one of King Solomon's numerous wives; and boxes for the most part opened and overturned with scattered contents, which had been full of beads and ushapti figures of the same dynasty. So far it was possible, as far as these objects went, that the burial might have been of a royal Egyptian, but there were other objects which made that impossible.

There were vases and earthenware jars which were not of Egyptian origin at all, being exactly similar to those which were even now constantly brought into Assouan by caravans coming from the East, rough in workmanship, with the marks of fire on them, showing that they had been used for cooking utensils. By no possibility could they have been associated with an Egyptian burial.

Then quite early in his preliminary scrutiny Professor Burnaby had come across a sculptured slab, bearing on it in bas-relief a representation of a seven-branched candlestick similar to that shown on the arch of Titus in the Roman forum among the spoils from Jerusalem. On the same day he had disinterred, from the heap that lay in front of the entrance to the inner chamber, a box similar (though not so fine) to the one he had obtained for the British Museum. But it bore on its lid, inlaid in blue faience, a royal cartouche in which was the name Shep-ba.

This was so significant and suggestive, fraught with such wonderful possibilities, that it was with the greatest difficulty that he refrained from making it known at once to the world. But before doing that, he penetrated into the inner chamber. That, too, had unfortunately been entered by the pillagers, and the slab which formed the door had been chiselled through to make an entrance. But on it again was found, sadly obliterated, but just legible, the seal of the necropolis. Within all was confusion: objects not yet examined or identified bestrewed the floor, and close by the entrance was a mummy that had evidently been torn from its case, and partly unwound.

He continued the unwinding of it, and found it to be that of a woman. On the third finger of the right hand was a ring with an amethyst scarab set in it. On the face of it it bore a royal cartouche, and the hieroglyphic characters spelling 'Shep-ba, royal queen of the South lands.' There was no such queen in the whole genealogy of Egyptian monarchs, and the title Queen of the South lands could not apply to such.

Then came a short summary. Here was a royal tomb, certainly not Egyptian. In it were found vessels of Eastern manufacture, and a slab clearly bearing the bas-relief of the seven-branched candlestick in the temple of Solomon. In it was found a box bearing the cartouche of a queen Shep-ba, and the mummy of a woman wearing the ring of Shep-ba, queen of the South lands. Without doubt, when the Queen of Sheba visited Solomon, she passed through Egypt, which was then the highway from these lands of the South (as the sculpture on the famous terrace of Punt proved), and on her return, so it might be certainly conjectured, journeyed home by the same route as far as El Nefer.

Here, so these remains testified, she died, and was accorded burial with the splendour befitting a foreign queen. In the Egyptian manner there were interred with her her personal belongings, among which was the bas-relief of the candlestick in the temple of Solomon, and these funerary objects of the twenty-first dynasty.

In another part of his dispatch Professor Burnaby besought the public to have patience. Immediately after he had made this discovery in the tomb chamber, he had sealed it up again, and it would not be reopened until the contents of the outer chamber had been cleared. Assistants, skilled in the preservation and restoration of antiques brittle and friable with age, were already on the spot; they would suitably treat the more fragile objects before moving them. The more robust would be taken at once to the Hotel Pi-netem, where Mr Christopher Heaton had placed at his disposal a large empty upper room in the annexe, which had previously been occupied by himself and his wife, who were both intensely interested in the work.

The effect of the lucid and unemotional statement was stupendous. The demand for copies of the Old Testament was unprecedented; the boat-train for the cross-Channel service was duplicated and triplicated; all berths were engaged weeks ahead in steamers going to Port Said or Alexandria, for everyone who had meditated a winter in Egypt was agog to be off.

Daily the floods of telegrams poured in for accommodation of any sort and at any price, and before the middle of December the garden of the Hotel Pi-netem was covered with the tents of those who could not get into the hotel. Morning by morning the road up to the tomb was black with sightseers, through whom a lane had to be made for the bearers who carried objects to the upper room in the annexe. Round the mouth of the entrance a strong iron railing was erected, electric light was brought up to illuminate the toil of those who repaired and sorted out inside, and the horde of newspaper correspondents stood in queue all day outside the small telegraphic office in the village. Special steamers ran excursions from Luxor for those who could not find lodging here, and Professor Burnaby was surrounded by a guard of Egyptian police, who kept him from being mobbed and secured for him an entrance to the scene of his labours.

Sometimes a couple of days would pass without anything being taken out of the tomb, but the delay only whetted the appetites of the curious, and the corps of camera-bearers would wait from morn till night round the railing, ready with the volley of their quick-firing shutters on the emergence of any object whatever.

Meantime the excellences of the Hotel Pi-netem were making their due impression on the visitors. The commissariat was admirable, the tennis courts superb, and pleasant it was after a hot day on the white road that led to the tomb to wash off dust and fatigue in the swimming-bath. Indeed, tourists who had been accustomed to spend their winter months at Luxor or Assouan stayed on here long after their interest in the Queen of Sheba had evaporated; and Christopher Heaton had plans and an estimate made for the proposed new wing.

At length the day arrived for the re-opening of the tomb chamber, and the excitement, already steadily burning, leaped high in flame as the most entrancing personal objects belonging to the great Queen were extricated. It was conjectured that the robbers had carried off whatever was made of precious metal, for none such was discovered; but a thrill went through the world at the thought that certain articles of underwear (though sadly perished in the course of three thousand years) had been worn by the queen, that this glue of leather gloves had once covered her hands, and a small cylindrical article, conjectured to be a thimble, the tip of her finger. The coffin-case, the inscriptions on which were much obliterated, was in a thousand fragments, but Professor Burnaby, talking one night to Christopher, told him that he did not despair of reconstructing it.

Norah was present at this chat, and she saw her husband look across at her with a certain dismay in his eyes. A preoccupied air had also come over the Professor as he spoke of the coffin-case.

'I have already made out certain pieces of the hieroglyphics on it,' said he. 'It puzzles me greatly.'

Again Christopher's eye sought his wife.

'I did not know that anything was legible,' he said.

Professor Burnaby got up.

'In the state in which I found it it was not,' he said, 'but by applying a certain solution I have managed to bring out indications of the characters which were originally invisible. Well, goodnight; you will be up at the tomb tomorrow?'

As soon as he had gone Christopher turned to his wife.

'We've made a frightful mistake,' he said. 'I never thought the case could be restored, for I smashed it to atoms, nor that it would be possible to read a word of the inscription on it. It's probably Ptolemaic in date, just about seven hundred years too late.'

'What's to be done?' she asked.

'I can't conceive. But it has nothing to do with us; it's up to Burnaby. Supposing he deciphers enough to show that the coffin-case is of Greco-Roman date?'

'But it does concern us,' said she. 'If the whole thing is found to be a fake, all the future of the place will be gone.'

'And Burnaby's reputation,' said he. 'Not that I mind about that.'

He walked up and down the room, deep in thought.

'We must wait and see what happens,' he said. 'Burnaby is already anxious about it. Luckily he minds very much about his reputation.'

During the next few days it became clear that some very deep perplexity was troubling the Professor. He became morose and silent, had no news to give to the special correspondents, and it became a certainty in Christopher Heaton's mind that he was making the most disastrous discoveries about the date of the coffin. Christopher had a key of the iron gate that now closed the entrance to the tomb, and after prolonged thought he came to the conclusion that the wisest plan would be to go up there some night, when all was quiet, and destroy these incriminating fragments, or at any rate completely obliterate their damning inscription. With the approval of his wife he set out, three hours before dawn one night, with a bottle of strong corrosive acid in his pocket and the key of the tomb.

The clear darkness of a moonlight night was over everything, and, quite unobserved, he made his way to the sepulchre. But, peering in at the entrance, he saw to his amazement that a dim light shone out of the inner chamber. He noiselessly turned the key, and on tiptoe crossed the sandy floor of the ante-chamber, and looked in.

Professor Burnaby was sitting by the table on which he was

reconstructing the coffin-case, with a look of abject despair on his face. His eyes were fixed on a piece to which he had applied his reintegrating solution, and his mouth twitched with some nameless agony. A rustle of movement must have betrayed Christopher, for he looked up and saw him. He sprang up with a squeal that testified to his jangled nerves.

'Heaton?' he cried.

He sank down on the floor, a collapsed heap.

'Heaton, I'm ruined!' he said.

He remained there a few seconds, breathing heavily.

'What's to be done?' he said. 'This coffin-case . . . Ptolemaic . . . it's the woman in charge of the female slaves in the house of some overseer at Assiout . . . the corpse, too . . . I never liked the way the corpse was wrapped up. . . . But this settles it. . . .'

Christopher pored over the hieroglyphics, now terribly legible.

'Good Lord!' he said, completely forgetting himself. 'I never thought it could be read. I didn't know anything could restore it.'

Some faint surmise gleamed in Burnaby's eyes.

'What?' he whispered. 'You didn't know. . . . You didn't think?'

Christopher faced him.

'Never mind about that,' he said. 'I'm thinking about you. You're ruined, you know, if this comes out. I don't want it to come out, either. I want to have the Queen of Sheba's tomb without any mistake at El Nefer. . . . Look here! I suspected this, and I brought up a bottle of nitric acid. One application of it, and that inscription's gone.'

'No, you mustn't,' said Burnaby, without the least conviction.

Christopher drew the bottle from his pocket.

'But I must,' he said. 'You know that as well as I do. Give me your brush. . . . Are all the legible fragments here?'

For one moment only Burnaby wavered.

'Yes,' he said at length.

The paint fizzled and an acrid smoke went up.

'About the mummy,' said Burnaby, ten minutes later. . . .

He pointed out to Christopher the details of the way in which it was wrapped, which was unsatisfactory. A close examination by experts would certainly reveal these, and throw a fiery searchlight of scepticism on the whole affair. After that they sat down and talked till dawn.

* * *

The following week—for April was already here—the tomb was closed again till the resumption of work in the autumn, but Christopher and his wife remained at El Nefer to superintend the building of the new wing of the hotel.

Towards the end of May the world was startled by an appalling and sacrilegious outrage. Mr Christopher Heaton, making one of his constant visits to the tomb, was horrified to find that the great steel door, of a pattern recommended by the antiquity department of the Egyptian Government, had been forced, the tomb entered, and the body of the great Queen stolen. The most minute search was made throughout the district of El Nefer, every port was watched, no luggage of any considerable size was allowed to leave the country without being examined, but no trace whatever of the missing mummy was discovered.

Professor Burnaby, when interviewed, seemed quite staggered by the news.

But the next season proved one of remarkable prosperity for the augmented Hotel Pi-netem. Thousands of visitors flocked to see the tomb, though its occupant had been sacrilegiously removed, and followed the further progress of its clearing with the warmest interest. The hotel was so comfortable and well-appointed, with its excellent cuisine, its new ballroom, its swimming-bath, and *en-tout-cas* tennis courts, that its success was quite assured now that there was that thrilling expedition to be made to the tomb of the Queen of Sheba.

SARDONIC
STORIES

The Exposure of Pamela

PAMELA PROBYN was bowling along in her motor to the house of the great novelist with exultation in her heart and a fountain-pen in her hand. It was no wonder that she allowed herself a brief gloating review of the wonderful campaign which had been crowned with so signal a triumph, for many as were the social heights to which she had climbed (and on which now collectively she was seated) there was no peak of which the conquest had given her so heady a gratification as that of the aloof and hitherto unscalable cliff of intimacy with Alan Graham.

Pamela was by no means of the stale type of common climber whose ambitions are satisfied with having her hospitable table surrounded by marchionesses and fashionable folk. She was an intellectual aspirant, and what she desired with the full force of her unbridled passion was solid intimacy with people of real distinction, people with critical or creative power, or those who swayed the destinies of nations.

Mere conversation with even these was of little value in her eyes, except in so far as it paved the way to things of better worth. Naturally she wanted everybody else to know on what terms she was with them, for in spite of her steely efficiency she was but human, and it was pleasant to give large parties to the justly envious with a star of the first magnitude seated on either side of her whom she called by their Christian names. The goal of her indefatigable energies was real intimacy with the truly great, and she esteemed her acquisitions in the main in proportion to the difficulty of their attainment. If the capacity for taking infinite pains is the criterion of genius, there could be no question about her quality.

She had long turned aspiring eyes to this virgin summit, but it seemed almost impossible to get near it, far less ascend it. Alan Graham lived a completely sequestered life in Barton Square with a wife who entirely devoted herself to him, and among the hosts of Mrs Probyn's friends there was none who could suggest the most devious chain of introductions which might lead to acquaintanceship. The two could be seen in isolated distinction, he hawk-like and abstracted, she with the calm protective presence of a Madonna with a humorous mouth, taking a daily walk of an afternoon round the Serpentine; but, short of falling into the water in the hope of being rescued by Alan, poor Pamela did not see how to make use of that. Equally futile had been a couple of rhapsodies which she had written him faintly expressing the epoch-making nature of his rare publications, for these had merely called forth a short reply from Agnes, thanking her for her nice letter. . . .

Then fortune, ever ready to help the deserving, caused her to meet at Bath the sister of Mrs Graham, to whom she confided her ambitions. Lady Lorimer, who resembled a dissipated bird of Paradise, marvelled that anybody should want to know poor dear Agnes or her husband, but gave her the opportunity to meet her mother. She, after being richly and constantly fed, asked Pamela to tea on her birthday, which was the one annual occasion on which Alan visited her.

After that all was comparatively simple to such a Field Marshal as herself. She wrote to Alan telling him that this tea-party was the crowning moment of a happy life, for his books (as she had already informed him) were a religion to her; and to have met him. . . .

There was a wistful 'Nunc Dimittis' note about these opening sentences, silenced immediately afterwards by the hope that, instead of sighing her happy soul away, she could persuade him to dine ever so quietly one day next week. He refused, and she continued to ask him until, in obedience to the immutable law of attrition, he accepted. She had already divined that behind his genuine shyness and the carefully drawn curtains of his seclusion, there burned a fire of egoism which hungered for the fuel of flattery, and she procured a second-hand copy of *The Tyro*, and asked him to glorify the glorious by writing her name in it. It was a well-worn friend, she truthfully observed, and, when she had scratched off the library label it was impossible to tell who had worn it. . . .

That night, too, she tried the eminently successful experiment of calling him 'Master'.

She ran over her victorious course as, fingering her fountain-pen, she thought of the exquisite task which would presently engage it. . . . Very soon she had been bidden to dine with him and Agnes, and had been shown the sanctuary where he worked and learned the manner of his creative hours. Every word of these wonderful books was dictated to the devoted Agnes, while he walked up and down between window and fireplace holding in his hands the paper-knife which had once belonged to Flaubert. There was the table at which Agnes sat; there, too, the manuscript book into which she transcribed his utterances. Pamela was permitted to peep into that. . . .

These dictations took place every day after their walk ('by the Serpentine' interpolated Pamela) from tea-time till dinner-time, and usually for another hour after dinner; the Master's mornings were spent in solitary preparation. He sat there in his armchair (yes, that chair) and made notes for phrases or sentences which would be used in the process of the book, on little slips of paper.

When dictation began the table would be paved with these, and he pounced now on one and now on another, and embodied it. . . . By a very happy thought Pamela turned to Agnes, and spoke loud enough to ensure that Alan would hear her.

'Ah, you lucky, lucky woman!' she said. 'To think that you take down all the Master's thoughts as they come straight from him, while we, poor public, have to wait months and months till all the copying and recopying and revision is done. If you were not so wonderful yourself, and so worthy of it, I should be mad with jealousy of you.'

Thereupon it was promised her that she should be permitted next day to sit in the workroom while dictation was going on. She sat, ecstatic, gasping and purring as Alan walked up and down, stroking the Flaubert paper-knife, while the exquisite sentences were enunciated.

Sometimes a phrase did not satisfy him, and he said: 'Erase, please, dear.' Now and then he said: 'Read over, please, from the beginning of that paragraph.'

But best of all was it when he said, as the clock chimed the half-hour after seven: 'Just two sentences more. Perhaps, dear Agnes, Mrs Probyn would like——'

She bounded from her seat, so that whatever he was thinking she would like, it was clear that what she did like was to be amanuensis for the two sentences more.

'O Master, may I really write those two sentences for you?' she asked, in a voice trembling with emotion. But she had sufficient command of herself to prevent any trembling of the hand, and in her beautiful calligraphy, which made Agnes's look quite coarse by comparison, she indited the final words.

After that her attendances at these sessions were numerous, but she was not satisfied yet. It was delightful to tell everyone that she was late for dinner because she could not tear herself away from the Master's work-room, but she wanted more yet, and of course she got it.

Only this morning poor Agnes had slipped on a banana skin (a fruit for which Pamela had previously held no brief) and sprained her right thumb. An hour later Pamela was rung up and asked if she would be so wonderfully kind as to take her place in the evening's dictation and stop for dinner, and resume her labours afterwards. She was as a matter of fact engaged for a very mediocre kind of dinner, and of course was suddenly and urgently called away.

So now with joy in her heart and her fountain-pen in her hand she sped towards Barton Square, about to take part in those sacred dictations at which no one but Agnes had hitherto been present.

Agnes's sprained thumb proved an obstinate injury, and for the next week Pamela was a daily amanuensis. She made great capital out of it, and represented herself as waiting all day at the telephone in case she was wanted to take down Alan's dictation. She became aware, however, that her experiences did not quite provoke the thrill in others which she was conscious of herself.

Certainly Alan's early books—*The Tyro*, *Collisions*, and *Simpler Ways*—had produced a great sensation in their time, but it was now four years since he had published anything, and these books, for all their exquisite clarity of style, and their detached lucidity of imaginative vision, had become an inheritance rather than remained a living and palpitating reality.

But as she could confidently inform everyone, a new book of his, which had occupied his last three years, was on the point of appearance, and then there was this further work with which she was having the privilege to help him. She made herself his champion, and with her elbows on the table and her distinct, well-modulated voice audible to all, she rhapsodized to her numerous luncheon parties on the glory of him.

'He gave me the proof-sheets of *Ages Past*, the book that appears next month,' she said, 'and I read it straight through the night. I am glad to be alive when such a book appears. Marvellous as *The Tyro* was—how well I remember its publication, and how we all talked of nothing else!—it is not to be compared with *Ages Past*. You will all see when it comes out. And then there's this book which he is dictating to me now; he hasn't got a title for it yet, but I tell him that it must have no title. It must just appear.... You can't describe it; there is no word for it at all. It's just perfectly perfect, as I told him; the word "a novel" will take on a different signification when it is published. Finished— when will it be finished? Ah, who can tell that? Sometimes for a whole hour together there is not a pause. Gem after gem comes out, each flawless and luminous. Ah, there is the telephone! I must run and see whether it is a summons for me. Alan is like a child with the telephone; he calls it "invoking the wizard". Oh, wrong number! ... As I was saying the new book is magical. Of course, my lips are sealed about the plot——'

Mr Blewitt, the famous critic whose lifelong *métier* was to translate all that was unreadable in foreign languages into English, and, above all, to discover new stars in the literary heavens, was her guest today. Discovery was his forte; he had discovered Alan when *The Tyro* was published (and had even written a charming little sonnet to him beginning 'Spontaneous lark who quivering in dawn'), but he was almost as good at demolition, for there was not room on the top shelf for all his discoveries, and Alan had long ago been consigned to the dustbin.

'Dear lady,' he said, 'our revered old friend is fortunate to have such an evangelist. Well do I remember in the dark ages those graceful ephemeralities of his, which at the time roused our juvenile enthusiasm. But I almost regret to hear he is writing now. He had become to me, at least, a beautiful legendary figure ... It is rather as if some marble crusader got off his tomb, and began laying about him with an obsolete battle-axe.'

'Ah, wait till you read *Ages Past*,' cried Pamela.

'I will wait with the utmost patience. But unless I am greatly mistaken the name of Graham will soon fly from mouth to mouth again. We shall all have our noses buried in Graham.... At last there has come out of the agonized years of the Great War a monument worthy of it.'

For the moment Pamela thought that Mr Blewitt was referring to his own book of poems which had lately been published. A distaste for air-raids, and a passion for Devonshire cream, had led him to pass these years of agony in salubrious retirement at Torquay, where he agonized in comparative comfort, and emitted these lyrical interjections. . . . But he dispelled the impression.

'I have been privileged to see a little volume of stories which will appear in a week or two,' he continued, 'and without any hesitation I pronounce them to be a work of supreme genius. They are by a young man who was for four years in the trenches in France, and is the nephew, I believe, of the veteran we have been speaking of. His name is Timothy Graham. The stories have already been appearing in some magazine, and rarely though I look at such periodicals, I happened to see one of them, and recognized its superlative merits. I waited on the gifted young author, hat in hand, and was the humble instrument of getting them published.'

'Timothy Graham?' said Pamela. 'I seem to recollect. . . . Ah, yes, why, of course, he came into dinner at his uncle's the other night.'

'His stories, I presume,' said Blewitt, with singular acidity, 'did not form part of your intellectual treat.'

On her way back to dictation that afternoon, Pamela began putting up more social scaffolding. She had established her intimacy with Alan; she could produce him at little luncheon parties, and call him 'Alan' and 'Master' quite naturally; in fact, the goal was attained. But if Blewitt was right (and she had every reason to trust his shrewdness) about the superlative merit of Timothy Graham's book, above all, if, with him to aid and abet, it was likely to make Timothy talked about, it would be well to set to work on him.

Mr Blewitt's last remark on the subject might have warned her that it was delicate ground to venture on with Alan; but, with her, a ruthless trampling advance was a more favourite method of attainment than diplomacy or tact, and as they sat at tea before going to the workroom she made enquiries.

'And I hear that nice Mr Timothy whom I met here the other

night has written a book of stories,' she said. 'Have you seen any
of it, Master?'

Alan gave a shrill little laugh, and pointed to a magazine that
lay on the table.

'Oddly enough,' he said, 'Agnes and I had just been talking of
a story of poor Timothy's which appears in that periodical. It
will be the first, I imagine, in his book, for it is called "Cricket",
and his book is *Cricket and Other Stories.*'

'And what do you think about it, Master?' asked she.

'My dear Pamela, I do not think about it at all,' said Alan.
'There is nothing to think about. A crude, violent little tale; I
could not detect any evidence of style or literary perception.
Odd, is it not, that the short story, by far the most difficult
achievement in fiction, should be invariably attempted by the
inexperienced. A short story, I may say, is altogether beyond the
powers of a humble worker like myself. Even Flaubert could not
always succeed; the third story in *Trois Contes* is by no means
a masterpiece. Timothy is fortunate enough to have written
twelve. I think I am right, Agnes, in saying twelve? You have
read them all.'

The humorous Madonna laughed.

'Alan and I do not agree about Tim's stories,' she said. 'He
sent me the proof-sheets, and I was thrilled at them.'

'Ah, but I see the Master's point of view,' said the nimble
Pamela. 'He judges everything by the standard of perfection which
he demands of himself. Anything that falls short of that is a
crime against art.'

Alan made a deprecating gesture which yet accepted the
homage.

'Well, there is no use in the discussion of what to me does not
exist,' he said. 'Bristowe, my own publisher, has accepted Timothy's stories and thinks highly of them, and Agnes endorses
him. I therefore must take refuge in my ignorance. And now,
dear Pamela, if you will give me ten minutes to con over some
notes in my work-room, I shall be ready for your help.'

Agnes waited till the door had closed behind him.

'Alan is a good deal upset at my admiration of Tim's stories,'
she said. 'He is frightfully sensitive; he said just now that he
could not understand how I, who have been so closely associated with his work all these years, could see anything in Tim's

except crudity and want of style. But he is always rather on edge when a book of his own is just coming out.'

Pamela threw up her hands.

'Ah, that's the supreme artist all over,' she said. 'He is never content with perfection even; he aims at something transcending perfection.'

'Well, you're a godsend to us just now,' said Agnes. 'Your admiration for his work stimulates him immensely, and today, knowing my appreciation of Tim's stories, I don't think he could dictate to me; he would dry up altogether. But with you he puts out his best.'

'Ah, the joy!' cried Pamela.

'That's charming of you. But really my thumb is quite well now; tomorrow I must take my place again.'

Pamela paused a moment and became professional.

'I quite lost my heart to Mr Tim,' she said. 'I wonder if he would come and dine some night. Would you give me his address, dear Agnes?'

The two books were published on the same day towards the end of the week; this, too, was the day on which in the pages of the leading literary paper Mr Blewitt's column on books new and old made its weekly appearance. His influence as a critic was undeniable, and Agnes coming down to breakfast that morning made haste to open the paper, and ascertain whether he gave *Ages Past* a friendly launching.

It had not occurred to her as within the bounds of possibility that he would notice the short stories of a debutant author who according to Alan was so totally devoid of literary merit. There in its accustomed place was Blewitt's signed article, extending, as she saw at the first glance, to a couple of columns. Then there flitted across her eyes the name 'Mr Graham', and again and again 'Mr Graham'. Still, in this first impression, before she began consecutively to read, she hovered with growing pleasure on a word here and a phrase there: 'a masterpiece of subtle observation'; 'the firm, true touch which has long been absent from our literature . . . exquisite handling. . . .' Simultaneously she saw also near the beginning of the first column, 'a new star in the literary firmament,' and found herself wondering what the title, 'The Mantle of Elijah', signified.

Then in a blink of perception she grasped the whole. The entire article was devoted to Tim's book of stories. Elijah, symbolizing the inspired artist, let drop his mantle on to Tim's shoulders. Mr Blewitt unsealed his soul, and poured out a torrent of sparkling admiration. . . . Right at the end of this exultant rapture came a sundered paragraph.

'We believe that Mr Timothy Graham is a nephew of Mr Alan Graham, whose gracefully conceived tales have in their time diverted the lazy leisure of so many readers. By a pleasant coincidence, by the same post that brought us the first-fruits of Mr Timothy Graham's genius, we received a copy of a new book by the veteran author, appropriately entitled, *Ages Past*. The many admirers of Mr Alan Graham's industry will probably find here a volume much to their taste. For us who prefer the fresh savour of the full tide to the faint odours of a backwater. . . .'

There was Alan's step on the parquet outside, and he entered.

'Aha, dear Agnes,' he said. 'I see you remember that our good Blewitt— Yes, "The Mantle of Elijah" . . . Mr Graham.'

Agnes was conscious of a complete emotional blank as Alan gently shouldered her away from the paper, and watched him hovering on it much as she had done.

'I see,' he said. 'Not about *Ages Past,* is it? That little book of Timothy's . . . wretched rubbish. . . .'

He took the paper across to the window for greater illumination, and she waited through a long silence, making the tea and opening letters. Presently she heard behind her the rustle of the discarded paper, and he sat down at the table.

'That article will please you, dear,' he said. 'You thought highly, I remember, of Timothy's little tales. I cannot profess to say what you found in them. But that is your concern.'

Throughout the next week, morning and evening papers alike hailed the new-risen star, and let the other sink unregarded to its setting. *Ages Past* would be mentioned with briefness and tepidity among 'Novels of the Day', as a book likely or not (it did not matter which) to add to the reputation of the author, while *Cricket and Other Stories* evoked columns of signed articles. That inexplicable phenomenon 'a boom' took place, and a boom throws all else, good or bad, into shadow.

Alan, except for the one word that Blewitt's article would please Agnes, made no further allusion to it. Day after day he was busy with the dictation of his new book, with his slips spread over the table and Agnes installed there, but he made hardly any progress; the dictation of one day was mostly erased the next.

What chiefly stood in the way of his progress was the knowledge, intolerable to his egoistic sensitiveness, that Agnes, who was privileged to take down his work, had appreciative sympathy for the sensational rubbish which all the world was hailing as the creation of a master. There was this too, that for ten days he had dictated to the ecstatic Pamela, who purred and sighed with rapture at her task, and he missed the exclamations: 'Oh, Master, how perfectly perfect!' 'Oh, the wonder of it!' Yet he could hardly suggest that his wife should vacate the office she had held for all the years of their married life, and it was Agnes who, one evening when scarcely half a dozen sentences had been the outcome of a couple of hours' work, suggested what he could not.

'My dear, we're not getting on at all,' she said, as she rose at the conclusion of this nightmare session, 'and I have an idea as to why that is. You see, you have been dictating to Pamela; you associate her with this particular book. Can't we get her to come back, don't you think? It would be a tremendous treat to her, too. You know how enraptured she was at being allowed to take the dictation down.'

Pamela received the SOS with temperate enthusiasm. She had had a great disappointment over the reception of *Ages Past*, for there was nothing exciting or wonderful in being amanuensis for Alan, and spending precious evenings in the work-room, if the sole reward for her industry was that it should be known that she had been scribe for a book which might prove to fall as flat as *Ages Past* had done. It would be no social achievement to enjoy this literary intimacy with one who no longer 'counted'.

Already she had pounced on Timothy, and after several failures had induced him to come to dine on the following Sunday when she would display him to a very select and important group of friends, and she felt herself to be too busy a woman to continue spending her evenings over the taking down of interminable chapters which would not, when published, secure her the smallest distinction. But she was quite good-natured when she had time for it, and she promised to take her place again in the work-room on the next day. Immediately the book began to prosper.

'Aha, we've got on famously tonight,' he said, at the conclusion (he always included her in the achievement). 'We needn't, I think, dear Pamela, be ashamed of our output.'

'Marvellous, marvellous,' ejaculated she. 'Perfectly perfect, as I was telling Mr Blewitt the other day.'

Over Alan's face there passed a shade of grimness.

'Ah, poor Blewitt,' he said. 'We have not the felicity of arousing poor Blewitt's admiration. But perhaps we are none the worse for that. Blewitt seems to me to have lost all critical faculty. My nephew's stories, for instance. I do not know if you saw what poor Blewitt said about them.'

'Quite idiotic!' she said. 'But Master, more idiotic was what he said about *Ages Past*. Luckily you can afford to treat such blindness with the contempt it deserves.'

His face cleared again.

'Yes. I do not think we need mind much what poor Blewitt says,' he remarked.

Pamela had already rough-hewn in her mind a plan for escape from this unprofitable dictation, and she began to outline it.

'Oh, this delicious room,' she said. 'What hours of illumination I have passed here! But I mustn't be greedy, dear Master. Now that Agnes's hand is well, I mustn't altogether usurp her place. She's so wonderful that she would not let it appear by the smallest token that she felt her exclusion, but she would feel it terribly. . . .'

His face grew troubled.

'But, dear Pamela,' he said, 'must you not think of me as well? I find that with you as amanuensis, and your eager admiration of my poor work to stimulate me, I am, as today has proved, at my very best. These last days with Agnes have been an utter blank. It was at her suggestion, too, that you resumed your place here!'

Pamela's eyes lightened with appreciation.

'Ah, that is so like her,' she said. 'She would do just that, leaving her own feelings altogether out of the question. But I mustn't take advantage of her unselfishness. . . . No, Master, I have thought it all out. I will take it all on myself. You must tell her that it is I who have said that I cannot be here every day. Put the blame on me.'

It was settled so. Pamela was to be dictated to on alternate

days. As she went away, in a positive halo of altruism, she felt
that the thin end of her complete abdication had been successfully introduced.

But her abdication came in a manner totally unexpected. Sunday, the day on which Pamela had planned a very special dinner
party of eight in honour of Timothy, with a small evening party
to follow, was a holiday for Alan, and the dictation-book lay
unopened.

The day had been wet, and the two had not taken their usual
walk, but nightfall showed a clear moonlit sky, and after dinner
Alan suggested that they should stroll out for an hour. They
went up towards the park, and passing Pamela's house he proposed that they should look in on her in case she was at home.

This, in their intimacy, was nothing out of the common; her
servants were charged to admit Alan whenever he appeared. Tonight he and Agnes were not even informed that a party was in
progress (Pamela had not of course invited him to the glorifica-
tion of Timothy), for the footman supposed that they were the
earliest arrivals of the evening party. He accordingly threw open
the door of Pamela's drawing-room, but did not announce them,
for there was something in progress. . . .

The select party of eight were assembled in a semicircle at the
far end of the room. Timothy, the centre of them, was standing
with a book in his hand and reading aloud to them. It was with
great difficulty that the entreaties of Pamela and Blewitt had
induced him to give them the first story of his book, and it was
now drawing to an end. Pamela had vaguely heard behind her
the sound of the opening door, but whoever the earliest of the
evening party might be, nothing would have made her interrupt
Timothy by welcoming them.

Timothy read the last words and closed the book.

'Ah, wonderful, wonderful!' said Pamela. 'Thank you, dear
Mr Timothy! Perfectly perfect!'

She turned to see what the discreet entry had been. She saw.
She clearly remembered also to whom and of what she had last
used that phrase.

She disengaged herself from her circle, with her mind quite
made up to give Alan and Agnes a welcome precisely calculated
to get rid of them.

'Ah, how sweet of you to have dropped in on my party!' she

said, knowing that they knew she had not asked them. 'That is nice!'

Alan turned to his wife. The situation of finding Tim reading his works to Pamela's party had fully impressed itself.

'My dear, we have done a terribly awkward thing,' he said. 'Pamela has a party. . . . We must make our apologies and go.'

Pamela, who a few weeks ago was moving heaven and earth to get Alan to her house, would not have moved a little finger to keep him there. It would be very awkward to have the old lion present at the assembly in honour of the new one. She did not quite admit that to herself; she put it that her guest, Mr Blewitt, would not care to meet Alan after that article of his. . . .

The two walked silently home. Alan spoke as they entered.

'I think, dear, we might invoke the wizard tomorrow morning,' he said, 'and postpone. . . . The dictation, you know. We must not take up her time. . . . She is busy with other things.'

Miss Maria's Romance

THOUGH both the Misses Chermside might be described in stable parlance as 'aged', there was, perhaps, a difference of ten years between them. The elder one, Miss Jane, was of strong mind and feeble body; Miss Maria, the younger, was of a romantic turn and swarthy. Morally, Miss Jane was in the habit of sitting on Miss Maria; in effect, Miss Maria had been known to burst into tears at the moral weight of her sister, leave the room with the tread of a grenadier, and bang the door behind her with such force that the pictures trembled.

They lived in a charming old red-brick house in the city of Winchester, a house too large for their needs, but enabling them each to have a separate sitting-room, to say nothing of the joint drawing-room and a small dark cupboard domestically known as the study. Miss Jane was not much of a reader, and only one shelf of the handsome oak bookcase which stood between the windows of her sitting-room contained books. These consisted of the complete works of Charles Lever and a few volumes of the modern and preposterous English school. A galaxy of medicine bottles occupied the lowest shelf, and the other two were empty except for a box containing four and twenty mild cigarettes. Originally this had been a box of twenty-five, and its purchase was induced by a perusal of the preposterous novels referred to above. She had smoked the larger part of one, she had no immediate intention of smoking more. The twenty-four cigarettes and the row of medicine bottles were, in fact, the projections of Miss Jane's feebleness of body. The rest of the furniture was the product of her strong mind. She had a knee-hole table, with a stout, mannish, military desk on it, and by its side stood an ashtray in which she kept nibs, no less. Two or three sporting prints hung on the walls, and on a side table was a mounted hoof of a horse, which she had bought for one and ninepence in a pawnbroker's shop off the High Street. She ordered dinner, and wore brown shoes.

Miss Maria, the younger, wore ringlets and wrote poetry. Poems formed the staple of her small but well-assorted library. Her favourite authors were Longfellow, Mrs Hemans, and in her wilder moments, Lord Byron. The diction of Shelley she found obscure, and she considered Keats coarse. In confidence she would have intimated that she thought Shakespeare very coarse, for she sat in unbiased judgement on the socialist authors, and took none in hearsay. Not that Miss Maria would ever have uttered the word 'coarse', for her method of intimating it was to shut her lips very tightly, and take down from her shelves a volume of Maria Corelli, who to her mind ranked almost as a poet. She had an enormous admiration for what she considered powerful; she considered *The Sorrows of Satan* very powerful indeed.

For the most part Miss Jane and Miss Maria used to live together in the most sisterly harmony. Their breakfast hour was five minutes past eight, or, as Miss Jane said on one occasion, when Miss Maria had been left waiting, 'Call it a quarter past!' They passed an industrious, even an arduous, morning; for while Miss Jane was ordering lunch and dinner, washing up the breakfast service of Crown Derby, and truculently looking for snails in the garden, Maria retired to her room, and read simply masses of poetry, the greater part of which she transferred in a fine angular hand to a prodigious folio extract-book. Indeed, should the works of Longfellow, Mrs Hemans, and Lord Byron be ever lost to the world, the bulk of their masterpieces will be found by the delighted antiquarian in Miss Maria's extract-books.

An hour or two of such inspiring labour produced, as was natural, inspiration, and for some two hours before lunch (they lunched at a quarter past one) Miss Maria would write poetry. Years ago she had used a rhyming dictionary, but by now, it may be fairly stated, she was acquainted with all the suitable rhymes of all the words she was likely to employ. She was at the present time employed on a tragedy of the most surprising nature, which was to be complete in five acts. The names of the principal characters were Orlando and Amabel; they met in a grove. There were among the dramatis personae a perfect legion of shepherds, shepherdesses, executioners, armed mobs, nobles, foreigners in exile, and princes in disguise.

After lunch, Miss Jane went out on her bicycle, which she rode slowly but firmly. The bicycle had been the cause of the last great disagreement between the sisters, for Miss Maria held that a bicycle was a modern and detestable development, and that the great women of romance would never have ridden such things, even if they had been invented in their day. Miss Jane had retorted rather unkindly, saying she didn't care a pin's head (which was true) for the great women of romance. 'You and your tragedies!' she wound up. The door had slammed.

The country round Winchester is charmingly rural, and red-roofed villages nestle exactly as they should in green hollows of the swelling downs, but it is not designed for bicyclists of fifty years and feeble body. Thus in Miss Jane's excursions the chief ingredients were trudging up hills up which she could not otherwise force her bicycle, and trudging down hills down which her bicycle would otherwise force her. But as long as a bicycle remains the most modern development in the history of individual locomotion, there is no doubt that, however hilly the country, Miss Jane will continue to employ it. The disagreement between her and her sister she did not regard as a reason for its abandonment. She naturally supposed that it would pass, as other disagreements had passed, and to all appearances, it did so. But the danger of superficial judgements is proverbial, and whether it was that Miss Maria's reflections on the occasions of her fortieth birthday warned her that it was time that she too took a line, or whether the bicycle was the last straw, which did not break the camel's back, but rather led him to revolt against all the other straws, it happened, at any rate, that it gave Miss Maria an idea. Such ideas had occurred to her before (for she was romantically made), but as theory only; this one she should put into practice.

The Misses Chermside were not letter-ridden folk, and the handwritings of their few correspondents were reasonably well known to each other. Consequently, when on a certain morning, some three weeks after Miss Jane took to her bicycle, she saw on coming down to breakfast a letter laid by Miss Maria's plate, it was a matter of course that she glanced at the handwriting to see who the author was. It both puzzled and piqued her that she did not recognize it, and the first ruminating sip of coffee did not make matters clearer. To so sound and practical a brain this was very annoying, and Maria, who was very late that day (the ringlets had been exceptionally tiresome) got but a sour greeting.

'Good morning, Maria,' said Miss Jane, 'or rather, good after-noon. You may call this a quarter past eight, but it isn't. There is a letter for you; and whom is it from?'

Miss Maria took up the letter languidly, and examined the address; then she laid it down by her cup.

'Good morning, Jane,' she said. 'A little butter please.'

Jane flapped (there is no other word) some butter on to her outstretched plate.

'Whom is it from?' she repeated.

'I haven't read it yet,' remarked Miss Maria, just as if she did not know the hands of all her correspondents, but she cut the envelope with her knife, and took out the letter. Then she be-came abstracted (a habit abhorrent to her sister), and forgot to put sugar in her coffee; she sipped it, and with an absent hand scattered half the crystals into her saucer.

Now it was not Miss Jane's habit to ask twice, still less three times, so she merely emitted a gutteral interjection, which would probably be written 'faugh', and went on with her breakfast in silence.

Later, Miss Maria helped herself to some marmalade, tethered a roving eye, and read the letter through again. Then she thrust it hastily into her pocket, and began to chatter with vivacious incoherence about snails, bicycles, cold mutton, and poetry. To Jane this vivacity was a degree more contemptible than her ab-stracted silence, for her powerful mind had grasped the fact that Maria's letter contained something out of the common, and such devices were fitfully transparent. However, curiosity conquered pride, and when they rose from the table, Miss Jane said a snappish grace, and seized the envelope which was lying on the table. After examining it carefully, she transferred a gorgon gaze to Maria.

'I don't know the hand,' said this remarkable woman.

'I daresay you don't,' replied Maria, for the worm had turned.

Harmony being thus a little jarred, and Miss Jane being pos-sessed for the time being by that subjective phenomenon, which when it occurs in children is termed crossness, the two parted as soon as they left the dining-room. Miss Maria went straight to her room, and Miss Jane having ordered an ascetic dinner, marched with more than usual energy out into the garden where she collected snails with fanatic vindictiveness, sparing none, and spudded up plantains with the zeal of an Indian chief on a scalp-hunting expedition.

Now Miss Maria's sympathies, as has been remarked, were with the great women of romance, and beneath her ringlets in spite of her forty years, lay the shapes of surprising and marvellously coloured idylls in no abstract guise, but touching herself. Thin and tawdry little day-dreams would there appear to the alien eye, and he who should play hero to her heroine was builded of the same stuff as herself. He had a crooning tenor voice (croon was a beautiful word and rhymed obviously), an apollo curl to crown an intellectual forehead; he was slim and dark and Italian looking, but she did not think him insipid. They met for the first time in the street, and eyes flashed an answering fire. Miss Maria (so these dreams told her) beat a chaste retreat, and looked not back till she could naturally do so, as she opened the front door of the red-brick house, yet, oh! what pleasing sacrifice was this renunciation. Then glancing carelessly over her shoulder, she saw that the slim unknown had stopped and was looking, gazing rather, after her.

Next day, and the day after, they would again encounter each other, ever with the same confusion and fluttering of the heart. He sat opposite her in the cathedral, and his crooning tenor called echoes from the vaulted roof, and thrilled her through and through. He would ride a fidgety horse down the High Street, displaying the most consummate mastery of the unruly brute (she would make him give up that horse for her sake), and at the end they met most conveniently at dinner in the house of a minor canon. Here it transpired that his name was Percy Elphinstone, and that his great-uncle was a baronet. He asked leave to call, and leave was given him, and thus in the fullness of time, the rosy-faced children who lived in the cottages round the baronetical manor house, curtsied with grateful humility to Sir Percy and Lady Elphinstone.

Such were the main features of that visioned world in which Miss Maria passed so many happy hours, now so familiar to her that she regarded its sumptuousness with calmness. Embellishing details were always hot from the mint of her brain, but the broad outlines of the vision were invariable. Yet this morning, after the affair of the letter, it was with some excitement that she went to her room, and with a new sense of the beauty of that much admired piece that she read Mr Longfellow's 'Golden Legend'. For, indeed, her romantic weavings seemed extraordinarily real to her, and her heart went out with a feeling of akinship to the creatures of the poet's brain.

Now, it must be understood that Miss Jane's seeming impatience with her sister at breakfast sprang from no more vital or intimate emotion than curiosity. Hot and burning curiosity it is true, but no more than that. It was, therefore, no great concession when, an hour later, she saw Miss Maria drifting towards her across the lawn with a letter in her hand, that she was fully prepared to welcome her possible revelations in a sisterly and sympathetic spirit; she even at the moment spared a snail because it was so little a one.

'I have come to consult you, sister,' began Miss Maria, in some confusion, 'about a matter—about a matter in which I should wish, if possible, to be guided by your judgement and your longer'—(she could not deny herself this little thrust)—'your longer experience of life. This is the letter I received this morning.'

And, stepping back after giving Miss Jane the letter, Miss Maria, in her maidenly confusion, upset the basket of snails. But there are more poignant emotions than snail-catching, and greater issues than their destruction, and Miss Jane took the letter and let the snails lie.

She read it through and then again.

'Most extraordinary,' she said, still retaining it.

Maria bridled.

'Most extraordinary,' repeated Miss Jane, calmly oblivious of her sister's feelings.

Then for a moment she stood in silence, and her intensely practical mind reviewed the situation and grasped its issues. An unknown gentleman, Percy Elphinstone by name, had written to Maria in a neat, almost copperplate hand, asking her to grant him the favour of an interview that afternoon, or the next afternoon, or any afternoon, in the Cathedral close, opposite the west door. He might be known, he said, by his wearing a piece of heliotrope in his buttonhole, and he would be dressed in a grey frock coat and a top hat. His intentions were honourable, his heart was not his own, though otherwise disengaged, and he threw himself on his charmer's mercy.

A mind less remarkable than Miss Jane's might have failed before the magnitude of the situation, but she remained herself. For Maria's sake she was delighted, and then there was something about the heliotrope and the frock coat of Percy which fairly enslaved the imagination.

'Where is Percy's top hat and the heliotrope?' How the sentence tripped off the tongue!

Thus sentiment stated the case, and business answered. If all went well with Maria, Miss Jane would be much better off than she was now, for she would sell the house which belonged to her and buy a smaller and more economical habitation. That would leave her less fettered in many ways; she could get a second bicycle, though indeed the first had scarcely enough exercise, and if ever she purchased more cigarettes they should be gold tipped. She had often surmised that it was only their cheapness which was so indigestible.

She looked up at Maria. Her reflections had been almost instantaneous.

'You must go,' she said, 'you must certainly go.' Then, with an air of fine resignation—'It is better that I went with you. Though I am pressed for time today, I will go with you. We will go together this afternoon.'

'Thank you for being willing to give up so much of your time,' said Maria with a faint acid note in her tone, 'but I think that will be needless, sister. Percy—I mean Mr Elphinstone—might feel less able, more timid I should say, if he found two of us. But do you really think I had better go at all? It would be so dreadful for me, Jane, if he was not quite all that one would naturally expect from his note.'

'Most certainly you must go,' said Jane with decision, 'you are getting on in years, Maria, you are no longer quite young, and it is time that you began to think of settling down.' Then as curiosity rose like a torrent over her: 'But I think—I am sure I had better come with you.'

'I cannot consent to go on such terms,' said Maria with finality.

Miss Jane stood awhile in thought.

'It would be more regular,' she said at length, 'if I went first and got a good look at him. Then if he turns out to be the sort of man whom I could fancy for you, Maria, I would say you had a cold, or something of that kind, and ask him to tea. That would be the more prudent plan.'

'But I haven't got a cold, Jane, and I would drab you,' replied Maria. 'Also, it would look as if I distrusted him.'

'I don't know that you have any reason for trusting him as yet,' retorted Jane; 'he may be a mere adventurer.'

'Percy Elphinstone!' murmured Maria, as if the mere sound of the name were sufficient to banish suspicion.

Miss Jane was not unmoved.

'It certainly has an aristocratic ring,' she conceded. 'Most extraordinary!'

The third repetition of so uncomplimentary an ejaculation stiffened Miss Maria, and with starch in her tone:

'I shall go and see him, since you recommend it, Jane,' she said, 'but I shall go alone.'

Miss Jane was silent a moment, for she was an honest woman, and she wished to make clear to herself exactly how much of her anxiety to see Mr Percy Elphinstone, his hat and his heliotrope spray, from a sisterly desire to shield Maria from the wiles of possible adventurers, how much from pure curiosity, a defect in her nature, which she acknowledged to herself, though to no other. This analysis was complicated, but eventually honesty prevailed, and she yielded.

'If you bring him to tea, then, Maria,' she said, 'there will be a cup ready for him, and I shall be glad to see him.'

The snails for the most part had made good their escape during this conversation, but Miss Jane was at pains to collect only the least distant of the truants. Romance had stooped from heaven and touched them, a sudden flower had opened on the bloomless stem of their quiet cathedral-town lives, and though Miss Jane had no great opinion of men in general, it would be hard to say, though beyond doubt top hat and heliotrope written in a copperplate hand retained some subtle aroma even through the post.

She wondered whether if she too had gone in for ringlets, and had stood like a sentinel on duty, ever listening for the footfall of romance, and ever ready to salute it, she too might have had her Percy Elphinstone. Both she and her sister bore time's stigmata in corners of eyes, and fading hair, but to the casual observer she would have appeared at least no older than Maria. But Percy was evidently no casual observer; like the digger of an artesian well in a soil of uncompromising dryness, he had conjectured and struck that perennial fountain of romance, which irrigated and flushed with the green of youth, the imaginings of one whom a not unkind appraiser would call of middle-age. And she stifled a sigh of regret for the days when she too had been only forty years old, and thought to herself that she would go for an unusually long bicycle ride that afternoon, and perhaps even reduce the contents of her box of cigarettes to twenty-three.

Miss Maria was trysted for four o'clock opposite the west door of the cathedral, and, strange though it may appear, she set off in a state of greatly excited trepidation, for her romance was very real to her, and in spite of, or in consequence of her day-dreams, Percy Elphinstone seemed to her a quite possible contingency. Also she had a strong dramatic sense, and certainly at this moment she held the stage. The play might be Hamlet, with the title role omitted, but whatever it was, she was acting in it.

The day was brisk with autumn, and a bright sun made the air crisp and sparkling, and for half an hour or more, she walked to and fro about the close, now stopping to read a moss-grown epitaph, or watch the gathering of the swallows, but busy all the time with the thought of Percy Elphinstone. Indeed, had he suddenly appeared in the lime avenue, top hat, heliotrope and all, she would not have felt it to be strange. Since she had received the letter signed with that magic name, he had become more vividly corporeal, her own fiction was convincing, and had certainly all the strangeness of truth about it.

Meantime, like the poet, Miss Jane had passed through the town and out of the street, in something resembling a tumult of soul. The sun of romance had shone on the red-brick house, she was invigorated by his rays; snails, a bicycle, ordering dinner, and washing up a set of Crown Derby had hitherto been provender sufficient for her psychine needs, but now her capacity for spiritual adventure had suddenly been enlarged. Wider horizons were unfolded to her gaze, and life was really an affair that presented problems, that held the germ of the unexpected. She had never hitherto contemplated the existence of the unexpected, and the prospect was exhilarating. A new light was shed on the novels of Charles Lever; they described things that actually might happen to actual people. All this was illuminating.

She had left Winchester by Hyde Street, and the exaltation of her spirit was such that the milestones, so she phrased it to herself, literally flashed by her, and she was already four miles from the town before she knew where she was. Then taking a road across the river, she wheeled her machine up a hill on to the downs, and striking the Farnham Road, came back at a breezy pace by the golf links, and dismounted to walk down the steep hill leading into the lower end of Winchester. Once on the level again, she remounted, and rode with great caution up the broad street towards home.

Shops and lamp-posts and people were vivid to her eye; she noticed a hundred things she had never noticed before; the flash and exquisite whiteness of the river as it plunged out of the darkness of the mill, the graceful outlines of the trees already showing through their diminished foliage, the topaz of a retriever's eyes, and, lastly, as she neared the High Street hill, a new butcher's shop. The butcher himself, a young, good-looking man, was recommending a piece of loin to a customer. He held a chopper in one hand, and with the other he slapped the joint.

Now Miss Jane had been for years in two minds about adopting vegetarianism; the thought of dead sheep, especially if her mutton was a little underdone, sometimes caused her a strangling feeling in the throat-muscles, and this cheerful slapping of the meat sickened her. But before she looked away she caught sight of the name above the shop.

It was Elphinstone!

The world turned giddily round her. Who then was the slapper of the loin, the man with the chopper and the blouse, but Percy? Fresh from his tryst with Maria, he stood in the open shop, patent to every eye, and spoke of the price of mutton. Perhaps he had even killed that sheep with his red right hand—butchers did such things—and Miss Jane got off her bicycle, and walked by its side, for there was no more spirit left in her. Black anxiety was by her side, for the cheerful butcher was just such a one as might take Maria's eye, and no doubt he had not revealed to her that the hat and heliotrope were purchased with blood-money. He had a black moustache, and a fine open expression, and, even when employed on his dreadful business, his manner was engaging.

Miss Jane's great-uncle had been Mayor of Winchester, and

the pride of race was hers. Indeed, her stories beginning: 'My uncle, the late Mayor,' always commanded a respectful silence.

'My uncle the Mayor—my brother-in-law the butcher!' Oh, what a falling-off was there!

She let herself in by the garden gate and went straight to the drawing-room. Maria was there alone. Without preamble she plunged into the midst of things.

'My poor Maria,' she said, 'has Percy Elphinstone got a black moustache, and a cheerful manner?'

Maria was startled, but her romance glowed in yet more vivid colours. Was there then, after all, a real Percy Elphinstone? She was quite prepared for it. But why 'my *poor* Maria?'

'Yes,' she replied, 'his moustache is as black as the night.' Then, with a sudden gust of Mrs Hemans flooding her brain: 'And his manner is as bright as the day.'

Miss Jane bowed her head despairingly.

'Be a woman, Maria,' she said, 'and be brave; he is a butcher.'

'It is impossible,' said Maria faintly.

The interview was long and harrowing. Miss Jane advanced a phalanx of argument; vegetarianism, proper pride, *mésalliance*, my great-uncle the Mayor, all warred against the connection. And Miss Maria though fighting for romance, and torn by a hundred dramatic emotions, was in fact severely relieved. Eventual exposure, a thing, which even in the first blush of her romance, loomed ashily in the background, was no longer formidable.

What had passed between Miss Maria and Percy, her sister, in a spasm of unusual delicacy, forbade to ask; but towards the close of the painful scene Miss Maria promised with a gulp that she would never see Percy again. And at the end Miss Jane kissed her with peculiar tenderness, and said she was her own Maria.

Since then some years have passed, and Maria has had no practical romance. Time has brought a healing of the wound; and now if she speaks unkindly of the bicycle, her sister is not afraid of wounding her too deeply if she retorts with the butcher.

The Eavesdropper

ELIZABETH ALSTON was not really ill-pleased to have stepped backwards on to the lawn-tennis ball, and twisted her ankle the least bit in the world, for it gave her a valid excuse for resting it and herself, instead of carrying on with the strenuous exercise in which the rest of the party so indefatigably indulged. Between them and the duties of hostess she was feeling thoroughly tired, though not for anything would she have let that be known, for she was determined not to fall below the high level of vitality and animal spirits which were so natural to the others.

Indeed, it must have been a lucky providence that made her heel turn on the tennis ball, for it gave her a few hours' remission. She would not hear of anyone stopping at home to keep her company; besides she had an errand or two in the neighbouring town, and would drive over and transact her business without leaving her car. So presently they had trooped out again, her husband and Dinah Challis to play golf, the others to cut in and out of a tennis four.

Elizabeth did not at once set out on her errands; indeed, the errands had been an excuse, for all she wanted was to be quiet and alone. Perhaps she would have to think, but she hoped that she would find that there was, when she came to grips, nothing special to think about. But she was aware that she had to close with the enemy that troubled her before she could ascertain whether it was substantial or only a phantom of her imagination. Her own sitting-room was upstairs, and in order to save her foot she selected as her solitary arena her husband's room on the ground floor. At one end of it was a big alcoved window with a screen drawn half across it, and there she ensconced herself with a book, in case there was really nothing to think about.

Of course originally she was responsible, for in her widowhood she had first of all allowed herself to fall in love with Reggie Alston, who, just thirty years old, was fifteen years her junior. She had known that it was unwise, but it was so ineffably sweet to be in love again. And by degrees she had seen that this love of hers, impalpably surrounding him, was having its due effect on him.

He was already a friend of old standing, he had always liked her immensely, but now her love for him began to kindle their comradeship into something more fiery. It rejuvenated her, and thus blinded him to the length of that span of years which separated them. She was handsome, she was vigorous in mind and body. She deliberately stifled the voice of reason which told her unmistakably that though she was undoubtedly free to fall in love with him if she chose to make herself unhappy, she had no business to let him fall in love with her, and make him (not now, but presently) unhappy too.

Instinct, the claim of her womanhood, had silenced that nagging voice, and when he proposed to her she accepted him. She knew she was doing wrong, or at any rate, doing what was dangerous, but having gone so far, it was mere cowardice to consider dangers and safeties. Certainly she would be old while he was still in the full vigour of manhood, she would be ash to his fire, but that would not be yet, and the ultimate future was dim behind the sunshine of the present. She even told herself that she would be satisfied, when that time came, that she should be allowed to love him; she would ask so little, indeed she would ask nothing in return.

Her own love by then would be a serene and tranquil thing, and she would not be exacting. Her love would have mellowed into friendship, his affection, not ardent any more, but kindly and steadfast, would be enough for her. And if his flame in those far-off days burned for another, she would be wise and indulgent.

And had those far-off days arrived? she asked herself. And was she going to be wise and indulgent?

She could not answer this at present, for she told herself at this point, the enemy, phantom or real, with which she had to wrestle was, so to speak, ready for her.

Of course Reggie and Dinah Challis had always been great friends, but had the quality of their friendship altered? Dinah was married now; she had been married six months to Colonel Challis, who, as well as his wife, was staying in the house now. He was considerably older than her, and the marriage certainly did not seem to be a very happy one. There was no mistaking the quality of his affection for her; it was real enough, but it had mingled in it some dreadful propriety element. He was the owner, so to speak, of some unique piece of china from which all possible purloining figures must be kept at a distance. He alone might go near it and run his complacent fingers over its fine surface, and feast his eyes on its exquisite colouring.

There was something hectoring and bullying about him too; she must be not only his unique and cherished possession, but his most obedient servant. And Dinah, so it was easy to see, was not intended by nature to be either a piece of china or a slave. Elizabeth wondered why on earth she had married him. But women, she reflected, are the most incomprehensible of animals, and it was her business just now to fathom herself.

Of all the despicable emotions, to her mind jealousy was perhaps the meanest, and she saw that her hatred of it must arise from some intimate knowledge of it; she could not so dislike a thing of whose nature she was ignorant. Last night Dinah and Reggie had strolled about the garden after dinner, and she (she saw and judged herself) had sat playing piquet in the drawing-room window with Colonel Challis. They had sat like two green-eyed monsters, yawning and fatigued with their game, and everlastingly glancing out into the garden spying no less on their partners.

It was too degrading, and presently Elizabeth, seeing herself in the odious mirror of her companion, had revolted at her own image, and gone up to bed without waiting for the wanderers' return. But though she was sufficiently mistress of her limbs to make them carry her upstairs, and of her eyes to forbid them to look out of the window, she was not mistress of her mind, which continued its prowlings. And the food of jealousy was suspicion; suspicion that made it wax fat, and as for suspicion, everything fed suspicion. It drew its nutriment everywhere; it battened on a word or a glance, and if there was neither word nor glance to feed it, it battened on their absence. Those whom it watched were cautious, that was all, and their secret betrayed itself in their reserve.

And how natural it was that these two should seek in each other what their marriage did not give them. Youth, like jealousy or suspicion, must be fed; without its food it died of starvation; it ceased to be young and became old, for age was the ashes of youth that smouldered still but could not flame. And it was for his youth, so largely, that she had loved Reggie; now she was bitter against him for the very qualities for which she had loved him.

'All women ought to be painlessly put to death at the age of forty,' she said to herself; 'they torture themselves. They become like me, and I'm like Colonel Challis.'

There came the sound of a rattled door-handle, and she heard her husband's voice.

'They're all out, Di,' he said. 'Come in and have a talk.'

Then came Dinah's laugh.

'We ought to go down to the tennis-court,' she said.

'That's just why we won't.'

Elizabeth heard the door shut and the key turned.

'Oh, Reggie, why lock the door?' said Dinah.

'In order to be sure that no one will come in,' said he.

Again that bubble of laughter sounded. How young it was; it reminded Elizabeth of a spring brimming up among grasses and ferns. Reggie's voice, too, was of the same quality.

'Juggins!' she said. 'Why shouldn't everybody come in?'

'Well, I don't want them. Look here, about next week. You'll be in town, you say. So I shall come up for a couple of nights. That's settled.'

Elizabeth knew that on the moment of the opening of the door she should have come out and disclosed herself. Now it was too late, for Reggie had announced as settled an arrangement that he had told her nothing of. Now, too, in the evil ways of jealousy, she wanted to hear more. She was powerless in the grip of that desire—she had to hear more.

'Oh, my dear, what fun!' said Dinah. 'But what about Elizabeth?' She heard the creak of the sofa springs, and she imagined them sitting there side by side as clearly as if she had seen them.

'Good heaven! Can't I come up to town for a couple of nights without asking leave?' he said. 'If it comes to that, what about the Man of War?'

'And can't I come out to have dinner with a friend without asking leave?' she said.

There was a long silence, broken by the fizzing of a lighted match. 'It's all pretty rotten,' said Reggie.

'And that's such a helpful remark,' observed Dinah.

'Is it? I'm glad. It wasn't meant to be. It was meant to be a plain statement of the case.'

Elizabeth found herself noticing the small and insignificant details of her surroundings with extraordinary vividness. In the window just in front of her was a tortoiseshell butterfly flapping up and down the pane in the hopes of discovering some outlet through the glass into the sunshine outside. It was utterly in vain of course. The bright, lovely thing was completely imprisoned there—just as Reggie was completely imprisoned.

Beyond lay a stretch of grass, bounded on the far side by a thick yew hedge; over the top of it there appeared from time to time a high-lobbed tennis-ball. The others were therefore still engaged with their game, as if nothing was happening. Below these surface-perceptions was the real self, listening quite quietly to the development of a situation which, though it concerned her so vitally that it seemed as if her whole life was bound up in it, yet seemed strangely external to her. She listened as she would have listened to a play, immensely interested in what happened to other people.

Dinah laughed again. There was not that limpid enjoyment now in the sound of it. It was a bitter spring, not outwelling sweetly among ferns and grasses, but tinged at the tips with some acid corrosion.

'Yes, it's a plain statement of the case,' she said, and again there was silence.

Elizabeth wished they would get on quicker with their scene; it was as if they had forgotten their words. Suspense, from the dramatic point of view, was well enough, but it was too prolonged. She had to remind herself that it was no play she was listening to, but the real thing, unhampered by stage convention or the feelings of the audience. Then Reggie spoke, just one word, and no more.

'Dinah!' he said.

There was no pause now; she answered at once.

'No, my dear,' she said, 'you don't mean it. You mustn't let yourself mean it, nor must I.'

Round the corner of the yew hedge came the figure of Colonel Challis walking straight towards the house, and Elizabeth's surface perception, which noted the insignificant sights round her, and her real, utterly absorbed till now in what she was listening to, joined forces and observed him.

Her husband's room, where she sat, was used by the men as a smoking-room; what if he came for some such trivial purpose as getting a cigarette, and found it locked? If they did not open to him, but sat there quiet, what if he went round to the window and looked in? And if they did open to him, these two alone behind a locked door. . . .

She heard his step in the hall outside, and the moment afterwards came the rattle of the door-handle. Somehow the situation must be saved. She could not bear that he should find Dinah and Reggie there behind a locked door. Her pride revolted against the idea of her husband being found like that, not for his sake only, but for her own. It was a rank humiliation for the wife as well as for him. Above all, there was Dinah to be thought of, who had said, 'You don't mean it; you musn't let yourself mean it.'

But what was to be done?

And then, clear as crystal, came the solution. She must discover herself as eavesdropper; that could not be helped. But the much worse complication could be helped, and there was no time to lose. She stepped out of her alcove, and crossed the room to the door. Out of the corner of her eye, for she did not look at them, she could see Dinah and Reggie standing there, and again came the rattle at the door-handle.

She took the handle in one hand, the key in the other, and turning them both together, so as to make one sound of it, she threw the door open.

'Why, Colonel Challis,' she said, 'what a hideous noise! You can't get into a room without turning the handle, you know. Here are Dinah and Reggie and I. Reggie was just going to the tennis-court to see if somebody would come and have just one rubber before tea. So now we've got you, we shall keep you.'

She turned to her husband.

'Ring the bell, dear,' she said, 'and tell them to put out the card-table.'

James Sutherland, Ltd.

THE gentle art of Advertising, particularly when it takes that delicate and difficult form of Self-advertisement, is perhaps not one of the most respected or altruistic accomplishments, but it is certainly one of the most lucrative. The advantage of the whole system is that it hardly matters at all what a man advertises, so long as his advertisements are sufficiently large and persistent; if one advertised earwigs in a really masterly manner, they would soon be found to supply some nearly universal need. Earwig-farms—Sir John Lubbock tells us they are excellent mothers—would become fashionable, and would prove indispensable at mothers' meetings. They only need a gifted advertiser.

These unimpeachable platitudes may serve to introduce one of the most gifted self-advertisers of this or any other century or country, James Sutherland, that pinnacled composer of fiction, whose voluminous works, dealing as they do with the great facts of life, command so envied a sale. Nowhere else does the enterprising reader find so uncompromising a foe to earls, bishops, and people of fashion, nowhere else so well-equipped a champion of struggling and heaven-born geniuses, scullery-begotten poets, and, in fact, what he himself calls the great heart of the country. He constructs on the gigantic scale; heaven, earth, and the things under the earth, are grist to his insatiable mill, so that with so various a feast spread afresh about every six months, it is no wonder that myriads of guests besiege and clamour for dinner tickets.

Three and sixpence is the (really nominal) price of these volumes, for James Sutherland considers that publishers are sharks, and that to publish in six-shilling form is but to throw an extra half-crown to these devouring fish. Why he brought out an autobiography at a guinea is harder to explain; but no doubt Mrs Eddy, of the Christian Scientists, could tell us.

It is, however, idle to speak further of his works, which are far too well known to need any gratuitous advertisement of mine; all I wanted to point out was that even so great an artist as this owes, or rather owed, far more to his brilliant self-advertising gifts, than to his meteoric style and range of subject. It was he too who brought to perfection the supreme method of all, namely, to advertise himself by expressing on all occasions, particularly public ones, his horror of self-advertisement. The principle is the same as that of the poster which says in large capitals DON'T READ THIS.

It was in the year 1896 that I first met him, playing golf with phenomenal inability at Brighton, and I could scarcely believe that this ruiner of gutta-percha, so infirm of execution, could be the voluminous Sutherland. Dressed in shabby flannels, with an anguished face which would have done credit to one of his detested earls, he smote and he smote, and the ancient County of Sussex flew in fits in every direction. Every now and then, however, when his stroke was less ill-directed, the lines of anguish melted, and a perfect peace irradiated his intelligent features. 'I think I'm improving a little,' he would say.

The fact was, of course, that there were two James Sutherlands—one the professional writer, the other the private individual, totally distinct from his uncongenial twin. And never have I met so delightful a person.

He was then about forty, all fire and vigour and general incompetence, enthusiastic to bursting-point over a hundred pursuits, going on tiptoe into the garden bushes to catch sight of a piping robin, always sneezing or stumbling resonantly at the critical moment and frightening the bird away, choosing investments for his money out of the *Financial News*, and losing it even quicker than he made it (which is saying a great deal, since his was the pen of a ready writer), always keen, always with a rose-coloured world to gaze at and admire.

But James Sutherland the professional writer! Words fail me to portray that dismal and pompous personality.

'Yes, I have a mission,' he said to me once. 'I know I have a mission. Look at the sale of my books! And I have just heard from my publisher that 150,000 of my new books have been subscribed for. That means Influence, and Influence means Responsibility.'

And he heaved an awful sigh.

By this time I knew him well, and sat down to make myself unpleasant.

'I should like to know exactly what you imagine your mission to be,' I said, 'if your published works contain the spirit of it. You sent me one yesterday, *Modern Babylon*, your last, I think. Well, I read it, I read every bitter word of it. Now let us take for a moment the Duke of Hampshire out of that work. Does he seem to you like a real person of any sort whatever, Duke or otherwise? Did you ever see or hear of a person like that? For myself I do not believe that any one drinks Chartreuse for breakfast, a table beverage it appears, or lights his cigarette with a banknote. That's not even original, it comes in Ouida, I think.'

'You don't understand,' said the professional James Sutherland. 'The lesson is this. I believe that the aristocracy of England is in a very bad way: it is loose in morals, extravagant, idle, vicious. I have to convey that to the masses. Perhaps one exaggerates; but the art of writing fiction, so I take it, is like that of the scenepainter. It has to be laid on thickly, boldly, in strong lights and deep shadows.'

'Another prominent character,' said I, dragging him back, so to speak, to his own work, 'is that of Enid, the gamekeeper's daughter. (By the way, the air is never really darkened at a *battue*.) She has eyes like Athene. Now is Enid with the eyes of Athene really characteristic of the gamekeeper's daughter? She says "Methinks". Why? She talks in hendecasyllables. She is waylaid by the Duke of Hampshire at the Achilles statue in Hyde Park, and is rescued by a banker's clerk with Apolline curls. Now what does it all mean?'

'Not Apolline curls,' said the real James Sutherland, peeping out for a moment as quick as a lizard. I hailed him with rapture, but the pompous twin had already whisked him back into the crevice.

'Yes, Apolline curls,' I said. 'Now when you are yourself you don't think about Apolline curls; you think about robins and golf balls, and children, and your dinner, like a proper man.'

'But I have also my work to do,' said he; 'and if I have not a message, why do my books sell so? People want them.'

'People want gin and other things as well,' said I; 'they want all sorts of things that are harmful, and all sorts of things that are nasty and stupid. But the gin-distillers, if one went to talk to them, would not make one sick with talking about their message or their mission. They would say, like honest men, "There is a demand for gin, which we propose to supply." They also advertise their wares; they know that advertisements mean sales. So do you.'

'My dear fellow,' he said, 'how can you be so unfair? I abhor self-advertising; I always set my face against it. If you knew the number of interviewers I refuse to see——'

'And the number of times you let it be known that you refuse to see them,' said I.

Again for a moment the real man peeped out.

'By God,' he said. Then the professional added, 'It is part of my system to let it be known that I strongly object to interviewers and advertisers.'

This was said with a certain dignity, so that I wondered afresh at the strange duality of the man. But almost without a pause he took up a formal-looking piece of foolscap and handed it me.

'I should like to know what you think of that scheme,' he said.

The scheme was one of the most extraordinary I have ever read.

It was the draft of the prospectus to turn James Sutherland, author, into a Limited Company. In other words, he was to sell his output of fiction to the company for a fixed annual income of £3,000 in addition to a thousand shares in himself. The company—I saw that his publisher, the editor of a well-known weekly, and the head of a thriving house in the City, were among his directors—would own, publish, sell, and reap the profits of all the fiction he produced, in which beyond his thousand shares he would have no interest.

Two stipulations only were made: one was that he should not part with the thousand shares he held in the company. This was reasonable, since it safeguarded the company against his laying down his pen and saying that he would write no more, for in that case his thousand shares would yield no dividend. The other was that he should embark on no other profession.

'I never heard of anything so extraordinary,' I said, 'and your directors are good people.'

'It seems to be sound,' said he, 'but I can make the advantage of it plainer to you. I earn on an average about £4,000 a year, but

I have to earn it, and I often feel that I want a holiday and can't take it. Well, under this scheme £3,000 a year is secured to me, and I feel sure that if I worked less my work would be better, and that I desire. Now here comes the psychological point. I am weak, and though I know my work would be better, I cannot stop. A firm writes to me and makes an offer. Well, I am in the mill, and I have to say "yes". I can't bring myself to say "no", and so I go grinding on, year in, year out, with scarcely a month's holiday in the year. Now under this scheme that temptation will be removed. I like my work far too well to be idle: I shall certainly not be that, but I shall have no monetary interest at stake, except the dividends from my thousand shares. That will be a great relief; my art,' he added with hideous pomposity, 'will be exercised solely for art's sake.'

He got up, and the real man, who had been peeping out at intervals during this speech, showed himself. 'I shall really try to do something decent,' he said; 'I shall study more, and, oh Lord, I shall have a cottage in the country, and keep pigs. I adore pigs.'

Then we went further into the figures. The company was a very small one, consisting indeed of only 20,000 shares of £1. Of these 5,000 were to be 4 per cent debentures, the rest ordinary shares.

Now at present James Sutherland earned £4,000 a year, and his publishers, according to the prospectus, earned as much more out of his works. Thus his present dividends amounted to about £8,000 a year, of which under the scheme £5,000 would be available for shareholders, after his assured income of £3,000 was paid. Without working expenses that would yield a profit of 25 per cent, of which, however, the 5,000 debenture shares absorbed only 5 per cent, leaving an extra 20 per cent on 5,000 shares for distribution among the ordinary shareholders. Then comes the question of working expenses, which, so the directors said, must be largely discounted against the increased prices they felt certain of getting for Mr Sutherland's work in America and the colonies, prices which he, as an artist and a gentleman, had been unable to ask, but which they, as businessmen, felt confident of obtaining. Furthermore, the estimate of profits given above were those which at present were made after all publisher's expenses were paid, and though the new company would have to spend a certain amount in initial ways, yet there was no development work, so to speak, to be done. The market already existed.

A private letter also from one of the directors told James Sutherland that they were confident of getting far more for his work, which would give a substantial value to his thousand shares. That, however, was their affair, a trade secret. Meantime, if Mr Sutherland saw his way to accepting their offer, the company would be immediately formed.

Within a very short time this was done, and the prospectus issued. The success of it was immediate. Applications for more than ten times the number of shares issued were received by the directors, and James Sutherland Limited began at once to be an active share on the Stock Exchange. The novelty of gambling in that which did not yet exist at all, i.e. James Sutherland's output for 1899 for instance, resident at present, if anywhere, in the beef and mutton he should eat in a year's time, was irresistible to the merry bears and bulls. The favourable reception of the prospectus had sent the shares up to nearly four, and then, before even the allotments were made, a sudden bear-raid was formed against it.

Private rumour was busy; it was believed in well-informed quarters that the subscription for Sutherland's new book, which had been acquired by the company, was a great disappointment; further, that it was altogether in a new style, a sober and un-hysterical, some said historical, work, and the reckless bears sold and sold. The shares, which had been dealt in on Monday at $3\frac{7}{8} - 4$, sunk in the course of a day or two to par, and by the end of the week were no better than $\frac{13}{16} - \frac{15}{16}$.

Now I was in the enviable position of being in the inner ring, for Sutherland had shown me his new book in proof, and he had also told me that there was a subscription of 150,000. I knew therefore that there was no truth in the bear-report that it was written in a new style: it was, on the contrary, quite in the old style: it teemed with sinister earls and Apolline bank-clerks, and was quite up to form. So, though I had not applied for shares in the first instance I now bought. But, for the time at any rate, the bears had it their own way, and the shares sunk still further. Then some began climbing in again, and the price went slowly up to about 2, where it hung, waiting for 6 November, on which day the new book was to be published.

As I have mentioned, the copyright of it, as well as that of all his previous works, had been acquired by the company, this giving them an appreciable asset. On the other hand, no one—except the directors—yet knew what price had been paid for it, and on this subject the market was divided. Some operators knew—so they said—that the price was a very heavy one, but against that one had to set the fact that the publisher was on the board of the new company. A reason for his being reasonable. In fact there was every opportunity for wide diversity of opinion.

But as the day of publication got very near—in accordance with James Sutherland's usual custom, no copies had been sent out for review—a perfect fever of excitement raged over J. S.'s as the Stock Exchange called them, and the price played up and down like the temperature of a typhoid patient. Here one was told for certain that the bears had immensely over-sold, and would, without doubt, be cornered, that there were heaps of shares in the market, and that the directors had already taken advantage of the rise, parted with their shares, and were now on the bear-tack themselves.

In fact, that which had begun as a sort of game, not as serious speculation, was speedily assuming somewhat grave proportions. I personally held a couple of hundred shares which I did not intend to part with just yet, but I did not buy more, since it was rank gambling to touch a market which was in so feverish a condition.

Then came the morning of publication, and as the early trains from the suburbs arrived, you might have observed the strange spectacle of thousands of City men hurrying along the platforms, each with a copy of *Aspasia* under his arm, some gleeful, some with faces of agonized woe. The directors had kept their secret well, and none knew what the book was like until on the morning of the 6th it was liberally stacked at all suburban stations for the benefit and enlightenment of City operators, bull and bear alike.

This excellent stroke of business was supremely successful: the City operators flew at it like swarming bees, and clamoured for copies. This in itself was a bull-point. Some thousands of copies, in addition to the subscriptions, were thus disposed of, while the affrighted bear on opening it was further confronted by a slip, saying that James Sutherland had completely recovered from his recent indisposition, and was hard at work again. Then to finish him off there was the perusal of the work itself: it teemed with wicked earls and noble housemaids, it was the essence and quintessence of the Sutherland whom the 'great heart of the people' so adored.

Indeed, it was a black day for bears, and they came tumbling in head over heels, while the price of J. S.s rose with the speed and effulgence of the midsummer sun. Violent fluctuations occurred during the day: at 12.30 for instance they stood at 8, then a reaction followed on realization, and they dropped to 6, rallied again, became buoyant on the number of the subscriptions (163,000) being made known, and closed very firm at $8\frac{3}{8} - \frac{5}{8}$. There was also some bidding in the street.

I, however, did not wait for this, and having sold at a fraction over 9, went home in order to dress and dine with James Sutherland. Him I found in a state of high febrile excitement.

'Why, I feel sea-sick,' he cried, 'just sea-sick. It's I who have been tossed in a blanket all day in the City. Shied to the ceiling, banged on the floor: I haven't known where I was for two minutes together. Total strangers came into the club and talked about me to my face: they said I was buoyant or drooping or a wild cat. I have never been called such names. And I can't sell the thousand shares I have in it. Man, it's pitiful! The shares are mine and it is me, and not a penny can I touch. But if I re-act I shall buy. What do you think of me?'

Then matters calmed down a little: the prices were put up to 10 for a day or two, just to give belated bears a lesson, and they crawled painfully in. To do the directors justice they had neither desired nor devised the extraordinary gamble which I have described, but finding it made for them, they took full advantage of it, and made a handsome profit. Then they turned to business again.

Now, the subscription list for *Aspasia* was, as I have said, 163,000 copies, and within three weeks' time upwards of 200,000 were sold. This far exceeded any previous sale of James Sutherland's works; and it was due, I think, to two causes, partly the excitement over the company, which induced people who never read a book of his to buy this one, in order to see what it was which had caused so great a commotion in the City. Also a sort of crusade in the Press helped the sale very much, for many earnest and thoughtful leader-writers felt themselves obliged to deprecate, in the sacred name of Art, a proceeding so derogatory to the interests of Literature.

But as they most of them wound up by saying that James Sutherland's works bore no relation to literature, they seemed to me to knock the bottom out of their own arguments. But they did not appear to mind this, and their solemn protests certainly stimulated interest.

The company also had great advantages in its directorship; for Sutherland's publisher was on the board, and he, like a wise man, saw a great opportunity for himself, as a large holder, of making a considerable sum of money. Having a publisher's business already in existence, with all its machinery of travellers and advertising, it was worth his while to conduct the publishing part of the business very cheaply. His agents, whom he was bound to have, did the business as part of their work, and the company did not have to pay that important middleman, the publisher, except as director.

Similarly, the editor of the *Friday Weekly*, who was also on the board, earned the thanks of proprietors by securing the serial rights of James Sutherland's next novel (he had hitherto always refused to appear in sections), and £1,200 had been paid for it. Thus when the balance-sheet for the first six months was brought out it read very pleasantly and as follows:

Debit	£	*s.*	*d.*
Salary of three directors for half year	600	0	0
To James Sutherland, Esq., for half year	1500	0	0
Rent of office	150	0	0
To Antrim & Co. for copyright of James Sutherland's previous works 2,000 f.p. Shares	2000	0	0
	4250	0	0

Credit	£	*s.*	*d.*
By profit on *Aspasia* at 1s. 2d. per copy (200,000)	11666	13	4
By serial rights of new work	1200	0	0
	13866	13	4

This left a very handsome balance of £9,686 13s. 4d., and the directors felt justified in recommending an interim dividend of 7s. 6d. per share. They also had great pleasure in stating that Mr Sutherland's next book would appear on 1 June. The subscription list had already been issued, and was meeting with a gratifying reception. There would be also in the next statement of accounts considerable profit on the sale of Mr Sutherland's previous works.

I saw James Sutherland a few days after this, and found him tearing his hair.

'They can pay,' he exclaimed wildly, 'the income of their directors, me, the rent of an office, and yet in a half-year earn nearly £20,000 profit! It is maddening, I tell you. Why couldn't I do it?'

I tried to point out to him that he was not a board of directors with the business capabilities of a publisher, an editor, and a City man, but only a soulful artist. But he refused comfort, and uttered ominous words.

'I'll cut down their profits,' he said.

'Then you'll cut down your own too.'

He sighed.

'I know, that's the worst of it,' he said. 'But even if they declare a 12s. 6d. dividend at the end of the year, I shall only get £4,000 altogether. I did that before without any of the City skylarking. Where do I come in? Of course, it's a great relief to feel there is no incessant need of grinding. And somehow, somehow—I think less ponderously about my mission than I used.'

'You mustn't do that now,' I said. 'You must remember that your own mistaken conviction about yourself is probably partly responsible for the public's mistaken conviction about you. Anyhow, I see you have been interviewed by three papers about this new book, and you seem to have taken yourself pretty seriously.'

He appeared rather disturbed.

'I know. These directors make a great mistake,' he said. 'If they would only listen to me, I could show them how much more paying it is to refuse to be interviewed. The public will get tired of me if they hear too much about me, and where shall we all be then?' he asked with enchanting naïvety. 'By the way,' he added, 'one of the interviewers was from the *Weekly Advertiser*. He was a man I had been to school with, always rather a smart fellow, married now and with three children. He had invested all he had in J. S., he told me.'

'What did he buy at?' I asked.

'Rather over eight. What are they now?'

'Six and a half, and rather weak.'

'Well, the new book will send them skying again,' he said, 'but I don't like feeling that Pearce's money, he with his wife and children, is dependent on me. It makes a sort of responsibility which I had not contemplated.'

'Not as long as you work properly,' said I.

'I don't like it,' he repeated. 'And there's another thing too. It's just this—I've been reading a bit lately, Thackeray and that sort of Johnnie, and I'm afraid, do you know, I'm really afraid that I write most awful rot. Somehow it never struck me before.'

This was more alarming for the company.

'Well, you've got to choose,' said I. 'Your feeling of responsibility for Pearce isn't compatible with your desire for writing what is not—well, as you said yourself, awful rot. Pearce will be all right if you continue writing awful rot. But if you go in for High Art, the Lord help poor Pearce!'

He continued his uneasy walk up and down the room, and I knew there was something more to come. At last it came.

'That's not the worst,' he said. 'I'm engaged to be married.'

Personally I never heard so depressing a mode of announcing this desirable condition, but commercially I saw a chance for Pearce. Next moment it was shattered.

'What is so dreadful is that—that, well, she likes me for myself, you know,' he said. 'She hates my books, she thinks them unreadable twaddle—her exact phrase—and, well, there it is anyhow.'

'Who is she?' I asked.

'Lady Helen Ascot,' said he.

Here then on the whole was one of the completest muddles I had ever the privilege to encounter. All his life poor James had devoted himself to the scarification of wicked earls; he was now engaged to the daughter of a real foe, and, so it was supposed, a wicked one. All his life too he had been singularly free from outside responsibilities; now, here was this company which drew its dividends direct from his brain, and paid them to people like Pearce. Add to this that Pearce depended on James Sutherland's rancid denunciations of the class to which his future wife belonged, who in her turn thought them unreadable twaddle (her exact words).

Her father, I may add, was Lord St Leger, a heaven-sent title, as I had always felt, for one of James Sutherland's works.

A few days after this it so happened that I was in our office in the City, neither of the senior partners being then in London, when a card was brought in, bearing Lord St Leger's name. He had before now dealt with our house, as a seller more often than a buyer of stock. A moment after he entered.

'I lately bought,' said he, 'some shares in James Sutherland Limited, and having some money to invest again I thought of adding to my holding. What is your opinion of it?'

Now he could not have asked me a more difficult question. Without inside information, that is to say without the announcement that James Sutherland had made to me the other day, that he was disposed to follow after Thackeray, I should have had no hesitation in recommending it. But supposing that James' conviction that all his writings were 'rot' was deep-seated, then the J. S. Limited had but a depressing outlook. Yet if this conviction was only transitory, if, with the added necessity of working to support his wife, he continued to write rot, standing, as it did now, low, with the prospect of a large rise in price on 1 June, when the new book appeared——

'I bought some for myself three days ago at 6,' I said, 'and I have no intention of selling them yet. You can get them now at $5\frac{1}{2}$. It is of course a speculation; it depends on one life, and on Mr Sutherland's continued popularity with the public.'

He thought a moment.

'Please buy me 200 shares,' he said, then paused again. 'I have a special interest in the material supplied by the company,' he added.

After his departure I sat down and reflected on the sinister dealings of Providence.

Here on the one side was James Sutherland confiding in me that he wanted to try to write like Thackeray; on the other his future father-in-law, investing his money, subject to my advice, on the chance, for that is what it came to, of his doing nothing of the kind. Then again there was poor Pearce on the side of the wicked earl, and Lady Helen ranged with Thackeray.

A month passed, and the new book was on the verge of publication. Again the market turned to the question of J. S. with an added zest, as to some revived game, for Consols and Home Rails and other heavy affairs had been to the fore for the last month or two. Again people at street corners had special information, and knew the book was doomed to failure; others, equally well informed, knew precisely the opposite.

This time the directors had tried a new policy, hazardous, but, if successful, likely to be extremely so. No discount of any sort or kind was to be given anybody; libraries, bookstalls and private purchasers alike would buy it at six shillings cash, and at no other price. This implied, of course, a solid confidence in the real demand for the book, but it was hazardous, since no library would take it on such terms. For instead of its being sold to the trade at three and sixpence or thereabouts, it would be sold, right through, at six shillings. Nor was boycotting of other goods possible, since the James Sutherland Company had no other goods.

But it was an anxious moment for the directors, since booksellers would naturally not deal in goods on which they received no profits. Some indeed supplied the book at seven shillings, but for the most part all orders were sent to the publishers, straight from the actual purchasers. And indignation found vent in meetings among the trade, the directors held their peace, and shareholders looked forward to the new balance sheet with hope and fear in about equal proportions.

But this hazardous policy was, as the event proved, abundantly justified. The sales of *High Places* exceeded even those of *Aspasia*, while each copy sold brought to the fortunate shareholders some half-crown extra. A meeting was held and everybody expressed the utmost obligation to and confidence in everybody else. A round-robin was even sent to James Sutherland, setting forth the immense approbation with which the proprietors contemplated their property. But the property, instead of returning a suitable reply, did not answer the letter at all. It was better employed with its well-beloved.

The marriage took place at the end of July, and for a couple of months I saw no more of James Sutherland, nor did the market particularly concern itself with the company. The first year's trading had been enormously successful, and it was judged imprudent to conduct blind banging attacks against an affair of so great stability. Naturally enough, the price was just a little lower in consequence of the decreased output which would temporarily follow James Sutherland's marriage; on the other hand, however, it was argued that so emotional a crisis in his life could not fail to produce a corresponding vividness and intensity in his works.

Then later in September they returned home, and staying with this divinely happy couple—the professional James Sutherland was not of the party—I had one night, after Lady Helen had retired, a long talk with her husband.

'And so now I suppose,' I said, 'you will set to work again for the good of the company.'

'Set to work?' said he. 'My good man, I've been working like a horse all this last month. In fact the next book is nearly ready. I sent it down to the office only today. I should have liked to show it you, but it had to go. I think—I think it will be rather a surprise. It is to be published on 6 November; that's a lucky day for me, and it's Helen's birthday.'

A sudden indescribable misgiving seized me.

'Why a surprise?' I asked.

'Because it is not the sort of book which the public associates with me,' he said.

'Poor Pearce!'

'I don't think so. Rich Pearce, I hope. Helen likes it a good deal.'

'What about the mission then?'

'I mistook it. It can be no one's mission to rave in public places as I have been doing. Rave, I tell you. But the mission is there all the same. I wonder if you remember telling me that I was a dual personality, or something of that sort—one side being occupied with rancid, I think you said rancid, imaginings, the other with proper straightforward humanities? Well, it was the other side that wrote this book. You see it has been living well lately; it fell in love very happily. That made it grow. And the rancid imaginings—I forget what happened to them—I think I left them behind somewhere.'

'For the sake of Pearce, send for them,' I entreated. He shook his head.

'I never saw any one so inconsistent,' he said. 'While they flourished you abused them, now they are dead you wish that they flourished.'

'Yes, for the sake of the company,' I cried. 'Oh, the thing is more complicated than you know. You have ceased to be the artistic and reposeful being, you have made yourself the driving power of a machinery. There is an office where intelligent men scheme how to make you more remunerative: you inspire the nightmares and the midnight dreamings of the innocent broker: widows and orphans put their savings into you—they have bought allotments in your brain. Other people have bought—your father-in-law bought quite a large estate there the other day. Secret cells of your brain belong to him by right of purchase. Be honest, give him a return for his money, or he will come down to my office again. Just think; because you want to write like Thackeray, which you will never, never do, you turn these confiding gentry into the street, so to speak. Pearce, perhaps, at present blesses you: his infant children will curse you in their cradles.'

He lay back in his chair, and laughed aloud.

'Wait till 6 November,' said he.

The publication of *Seed Time and Harvest* is still a recent event, and no one will forget for some time to come the effect of its appearance, how the public seemed to drop all it was doing, and concentrate itself on that wonderful tale. For after all, just as there will always be a universal demand for wholesome food to feed the body, so, to the credit of the human race be it said, there will always be a universal demand for wholesome food to feed the mind. No one ever denied that James Sutherland was a vigorous writer, and *Seed Time and Harvest* seems to me the most vigorously written of all his books.

Only here, for the first, though not for the last, time his vigour flowed in happier channels, and did not feed mills to grind the bones of people of whom he knew nothing, or supply chromolithographic effects of the limelight order for people who never existed at all. The 'great heart of the people' before which he had so often dangled his raving puppets, he treated here with respect and love and reverence. More than that, he made it beat full and strong by that stirring and human tale. Consequently J. S. Limited still flourishes exceedingly; so also does J. S.

Personally I was rather hard hit, for, on my inside information, I sold a bear. But I have crawled in again now.

Bootles

LADY MAIZIE FERRARS took a cigarette from the gold box by her and lit a match on the sole of her very high-heeled shoe. She had masses of the most beautiful golden hair, all quite genuine in both quantity and colour, deep violet-blue eyes which reflected her very various moods as rapidly and as correctly as an echo, a brilliant pink and white complexion, and the most marvellous faculty for enjoying herself.

'My dear, of course it is a success,' she said. 'If one has a grain of intelligence—and personally I have at least two—and only sits down to think, one can always make a success of anything one chooses to do. The people who fail either have no intelligence—that is the commonest cause—or else they will not or cannot sit down to think.'

Mrs Grantham drew the chair which she very completely filled a little nearer the hissing log-fire on the open grate.

'O, but even you have bungled,' she said. 'Think of your first marriage. No doubt it was made in heaven and all that, but it was not quite—quite at home under terrestrial conditions. You can't say it was a success.'

'I know that, dear. And that was because I hadn't sat down to think. I fell in love. Poor Guy! He was in love with me, too, and didn't sit down to think either. We each of us said, "Love is enough, darling", which was extremely sweet of us, but errone-ous. Love is never, under any circumstances, enough. Unfeeling tradesmen used to threaten to county-court us, though we were so sweet, and the mutton was always tough. It is absurd to think that because a woman is married to the man she loves she is necessarily happy. Love in a cottage, indeed! Cottages are either stuffy or draughty, and often both. Never, I hope, will I live in a cottage again, and, to tell you the truth, I don't think it's in the least likely.'

Mrs Grantham's large eyes, rather like a horse's, grew appreciative.

'He's enormously wealthy, isn't he?' she asked, in a reverential tone.

'My husband? Yes, quite enormously. O, my dear Pussie, it is such fun! And he adores me! If I have a headache, he asks me, so to speak, whether a few large pearls would do any good. So much nicer than pills, you know, and they always cure it at once. And when it is cured, he gives me some more to prevent it coming back.'

She paused a moment.

'In fact, really, it is a great mistake to marry the man you adore, whether he is rich or not,' she said. 'I adored Guy; I did, really. But in the natural course of things that grew less; it lost its original thrill, and he became to me like—like a picture-frame hanging on the wall with the picture taken out. I was always annoyingly conscious of its absence. One should not see too much of the people one adores, but there should be lots of them. I have heaps. I adore Jack, for instance.'

'My husband?'

'Yes, dear. He doesn't much like me, but that doesn't make the slightest difference. You don't mind, do you?'

Mrs Grantham laughed loudly.

'Not in the least. I adore him myself. I think it shows your good taste.'

'Dear Pussie,' said Maizie, 'you are really an understanding person. You know what a perfectly harmless little being I am. I only want'—and she spread her hands out—'nice things, plenty of them; nice people, plenty of them. But the secret is to adore people two or more at a time.'

'The secret of what?'

'Of—of not complicating matters. You talk to one, you see, and think about another.'

'That sounds fascinating,' said Mrs Grantham; 'quite a new philosophy, guaranteed safe. I think I must try it. Anyhow, I'm delighted your marriage is a success. You see, I haven't set eyes on you since it happened, and, as usual, I imagined the worst; I always do. One is then delighted if the worst hasn't happened; if it has, one has the consolation of knowing one was right.'

Lady Maizie threw her half-smoked cigarette away and took another. That was extremely characteristic of her.

'Of course, dearest, Bootles is——'

'Bootles?'

'Yes, because he's such a baby. Of course, Bootles is *too* hopeless for words in some ways, and he's too old to learn now. But it only makes me shriek with laughter. For instance, that dreadful old cat, Lady Dover, was here last week. I only ask her in order to keep her tongue quiet—I'm sure it's forked, by the way; if you keep her mouth full, so to speak, she can't talk about you. She only wants feeding—nothing else. What was I saying? O, yes. Well, Bootles, the last evening she was here, talked to her about alcoholism and crime in a loud voice, amid deathly silence all round. Now he has been all the autumn in this country, and he apparently didn't know that Dover drank himself to death, after doing absolutely everything else first. So all the fine work I had put in, asking her down here, giving her the entire use of a motor, having family prayers in the morning, was all completely thrown away. I might just as well never have asked her, for I know she thinks I put Bootles up to it, and *le bon Dieu* knows what she has been saying about me since.'

'You—had—family—prayers?' asked Mrs Grantham, with an impressive pause between each word.

'Yes, and a hymn. I sang about alto. I told her that Bootles insisted on it, and we all found it very helpful. You see, Bootles comes of Puritan stock—the people who sailed in the *Mayfly*, or something. Out over there, you know, if your people came over in the *Mayfly*, you have the pride of birth; your blood is *the* very bluest.'

Mrs Grantham laughed. 'What a country!' she said.

'Yes, but what a convenient one! What should I have done if it had never been discovered? Lived in a cottage still.'

'And this adorable husband of yours really talked about dipsomania to the Dover cat. Maizie, he must be very, very rewarding.'

'He did, indeed, and returned to the subject again and again like the moth to the candle. I know she thought I had told him to, for she gave me the tip of one finger to shake when she went away, and left an old pair of shoes behind, my dear—such shoes!—which she telegraphed for, by way of giving as much trouble as possible. But I didn't send them.'

'I know where she will go when she dies,' remarked Pussie.

'I know, too; we shan't meet. And you should see Bootles

shooting! He shoots from a sense of duty, because all landed proprietors in England shoot, and I'm told he has a range-finder on his gun which pulls the trigger automatically when it has found the range. Then he misses, and explains exactly why.'

'*Ben trovato,*' said Mrs Grantham.

'Yes, very likely; in fact, I think I made it up.'

Mrs Grantham got up, and stood in rather a masculine attitude, feet apart, in front of the fire. The attitude certainly suited her; being a very large woman, rather heavy of feature and big of limb, she took herself as nature made her, and was *bon garçon* with a loud laugh to all comers.

'I haven't seen him yet, so I don't know,' she said; 'but I think I am sorry for Bootles.'

'My dear, he is happier than the day is long. You will see.'

'Ah, days are not long in November,' said Pussie.

'I would say the same in June.'

'Because he adores you?'

'Yes: and because I am clever enough to play up.'

Mrs Grantham regarded her friend attentively.

'Every now and then, Maizie,' she said, 'you seem to me to have a touch of genius. Family prayers were genius. But I offer one point for your consideration. Some day you will find it literally impossible to play up, as you call it. You will find you really can't manage it. *Après?*'

'O, the deluge, I suppose,' said Lady Maizie; 'and I shall sail away on a neat raft. Gracious! we must go and dress. You know your room? Of course you don't; I will come up with you.'

But Mrs Grantham still lingered.

'I am delighted you are happy,' she said, 'and I think it's very clever of you. All the same——'

The door opened softly, and a large, pink-faced man came in. His hair was white and flossy like a poodle's, and a large moustache concealed both upper and lower lips. Heavy eyelids, half-obscured dark grey eyes of singular sagacity and kindness, they were faithful and amiable, like a collie's.

'Well, Petsie,' he said, 'not gone to dress yet, little woman? I beg your pardon; pray introduce me.'

'This is Bootles, Pussie,' she said.

'Charmed to make your acquaintance, Mrs Grantham. Your husband's been wondering where you were. Motor met you at the station? That's all right. And I guess Petsie's been telling you about Lady Dover. Wasn't it dreadful? And she said I'd spoiled it all. But I guess I haven't spoiled everything yet, eh, Petsie? You and I aren't a cent the worse, you know.'

He took his wife's hand, pressed it against his white moustache, and apparently smacked his lips. Mrs Grantham turned hastily round; these little connubialities were slightly embarrassing. Really, Maizie was very clever to make a success of this.

'O, little woman, little woman!' said her husband.

'Silence, you transatlantic monster!' she cried.

This tickled him enormously.

'Transatlantic monster?' he said. 'Why, if that's not real mean of you, after I've come over this side for good and all, too. She won't let me even look at a map of the States, Mrs Grantham.'

Maizie took her husband's arm, with a side glance at Mrs Grantham, as if to say: 'This is how we do it. Quite easy and perfectly infallible. One dose a day.'

'You horrid, selfish old Bootles!' she said. 'You've left me alone all day, and only come to see me when it's time to go and dress. I shall bring an action against you for neglect and cruelty. Come and show Pussie her room. We shall all be horribly late, but they can't begin without us. That, dearest Bootles, is a cause for deep thankfulness.'

Certainly Bootles seemed to himself to have many causes for deep thankfulness. He had devoted all his life to business, and in the matter of the affections he was as unspoiled and as unsatisfied at the age of fifty—his hair, though white, was abundant— as a boy. And through all these busy years he had carried about with him, like a miniature or a locket worn next the heart, a daydream, an ideal.

That he should ever find it seemed to him, even in his most sanguine moments, almost outside the bounds of possibility; and, as the years bore him through middle-age, he had begun to look upon his daydream as a thing which might once have been, but never now could be. Yet today, yesterday, tomorrow it was his: this wife of his, so gay, so charming, so exquisite, so human, and so tenderly fond of him. Even now, after four months of marriage, his happiness seemed sometimes to be too divine to be real; yet day by day but confirmed its authenticity, and he was quite convinced that no one had ever been so blessed. He had, in fact, that evening had a short talk with Mrs Grantham on the subject of his wife, and he convinced even that very critical and sceptical person of the ideality of his marriage. She really felt, in fact, that she had never done Maizie justice before. It would have been easy enough for her just to get herself married to this guileless millionaire, only to make him, and perhaps herself, miserable afterwards. But her achievement was of a much finer order. She had managed—she might perhaps be trusted for that—to make herself comfortable, but also she had made him blissful. For four whole months he had been blissful, and was unquestionably so still; and if it was possible for four months, why not for ever? Mrs Grantham freely confessed to herself that it required a woman, as she had said, almost of genius to have done that. No doubt Bootles was pleased with little, took her friendly little caresses as tokens of something deeper which did not exist; but how clever of Maizie to have caught the right note. Still cleverer was it to keep on singing it all the time. What a throat! But, but——

Maizie, with her eye for picturesque effects, had asked to this party all the men who had proposed to her, either before her first marriage or during her widowhood, and the house was full. Most of them, like sensible folk, had eventually married somebody else; but there was one who had really been charmingly faithful.

This was Vincent Ellison, who had proposed to her twice— once when she was still a girl, and, for the second time, after Guy's death had set her free again. She was really very fond of him, and his devotion had always flattered and even touched her. He was still not yet forty, had held a post in the last Liberal Cabinet, and was generally regarded as the only man who could possibly pick up and put together the very small pieces into which his party appeared to have been shattered. He was a man certainly of great power—quiet, rather reserved and sparing of speech—but what he said usually happened to mean something, a somewhat rare attribute of speech. He had the further distinction also of being probably the only person in the world of whom Maizie was afraid.

They had simultaneously cut out of a bridge-table that night, and had retired to a corner of the drawing-room to talk till the cards claimed them again. He was a little short-sighted, and looked round the room with a smile and a pince-nez.

'I see the legion of honour is largely represented,' he said.

'And what is that?'

'The legion of those who fruitlessly adored you.'

'And my husband?' she asked.

'Ah! he is the victorious foe to whom we have all surrendered.'

'Dear Bootles,' she said. 'Is he not a dear?'

Vincent let his pince-nez drop.

'I should think that described him excellently,' he said.

'How odious of you! One never knows exactly what you mean.'

'I mean exactly what I say. And I sincerely hope you will be very happy.'

His smile deepened a little as he looked at her. She was radiant, dazzling, and, as always, her presence bewitched him. He was too clever a man not to see the hundred shallows and smallnesses of her nature, but whatever they were, they were part of her, and for that reason transmuted. Critical and cool as he was in his judgements, there was one person in the world whom he was incapable of judging.

'And I think you will,' he continued. 'You have a great genius for happiness; in fact, you have the ideal temperament for it.'

She laughed.

'One used to be taught that if one is good one is happy,' she said. 'Now that seems to me such nonsense. If one is good one is bored, is far more often true. But I suppose it depends on what one means by "good". Now, Vincent, I'm sure you are good; do tell me you are happy.'

He looked straight at her.

'Not in the very least,' he said. 'Did you expect me to be?'

There was enough of the flirt in her to be pleased at this.

'But I want you to be,' she said.

'I asked you to make me so twice,' he said, 'but you refused.'

'You make me feel a brute.' She lowered her voice. 'But you're not jealous?'

He looked up, and his eyes rested for a moment on the calm, pink face of his host.

'No, not this time,' he said.

Six months passed, and Mrs Grantham had begun to wonder whether she had not rated Maizie's capabilities too high.

Brilliant as her achievements had been for the first half year of her married life, she had failed, so her friend saw, in 'staying' power. She was frankly, irredeemably bored with her husband; he got on her nerves, and slowly, but with certainty, he had begun to see this. It was made very clear to him about the middle of the season.

They were to have stayed from a Saturday till Monday at Vincent Ellison's, but only the day before a telegram came for Maizie announcing that her host was down with influenza and the party put off; and Maizie threw the telegram into the waste-paper basket with a feeling of disappointment, the intensity of which amazed her. She had seen a great deal of him in the last six months, and his society was beginning in some secret manner to be necessary to her. What was happening, she did not care to ask herself; she only knew that he absorbed her thoughts.

'It is too provoking,' she cried. 'I had set my heart on going, and here we are stuck in London till Monday. How maddening! I hope he is not very bad.'

Her husband was watching her quietly. Because he did not proclaim to the world what he saw, it was generally supposed he did not see anything,

'I expect he's pretty sick if he puts you off,' he said.

'Ah! how can you say such horrible things, Bootles?' she cried. 'You say them just to frighten me. And I wish you wouldn't use the word "sick" like that; it irritates me.'

His suspicions and fears grew deeper on this.

'I know it does, Petsie,' he said; 'and I guess a lot of things I do irritate you. Well, never mind that. Why need we stop in London? Let's go down to Hinton tomorrow till Monday.'

'My dear man, you can't get people at a moment's notice like that.'

He paused a moment, choosing his words, speaking with purpose.

'No. Why should we get people? Just you and I, I meant.'

She laughed, not very pleasantly; she was too absorbed in her own disappointment this moment to 'sit down and think'.

'Good gracious! We should yawn our heads off with boredom,' she said. 'And I prefer to keep mine on. Hinton with nobody there!'

'I shouldn't be bored,' he said. 'I should like it.'

'Ah, you perhaps. But you are in love with me, you see,' she said, going on with the note she had been writing.

He rose slowly.

'Yes, I guess I see,' he remarked.

She hardly heard him, and he walked up and down the room once or twice. Then he came up behind her and laid his hand on her arm.

'Well, I'm going out,' he said. 'Give me a kiss, Petsie.'

'O Bootles, how tiresome you are!' she cried. 'You've jogged my elbow; I must write it all over again. Pray go out if you are going.'

He left the room without more words, went upstairs to his own sitting-room at the top of the house, and sat down before his table, looking vacantly in front of him. But, at any rate, he had 'sat down to think', and for half an hour he thought. He went over in his mind all possible contingencies and combinations, all solutions which might make the situation bearable. But there was nothing in the least degree satisfactory.

'Yes, it's bad,' he thought to himself. 'And poor Petsie so bored with me. It's bad.'

Then suddenly he got up, with the air of a man who has thought out a difficulty, and walked on to the balcony outside the window, looking on to the stone-paved yard forty feet below.

'Poor darling Bootles,' said Maizie that evening to Mrs Grantham, who had come in answer to the dreadful message. 'He must have leaned against the railing of the balcony, which was very thin and rickety, and the whole thing must have given way. It was this morning, just after I had heard that Vincent had the influenza—how is he, by the way? It is too dreadful; I shall never get over it. And I had been so unkind to him in the morning. The last words I said to him were so cross—I did not think. It makes one feel as if I had killed him. Poor darling Bootles: he was always such an angel to me.'

Which was all quite true.

Julian's Cottage

FOR many years before this fatal tendency in Julian Hind really declared itself, the mischief must have been going on like some insidious bodily disease which is not detected till it has got hold of the sufferer. Indeed, for a long time his malady, instead of presenting itself as a morbid symptom, seemed rather to be one of good sense and prudence. He lived well within his income, making at long intervals some small careful investment. There was nothing wild or extravagant about him: his was a sober and steady life.

Every morning he walked across St James's Park from his flat in Buckingham Palace Road to his work at the Foreign Office— that was very good for his health: he never indulged in drinks at odd times, and he smoked but sparsely for the same reason. He was very popular. This was only to be expected in a youngish man of so agreeable an appearance, of so pleasant a geniality, of so ready an aptitude to enjoy himself, and the days were few when he dined at his club at his own charges. Consequently, since evening usually saw him seated at some well-appointed and luxurious table, he exercised during the rest of the day a wise frugality. That also was good for the health.

'Of course, if one is lunching out,' he said to his cousin Margaret Kelvin when he was dining with her one night, 'one has to eat for politeness sake, but when I'm not out, a plate of macaroni or something of that sort is all I ever touch. One good meal a day is enough for anybody, especially when it's such delicious food as you always have. I tell everybody that you've got far the best cook in London.'

This was not quite strictly true, for it was only when Julian dined with her that he said she had the best cook in London. But there was a sort of generic truth about it, for wherever he dined he paid, if at all possible, a similar compliment to his hostess. Such a plan was politic: every sensible, hospitable woman likes to be assured of that, and is inclined to ask to her table those who publicly appreciate what she provides.

'Nice of you to say so, dear Julian,' said Margaret. 'And what are your plans for August?'

Julian remembered having heard someone say that Robert and Margaret Kelvin had taken a villa at Le Touquet for a month or two this summer. It was worth trying . . .

'My plans are of the most economical,' he said. 'I wanted to go abroad to Deauville or one of those cheery little French places, but I simply can't afford it. The prices they charge in the summer are simply ruinous, and as a matter of depressing fact, I'm rather hard up just now. So I shall pay a few visits for a fortnight, and take the rest of my leave later, if I can arrange it. London's not so bad in August. Heaps of Promenade Concerts which I always love.'

'Oh, but that won't do at all, Julian,' said Margaret. 'We've taken a villa at Le Touquet for a couple of months. Spend August with us there. It would be delightful for us.'

'My dear, what a Heavenly plan!' said he. 'Do you really mean it?'

'Of course, I do. Robert will be kept in London, I'm afraid, a good deal, but he'll be backwards and forwards. It will be amusing I hope: people will be coming and going. Now if we're to see the beginning of the play, we must be off.'

Julian, therefore, had a very economical holiday, for it cost him nothing beyond the price of his ticket to Le Touquet. Later in the year his father died, and his income was considerably increased.

He had some money of his own already, and this with his salary had hitherto amply sufficed for his modest personal expenditure. But the additional two thousand a year did not tempt him into any ill-considered extravagance. He was very comfortable where he was in his small service-flat, and he decided not to set up an independent establishment of his own, for he was really happier and more carefree without the responsibility of a household. Your cook might suddenly give notice, your parlourmaid might get influenza: a service-flat made you safe from such sudden upsets.

But his disease had not yet so far progressed that he stinted himself in any way or deprived himself of anything that could add to his comfort. He had long wanted to have some modest little house in the country not too far from London, and, after going very carefully into the matter, he bought one on the slopes of Ashdown Forest, where he could easily get down for weekends. A man and his wife would look after it, and he could furnish it with stuff out of his father's house, which was too large for him, and which he proposed to sell.

'You must come down and see my cottage,' he said to Margaret, 'and stay with me often for weekends as soon as it is in order. I shall have the greatest fun with it. I shall go down there every weekend in the summer, and have little parties there: just two or three, for it is tiny.'

'And you'll have to get a car, Julian,' said she.

He shook his head.

'I've been thinking that over,' he said, 'but I shan't get one just at present. There's an excellent train service to Forest Row, and I'm not more than ten minutes' walk from the station or from the golf-links. And one doesn't want to lunch or dine out in the country, and having no car is a good excuse.'

This rather surprised Margaret. During that month at Le Touquet, Julian had been very sociable, driving any distance in her car to lunch or dine with friends in the neighbourhood.

'And then in London,' he went on, 'I always think that a car is a mere nuisance to a single man like myself. I'm at work all day, and I should only use it to go out in the evening. It's much simpler and cheaper to take taxis: the new taxis are excellent, quite like private cars. No anxiety either about your car breaking down or your chauffeur stealing the petrol. Also I know I should get lazy if I had a car. I should give up walking in London altogether, and grow fat. Anyhow, I couldn't afford one this year, for I shall have to spend a lot on the cottage, and there are all the death-duties to pay. I see I shall have to economize.'

With so many reasonable objections against owning a car, there was no use in pressing the matter, and Julian had many knotty points on which to consult his cousin about the cottage. A private bathroom for himself would be an expensive luxury, but he was resolved to have that. There would be another for his guests: as the cottage, as he persisted in calling it, had only three spare rooms, one bathroom would suffice for them. He thought he must put in central heating: there was an apparatus which ran that and also supplied hot water for baths. Dreadfully expensive, but the absence of central heating would mean geysers for bath-rooms, and he was terrified of geysers.

He had already got his couple, man and wife, to look after him. The woman had once been a cook, and the man would be valet and butler when he was down there, and work in the garden at other times. And what did Margaret think on the question of board-wages? There would necessarily be a lot of food left over when he was there: bits of fish, odd cutlets, milk, butter, and all sorts of things which his servants would finish up. How would it do to put them on board-wages when they were alone, say from Monday till Friday, and cut off the board-wages when he was there? Rather complicated, perhaps. But it was so important to get everything working in the most economical and sensible way from the first.

He did not mean to keep a regular housemaid. Three perma-nently in the house when he would only be there for a few days at a time would be ridiculous extravagance. He would get a girl in, if necessary, while he was down.

There were a thousand little problems of this sort to be solved. And would not Margaret come there on Saturday with him, and look at the place and give her advice on the spot? They could go down by train in the morning and lunch at the inn. Naturally, Margaret suggested that she should drive him down in her car, and take a basket of lunch with her: didn't Julian think that would be more comfortable?

Julian did.

Throughout the spring Julian's cottage was an obsession with him, and almost a nuisance to his friends. Sometimes, when con-fronted with estimates for painting and papering, for a gas-stove for cooking (this seemed the cheapest and best method), for the installation of electric light, for central heating, the magnitude of the enterprise appalled him.

There came a day when he seriously considered having no central heating but a geyser, in spite of its terrors, in his own bathroom. In this instance he might provide no bathroom for his guests, but to introduce in its place some hip-baths and sponging-tins which had been stacked away in his father's house: these would need repainting. Again, in the pantry-cupboard there, he had found some quite serviceable oil-lamps, and for a while the installation of electric light in the cottage hung in the balance.

But during this crisis, the sale of surplus furniture out of his father's house occurred, and it fetched far more than Julian had anticipated. Consequently both the central-heating scheme and the electric installation were proceeded with. But he decided not to furnish all his three spare bedrooms at once: they were rather small and most of the stuff out of his father's house was too big for them. One, therefore, though painted and papered ready for the time when he should be more in funds, was left empty for the present. He could thus still have a couple of friends down to stay with him.

On the other hand, there was an occasional oasis in this interminable wilderness of expense. For instance, the two Robertsons, the husband and wife whom he had engaged, had furniture of their own with which they did not like to part. They, therefore, asked permission, which he willingly granted, to furnish their bedroom and sitting-room with their own belongings. That was a considerable saving.

Of course, they themselves insured their property against fire: that was only fair. Mrs Robertson also had her own kitchen utensils, which would be useful.

It was during the month of April that Julian spent his first weekend at his cottage. The weather was bitter, but Robertson, in thoughtful anticipation of his visit had run the central heating for a couple of days in order to warm and dry the rooms. Julian thought that one day would have been enough, and Robertson must clearly understand that the furnace was not to be used at all in his absence. It was wicked waste, especially when broken coke was at its present price, to have the whole house warmed when he was not there.

Then Mrs Robertson's management had to be tested. Certainly she was a good cook, but she had ordered in a leg of lamb as well as a chicken for this Saturday and Sunday. It was a small chicken, it is true, but there would certainly be a great deal of lamb left over when he returned to London on Monday, which his servants would consume during the ensuing week while they were on board-wages.

Then Julian noticed that the lights in the kitchen, the pantry and the servants' sitting-room were all burning simultaneously. That surely was wasteful; if Robertson was working in his pantry, and Mrs Robertson in the kitchen, there was no reason why the sitting-room should be illuminated. He spoke about these points, but mingled his criticism with praise of the excellence of his food and of the valeting of his clothes.

After a few such weekends Julian was able to estimate what running expenses there would be. They were higher than he had anticipated, and if he brought down guests for the weekend they would be higher still. But the total annual cost would not, he hoped, be beyond his means: if it proved to be so, he could probably let so well-appointed a house occasionally for a month with his servants. But he had no immediate intention of doing so, and for the next two months he came down to Sussex every weekend.

He did not invite anyone else, for he was quite happy alone after a busy and social week in London. He told his friends that he was only picnicking in a corner of the house while he was getting it shipshape for them. In a few months now it would be in order, and he was looking forward to having his little parties there.

As he was busy in the garden, he did not join the local golf club. Often he did not play golf at all: if he did, it was cheaper to pay a green fee for the day, than incur the expense of entrance fee and subscription.

With the solid addition to his income caused by his father's death, Julian found that, in spite of all these outgoings, his balance at the bank was mounting in an agreeable manner, and he consulted Robert Kelvin, who was a partner in a firm of brokers, as to the investment of these surplus funds. Robert strongly advised him to put the whole of his thousand pounds into the ordinary shares of a certain Rayon company which he believed to be unduly low; there was almost sure to be a rise in them.

After agonies of indecision Julian followed his advice, and the shares thereupon had a sharp fall: he regarded his thousand pounds as lost. Fool that he had been to listen to so speculative a counsel! If ever he had a penny in the bank again, he vowed that he would make no investment of which the gilt edge was not of the broadest.

'It's awful; I'm perfectly crippled,' he said one night to

Margaret. 'I don't blame Robert in the least, mind you. I'm sure he thought his advice was good.'

'Of course he did,' answered Margaret, who was getting a little weary of Julian's finances. 'He put twenty thousand pounds of mine into the same company the other day.'

'My dear, what a sum!' said Julian. 'I hope the shares will recover for your sake as well as my own. I should have had fifty pounds a year, you know, if I had put my thousand into War Loan. Enough to pay for the fittings of my two bathrooms. I shall have to be very economical for the next year. And I was so hoping to have quantities of delightful little parties at the cottage in the autumn!'

Julian's malady now definitely declared itself. Hitherto, in the furnishing of his cottage, he had not stinted himself in any way, and provided that a man spends freely on his own pleasures, he cannot be said to suffer from malignant miserliness. But now under the ruinous impact of that investment, Julian began not only to cut off his own indulgences, but also to enjoy doing so.

Because it gave him a greater satisfaction to save a few pounds every Friday, he stopped for a whole month his weekend visits to his cottage. He also reduced the board-wages of his servants by two shillings a week, but allowed them to consume the fruit and vegetables from his garden, which would otherwise be wasted.

He found that he took a keener pleasure in his walks across the Park every morning, because he recognized that they were not only health-giving, but also that he saved eighteen pence by not taking a taxi: that economy alone brought in seven shillings and sixpence a week, or close on twenty pounds a year. If it was wet there was a bus that took him almost from his own door into Whitehall. Nothing that saved his purse did he account an inconvenience, for the joy of it left a balance in his favour.

How wise, he thought, was that proverb: 'Take care of the pence and the pounds will take care of themselves.' How admirable, also, the complementary maxim: 'Penny-wise, pound-foolish.'

So not only did he take care of pence, but of pounds also, and when his landlord intimated that he was raising the rent of his flat on June quarter-day, Julian gave it up and moved into a smaller one two stories higher. It was large enough, and looked on to a smaller and quieter street. He wondered why he had not moved there before. Strawberries were cheap now, and he gave a little tea-party to a dozen friends by way of a house-warming and several of them, before they left, asked him to lunch or dinner during the next week. A good investment in strawberries . . .

It was soon after this that two very important decisions demanded his attention. Rayons had been on the upgrade lately; he could sell his shares at the price he had paid for them, so that apart from the brokerage (which had always seemed to him a monstrous overcharge for making a purchase on the Stock Exchange) he would be no poorer than he had been before he embarked on the sea of speculation.

Robert Kelvin rang him up about it, and though he had vowed to himself that if ever he could get out of so unstable a piece of property without serious loss, he would do so, he hesitated. Robert's gay and careless voice down the telephone (for he had nothing at stake) was reassuring, and Robert strongly advised him to hold: there did not seem to be much point in buying shares, if you sold them for what you had paid. So he decided to stick to his Rayons, but peremptorily rejected the idea of buying more.

That very evening when he returned home on foot from a very pleasant dinner, the second of these decisions awaited him. He found a letter from the house-agent in East Grinstead, through whom he had acquired the cottage, asking him if he would consider letting it for the month of August. A client of very good standing thought it would just suit him, and the agent would like to know if Julian would give him an 'order to view'. With this rise in Rayons, he had contemplated being in residence there himself for that month, but now he saw that having decided to retain this speculative holding of his, it would be wise to have some definite counterbalancing asset, for Rayons might go down again.

There was, of course, the problem of what he would do with himself in August, but the Kelvins, he knew, had taken a house again at Le Touquet, where he had enjoyed himself so much last year. Margaret had already hoped that he could manage to pay them a visit, and it seemed very improvident to reject, straight off, this opportunity to let his house.

Next morning he telegraphed to the house-agent permission

for his client to see the house, and awaited the reply with some anxiety.

It came. The client of good standing was delighted with the house, but the accommodation was one bedroom short of his requirements. If Julian would furnish the extra room which stood empty at present, it would suit him excellently. It would also be a great convenience if he could take on the very pleasant couple who were in charge. The rent offered was sixty pounds for the complete month.

Julian lay long awake that night, and the small hours seethed with mental arithmetic. He got out of bed, and with a pencil and paper worked it all out.

The room could be cheaply but nicely furnished: a drugget on the floor, white enamelled wardrobe and table and washstand, rep curtains, an armchair from the drawing-room and so forth, but there would be little left of the rent. But the house would then be complete for future letting, and Julian would also be quit of wages and board-wages for the Robertsons for a whole month. Big Ben had just struck three when he made up his mind.

He had a plan of the house which gave the dimensions of the rooms, and he spent his luncheon hour next day at a notable furnishing establishment. The sympathetic shopman understood his requirements very well: simple, neat apparatus for a small bedroom at a cottage in the country, but no armchair. It would all be dispatched at once, and the sum to be paid on deposit was really trifling.

In the afternoon Margaret picked him up in her car at the Foreign Office to see the tennis at Wimbledon where she had two tickets for the centre court.

'Good news for you today, Julian,' she said. 'Those Rayons are behaving like perfect gentlemen. They have gone up three shillings.'

'Really!' he said. 'That's excellent, for I've been so bothered about them. Last night I lay awake till three in the morning thinking about my wretched money affairs. Dear me, if it had only happened yesterday!'

'You would have had a good night?' she asked.

'More than that. I've just let the cottage for August. I had a very fair offer for it, and with everything so uncertain, I didn't like to refuse it. Fearful expense though, for I had to buy furniture for my empty bedroom. So I'm out of it till September.'

'Come to Le Touquet for August again if you like,' she said. 'Robert's taken the same villa as we had last year.'

'My dear, how delightful of you. I should simply love to, and then I can spend my weekends in September at the cottage. By the way, Margaret, I've only just thought of it: when you let a house does the tenant have the garden-produce free? Robertson writes that the plums and cherries are wonderful this year.'

'I should think it depends on the terms of the lease you give him,' she said.

'I must see to it then. If I didn't give him garden-produce Mrs Robertson could make jam that would last me through the winter. You really must come down there when you get back from Le Touquet. Promise.'

Julian felt, as he watched the tennis, that it had been the greatest luck that the rise in Rayons had not occurred yesterday, for then he could have found no reason for letting the cottage during August. As it was, he would get his holiday free of expense, and would be reaping the benefit of his rent with all outgoings saved him. Quite providential! And this rise in his shares would bring him in, if he sold now, a profit of nearly a hundred and fifty pounds.

'Tell me, Margaret,' he said, at the moment when the match they were watching was in the most exciting state. 'Are you meaning to sell your Rayon shares? I feel in two minds about it.'

She seemed not to hear.

'Oh, Julian, wasn't that a wonderful shot?' she cried. 'That makes them five games all.'

Throughout August these Rayon shares continued to rise. It was almost too exciting to be pleasant, so fraught was Julian's enrichment with agonizing doubts as to whether he should take his profit or not. More than that, it took the colour out of other pursuits: he did not play golf with his accustomed keenness, for golf seemed to matter very little, and the great event of the day was the arrival of the English papers with Stock Exchange news. During the last week of his stay, he could bear the strain no longer, and regardless of expense, he telephoned to Robert to sell.

That very day the shares jumped another two shillings, and he did not know how much of that rise he had secured before the sale was made. That was on the knees of the gods, and it was no use tormenting himself about it, but that very evening he was plunged into fresh problems, for there arrived a letter from the house-agent at East Grinstead, saying that his tenant would like to know if he was thinking about selling his house, and if so, what he would ask for it. He would like to buy it furnished, just as it stood. In the interval which must elapse before all this could be settled, would Julian let him take the house for another fortnight?

A sleepless night followed, and innumerable addition sums. Julian noted down what he had actually spent on the acquisition and embellishment of the house: he added to that a fair estimate of what his father's furniture might have been expected to fetch at a sale, and then thinking that was too low put on an extra hundred pounds: he added to this what he had spent on the furnishing of the empty bedroom: to these items he added varying sums to represent a reasonable profit on the trouble he had taken over the place, and the dividends which his outlay would have brought him in if he had invested his money instead.

In the morning he wrote to the agent, and taking the largest of these totals, he said that this was the lowest figure at which he would sell. He also granted his tenant a fortnight's extension of his lease, for where was the use of occupying the house himself if he was going to part with it immediately? Thirty pounds more . . .

Margaret noticed how *distrait* he was, how worried his mien, but until the business was concluded he said nothing to her about the reason. But when the agent replied that his client offered three hundred pounds less than the sum he had named as the lowest he would take, Julian had to confide in her, for he could not bear the strain alone.

'I'm terribly bothered about something,' he said, 'and I must consult you. That cottage of mine at Forest Row. I've had it six months now, and I've hardly used it at all. Indeed, it has been nothing but a worry to me, and far more expensive than I thought it would be.'

Margaret seemed to wear a secret smile. Julian had noticed before, when Robert was here and he himself was agonizing over

Rayons, that Robert's eyes and hers sometimes met, and they both wore a secret smile.

'My dear, you mustn't laugh at me for being so worried,' he said. 'The cottage, as I say, has brought me nothing but anxiety, and I think I shall get rid of it. My tenant wants to buy it just as it stands, but he offers me three hundred pounds less than what I proposed. It still leaves me well on the right side, but all this bargaining is so hateful. What would you do?'

Margaret laughed outright

'Good gracious me, sell it and have done with it,' she said. 'But do take care, Julian. If you don't look out you'll get to think about nothing but money. You're rich enough, aren't you?'

'You're rather unkind,' said Julian. 'All I want is to be free from anxiety about money. It's all very well for you who put twenty thousand into these Rayons. If I had done that I should take my profit, and never think about money again. But I think I will sell the cottage. That will be something.'

Julian returned to England. London was very empty, but there were Promenade Concerts going on at the Queen's Hall, and he went there most evenings.

Often there was not much he wanted to hear, a Beethoven symphony one night, a Bach concerto another, or a couple of Wagner overtures. It was hardly worth while taking a seat for so short a time, and he stood with the crowd in the central area, where you heard very well. But he found his pleasure in music on the wane. He could hardly attend to it; his balance at the bank was a constant preoccupation.

The purchase money for his cottage had been paid in; the proceeds from his sale of Rayons was to his credit also, and it was most difficult to know what to do with this large sum. He was determined to run no further risks over speculative purchases, yet how dazzling sometimes was the prospect of another coup. If only he had held them a fortnight longer, for they had continued to rise . . .

Again Government stock was very high: if an election occurred in the autumn, it would doubtless go down, and that was the time to buy. Was it better to wait, sacrificing in the interval the accruing dividends? It was a serious loss of income to have seven thousand pounds on deposit, and before the month was out he invested the whole in Conversion Loan. He could not afford to let it lie idle any longer, though he foresaw he might have to sell part of it to pay the iniquitous demand on his income made by the Special Commissioners for surtax. An appalling sum: he would be poorer than ever.

All the various impulses of life seemed now to have flowed like tributary streams into the one broad river of his purpose. Like a malignant malady, the love of money drained his faculty for joy. He no longer cared about anything which did not make or save money for him. He still enjoyed what cost him nothing, but he denied himself, not with a sense of renunciation but of gain, whatever ran him into any expense.

A weekend in the country was enjoyable provided only that the cost of the journey was not greater than what he would have spent on his food if he had stayed in London: a concert or a play was only pleasant if he was taken to them.

His work at the Foreign Office he still performed quite efficiently because a salary was attached to it, and when, during the winter, he was asked to transfer himself to the British Embassy at Washington to take the place of a secretary there who was required in London for two months, he at once jumped at the opportunity, for all expenses of his journey were paid for him, and his salary would be more than sufficient for his living. There he speedily made his mark, and a caustic *mot* went round, that though America was justly proud of her Mr Washington who never told a lie, England could boast of her Mr Hind who never gave a drink.

A journalistic rag got hold of this acid piece of homage to his carefulness, and he received a marked copy of the issue. The virulence of his malady may be estimated from the fact that he did not resent it in the least.

The spring saw him back in England: he travelled second-class and found it quite comfortable. Presently he went down with a sharp attack of influenza.

It was an extravagance to send for the doctor who would merely tell him to go to bed and keep warm; for that he could do without paying a guinea for the advice. But this was one of his few mistakes in his management of his money, and his wisdom over pennies proved its foolishness as regards pounds.

Pleural pneumonia had already set in when the doctor was called, and the size of his fortune, when proved for probate, which so astonished his friends, yielded Julian, at the most, a posthumous gratification.

SOCIETY
STORIES

Fine Feathers

MR AND MRS ALTHAM sat open-mouthed and staring at each other across the breakfast table while the urn hissed unregarded, and little islands of grey grease formed in the gravy of the dish of kidneys. An event crude and melodramatic in the highest degree had just been made known to her through the stereotyped medium of a solicitor's letter. A shadowy uncle of hers had died intestate in some incredibly remote part of Australia, and she as next of kin came into a fortune of three hundred thousand pounds. At present all power of connected speech had left her, and for the last two minutes, after she had read the letter aloud and then passed it to her husband, she had sat with her arms on the table in front of her, exclaiming at intervals, in the manner of a bell tolling for the deceased, 'Uncle Simeon'.

But those who knew Mrs Altham best (and her husband, in virtue of twenty-four years of matrimony, knew her very well indeed) were perfectly aware that silence on her part implied that thoughts were pouring in riotous foam into the reservoir of her brain, and that it would be no matter of long delay before it burst out in spate of speech. He waited: it burst.

'Well, and to think that all these years poor Uncle Simeon has been working in those Australian bushes, and I never gave a thought to him,' she said. 'It would be idle for me to pretend to miss him, Henry, since the last time I saw him was certainly forty years ago, if it was a day, and then all he did was to take far too much of poor Papa's most expensive Madeira. But mourning of some kind I shall certainly wear for three weeks— I think three weeks is ample for an uncle, especially in Australia— and it would show a very proper spirit if you had a hat-band or something of the sort. But, anyhow, we shan't spend our evenings any longer wondering who will take Sir James Westbourne's place at Hinton, which he can no longer afford to live in. I shall step round to Coats' agency immediately after breakfast. And a yacht. You shall have your yachting, Henry, which you have always hankered after, since you were not seasick all the way across from Southampton to Havre. There are some caps with a white sort of covering over them in Bates' stores, which are just the thing. But Hinton I shall take lock, stock, and barrel. I should not even wonder if I asked Mrs Ames and her husband over for a shooting party, amongst others. Poor Mrs Ames! London! I think perhaps a little flat in London, but no more. I have always said that two great houses are more trouble than either is worth. And now if you feel equal to giving me a kidney! There is no reason why I should starve to death as far as I know at present.'

Mr Altham was an adept at disentangling the various topics that made up his wife's meteoric monologues and choosing one of the most important to respond to. Here, with unerring perspicacity, he chose the simple sentence, 'Poor Mrs Ames.'

For years his wife had disputed the leadership of Society in this little country town of Riseborough with that lady, and so far her efforts, maniacal in intensity, had not met with the smallest particle of success. Mrs Ames was plain and middle-aged, and not well off, whereas even if it was conceded that Mrs Altham was equally plain and not much younger, she was already, before the news of this morning, in far more comfortable circumstances. She entertained more lavishly than this detestable queen of Riseborough, she dressed better, she exerted herself more, but hitherto Mrs Ames had had things all her own way.

But now a revenge bitterly sweet was in her rival's power, for Sir James Westbourne, whose place, owing to Radical iniquities, was to let, was Mrs Ames' first cousin, and that lady's casual allusions to 'old days' and 'the rose garden on the south front' had at times been almost more than Mrs Altham could bear. To take Hinton, and occasionally be magnanimous enough to supply Mrs Ames with some 'new days', would be the completest retort to the annoyance of years. Mrs Altham almost determined to dig up the rose garden and plant it with grass, so that Mrs Ames could talk about that no longer.

Henry gave a little minute squeal of laughter, as he did when his opponent at golf hit his ball into an unusually deep bunker, or when at bridge his adversary forgot about the last trump or the ace of spades or some trifle of that kind.

'Dear me, that will be paying Mrs Ames out,' he said. 'I think, my dear, I should not even ask her to a shooting party, to begin with. Just a garden party next summer, when you will ask all Riseborough, doctors and auctioneers and what not. I expect if you really mean to take Hinton, you will have enough entertaining to do among the county families without bothering about Mrs Ames and her great fat Major!'

But Mrs Altham was of sterner stuff; there was something of the House of Atreus about her.

'No, Henry, shooting party,' she said. 'I want to single out Mrs Ames and condescend to her. I should like to see that great fat Major, as you so justly call him—though you cannot expect everybody to keep his figure as trim and slender as you— to see that great fat Major stumping about and missing every rabbit within miles. I shall like to see you wipe his eye every time you let your gun off——'

'I must get up my shooting again,' said Henry, charmed by these unusual compliments. 'I believe it is good practice to fire at clay pigeons.'

'I am sure you will be an excellent marksman,' said his wife, 'but it's much more than that I want you to do. You will have to take your place now as Squire, for I shall always call you that, of Hinton. Thank goodness we shall have no more of the trumpery tittle-tattle and nonsensical gossip of Riseborough, where all that anybody attends to is what entirely concerns somebody else. And, talking of gossip, it *is* true, and Dr Evans *has* got a motor-car with a man in livery. I couldn't get near enough to see what the device on his buttons was, but there was some sort of crest or coat of arms there: that I saw quite clearly. A couple of lancets supporting a stethoscope and a pair of pincers, I should think, or a bleeding bowl. And there is no doubt that that great stick of a Mrs Evans, who reminds me of nothing so much as a piece of French asparagus, all white and weedy, has launched out into a footman as well as a butler, though what with Dr Evans' practice going down, as I feel sure it is, and the little they entertain, for I don't believe they've given a dinner party since last spring, I should have thought their butler might have managed single-handed. But some people aren't happy without a quantity of cheap pomp like that. I wonder how many men we shall require at Hinton! Rose garden, indeed!'

Mrs Altham ate a quantity of food in a great hurry, and broke out again.

'I'm not going to let the grass grow under *my* feet,' she said, 'and nobody shall say I don't live up to my new position. Of course, we shall take rank with the county, Henry, and you will have to get an agent with leather gaiters, who comes in to see you after breakfast. I daresay young Martin, who always patronizes you so at the club, would be very glad to take that sort of place. He would not live in the house, of course, but you might ask him in sometimes to have a rubber in the evening. Mrs Evans, too, she is a cousin of Sir James's. She will not be so impertinent—for I assure you it was nothing less than that—on the subject of my lawn again. And now you might go round to the club, I think, and read *The Times* there instead of in your study, and drop a word now and then about the two or three hundred thousand pounds that we have come into. Don't be too definite, Henry, and depreciate it rather than exaggerate. You can say, too, that it is wonderful how things get round, and that you have been already asked whether it is true that we are going to take Hinton. It will be as good as taken by that time, for I shall be off to Coats' immediately. And if that young man there, who was so very superior when I consulted him about the letting of this house when we were at Sea View last year, gives me any more of his airs, it will be a nice set-down for him to know what I have come about.'

With the promptness, not to say fury, for action which characterized all Mrs Altham said or did, that lady actually left her second cup of tea untasted, and put on her walking-dress. She was always in a hurry, and the almost incredible fact, that dreams which seem to last the whole night occupy only a few seconds, became quite comprehensible with Mrs Altham as the dreamer.

The impertinent young man had a tremendous set-down, and became more than obsequious in his manner of giving information. It appeared that Sir James would prefer, if possible, to let the house half-furnished, so that with the rest of his possessions he might equip a big farmhouse near, which he proposed to occupy until it was possible for a gentleman to live in his own house again, and this arrangement admirably suited Mrs Altham, who would thus move into Hinton the furniture from her present abode in Queensgate Street. Indeed, in an hour's time, the thing, as she had anticipated, was 'as good as done'.

The hour was now about half-past eleven, and the High Street was full of the ladies of Riseborough, who, not having a club where they could meet, were accustomed to spend a considerable portion of the morning popping in and out of the shops, and exchanging news on the pavement.

Mrs Altham had not been there five minutes before the sensation lately created by Dr Evans' new motor with a driver armorially buttoned, which had been the subject of so much justifiable indignation, became utterly effete and savourless. She dropped a hint to Mrs Fortescue casually, as if it was an affair of no consequence, who swiftly crossed the street to tell Mrs Evans, whose husband had already been to the club, and had told her what was known there.

Two minutes afterwards Mrs Evans met her cousin, Mrs Ames, carrying a large paper parcel in her own hands. Only Mrs Ames could do that sort of thing without loss of caste. That was one of the infernally exasperating things about her. As usual, she looked like a comely toad.

'Good morning, dear Millie,' she said. 'Yes, a pair of shoes. They are big enough for—for—well, the largest feet in Riseborough, be those whose they may. I want to startle Mr Gilchrist by putting both my feet into one of them, and asking what he means by it. What is the news?'

Mrs Evans, who had been compared that morning to a stick of white asparagus, was in reality a very tall and graceful woman.

'You've not heard, then, Cousin Amy?' she said.

'Unless it's about your husband's new motor. Mrs Altham, whom I saw yesterday, seems to take it as a personal insult levelled at her.'

'It's about Mrs Altham. She has come into an immense fortune, four or five hundred thousand pounds. And she is going to take our Cousin James' place at Hinton.'

Mrs Ames dropped the parcel, which burst. She picked up the immense shoes, and stood with one in each hand, regardless of what Riseborough might say (as a matter of fact Mrs Fortescue was told an hour later that Mrs Ames had appeared in the High Street with a pair of her husband's trousers over her arm).

'Pish!' said Mrs Ames. 'Really, I beg your pardon, Millie, but it isn't the first of April, dear. You might as well tell me she had taken Westminster Abbey.'

'She is going to have a flat in London,' said Mrs Evans. 'And a yacht—Wilfred heard Mr Altham say so at the club.'

'My dear, I can't believe it. Look, there's Mrs Altham steaming up the hill towards us. She knows we are talking about it, but I would sooner bite my tongue out than ask her anything.'

Mrs Ames made a rather distant little bow to Mrs Altham, determined not to take the slightest interest in this colossal piece of news. That was how she was accustomed to treat Mrs Altham.

Mrs Altham, of course, was quite unable to pass without scattering careless, casual information, sufficient to whet anybody's appetite.

'Ah, dear Mrs Ames,' she said; 'how wise of you to do your errands yourself! Taking your shoes, I see, to have them made a little easier.'

Mrs Ames let her eyes rest for one second, no more, on Mrs Altham's feet. That was all. It was quite unnecessary to reply, and Mrs Altham hastily continued. She was not quite sure that the subject could be pursued with advantage.

'I declare I feel quite shy this morning with everyone enquiring and congratulating me,' she said. 'The very birds of the air seem to know about it.'

'Dear little things!' said Mrs Ames, contemplating a sparrow.

This was horrible; Mrs Altham was obliged to yield before this impregnable lack of curiosity.

'Of course, it's a great responsibility,' she said, 'and I'm sure I envy those who have not got such a thing thrust on them. Fancy poor Uncle Simeon leaving me all that money. Three hundred thousand pounds!'

'Dear me, a very comfortable little fortune,' said Mrs Ames.

'It will quite put us out of the fear of actual indigence,' said Mrs Altham, catching the ironical tone, 'and I fully intend to put Sir James' house in good order at last. I hear there is no electric light. Yes, I have practically taken Hinton, though I am sure there will be a vast deal to do to it. But it will suit me on the whole, and I am sure Sir James will be far more comfortable in the quaint little farmhouse that I hear he means to live in. And, of course, we shall only be too delighted to send him game, and I am sure Henry will often ask him over to shoot the covers. Does Major Ames shoot? I hope so, and that you will bring him over one of these days, Mrs Ames. You may be sure we shall not forget our old friends in dear, funny little Riseborough.'

Mrs Altham had worked herself up into a perfect frenzy at not being able to arouse the faintest sign of interest or curiosity in Mrs Ames, who was wrapping up her shoes in their brown-paper covering.

'I must try to remember to tell my husband,' she said, 'all about your good fortune and your kindness in proposing that he should come over. But my memory is so bad: I must tie a knot in my handkerchief. Then I shall remember. So glad, dear Mrs Altham.'

Mrs Ames gave her a little nod of dismissal, a habit which Mrs Altham found utterly odious, the more so since she found herself always obeying it, and Mrs Ames waited till she was quite out of hearing.

'Squire Altham!' she observed. 'Squire and Mrs Altham. Pish! They won't be able to live at Hinton, my dear Millie. They don't know *how*.'

Mrs Altham did not let grass grow anywhere, even on her lawn, and within a month she and Henry were installed in the great barrack of a house that stood eight miles out of Riseborough and of all that Mrs Altham had previously known of what is called civilization.

She found that a perfectly new art of living had to be learned, and even the alphabet of it, the mere passing of the hours, and living in large rooms, was unknown to her. She lost herself in the basement, until she made a small, surreptitious plan of it, and wandered disconsolate through the big drawing-room, the small drawing-room, her own vast sitting-room, the Chinese room, wondering what was to be done with it all, while Henry sat cowering in 'the study', a forlorn atom in a great, gloomy prison.

All the old landmarks were lost; the two were on a horizonless and uncharted sea. She who had been accustomed to know exactly what must be ordered from the butcher's and the fishmonger's and to order it herself, found that those pleasant household duties were completely taken from her. One night they had turbot for dinner, of which there was 'a great piece' left, and when she suggested a fish-pie for lunch, next day, she found to her bewilderment that the 'great piece' had been consumed below. A hot apple-tart for dinner, again, necessarily meant cold apple tart next day, a dish of which Henry was almost lasciviously fond, and when she made enquiries about it, she was met by blank incomprehension from the chef, who had been recommended as an excellent manager.

She found that, pending the completion of the electric light instalment, fresh candles were put in the drawing-room, where they sat only after dinner, every single evening, regardless of whether they were completely burned down or not, a thing that revolted her sense of economy, for it was odious to think of the best wax being used in still-rooms and pantries, even if it was used there at all. And the still-room! She had 'heard tell' of still-rooms, but she had not really grasped the fact that such things existed for the manufacture of a few buns and sweet cakes.

As for the rose-garden which she had almost determined to dig up in order to quench any further allusion to it on Mrs Ames' part, her spirit altogether failed at the prospect of digging up an acre and a half of rose-trees. Above all, there was this awful loneliness, and absence of the human interest that characterized Riseborough. Iron-masked servants, terrifying men, surrounded her who moved impassively about on noiseless errands, and spoke in low voices when spoken to, but not otherwise.

Henry fared even worse, and found the transformation of being stretched, so to speak, into a country gentleman, a process about as comfortable as days on the rack.

After breakfast the gamekeeper came in for orders, and in preparation for the regular shooting parties which were contemplated he had to go out with his new gun and trudge all afternoon through long, wet grass and sticky stubbles, to pick up the alphabet of shooting. He had to stand waiting while in some mysterious manner small outlying covers were beaten up to him, praying that the 'bird or two' which they would probably unharbour would fly in any direction rather than within range of his quavering barrels. Or, if he got off 'picking up a bird or two', a phrase which somehow appealed to his wife, he would have to walk round the gardens, or simulate a clumsy delight in a heifer, a colt, or a new piece of park paling.

In this dreary November weather he often came back home drenched and chilly, and thought with a sort of aching longing of the pleasant afternoons in the club smoking-room, where the rain beat innocuously on the windows, and bridge began early, and all was so cosy and snug and gossipy. But a fine autumn afternoon seemed even more irretrievably wasted in pottering about after those beastly pheasants when he thought of the briskness of a round of golf with a slightly inferior opponent on the high, invigorating downs, and the bridge and hot teacakes to follow, and the sense of companionship. Afterwards, perhaps, the evening might fall chilly, and he would walk quickly home to the house in Queensgate Street, to have a hot bath before dinner in the newly fitted bathroom, with its white tiles and gushing hot water.

Here the bathroom was an immense, chilly apartment, half a mile away from his bedroom, and the bath, put in by Victorian plumbers, let water slowly steal with moribund gurglings into a sort of sieve at the bottom of a huge grey coffin. Of course, that was all to be altered, if they took a long lease of the house, but it was a mournful affair at present.

Then there followed the stately dinner with his now sadly reticent wife. There was no enlivening gossip, for there was nobody to gossip about; there was no thrilling speculation to be made about neighbours, no small and cosy sitting-room with an armchair drawn up to the fire, and an evening paper to look at. Here, awed by gigantic footmen, they ate a succession of endless dishes, and sat in the big drawing-room afterwards (on this point Mrs Altham was firm), where a huge open fireplace with burning logs positively forbade a near approach, and where it was simply impossible somehow to smoke a pipe at all. Nothing *tasted* in these enormous rooms, and the evening paper did not appear till next morning. Then came bedtime, and he climbed into the great four-poster with tapestry curtains, and dreamed about Queensgate Street.

An awful Christmas followed with two shooting parties, which were unadulterated purgatory to the host. Occasional guests came from Riseborough, but Mrs Altham, though dying to know all the smallest details of everybody's life, was far too 'county' now to take any apparent interest in Mrs Taverner's new dining-room carpet, and the unaccountable rise in the price of bacon. All was stiff and formal, and though her visitors may have been impressed, the prevailing impression was that they were uncomfortable.

Worst of all, Mrs Ames refused five invitations one after the other, with excuses that a child would have laughed at. But she hoped that Mrs Altham found the 'dear old place' sufficiently roomy for her. Not being a child, Mrs Altham did not laugh, but it was true that she found the place very roomy indeed. Then winter was blown away by the gales of February, and March, coming in like a lion, proceeded to resemble a fish.

Mr Altham had driven into Riseborough one morning, lunched at the club, had a round of golf, and a good gossip in the clubhouse, and drove back again behind the new and nerve-shattering chauffeur, feeling utterly homesick. All sorts of cheery little things were going on: Queensgate Street and the people he passed, though he flashed through it, he could see at a glance would have furnished entrancing topics for the evening, and have produced a sense of exhilaration at the hour of awaking next day, and here he was going back to the great empty mansion, out of it all. He had seen, too, that the board of the agent was still in place over the gate of his old house, to show it was still to let. It was like looking on a dead child....

His wife met him at the lodge-gates, and he, eager to escape from the hurricane car, was delighted to get out and walk with her.

'Well, Henry, what news, what news?' she asked.

He looked at her with eyes of sudden comprehension. He guessed that she was so eager to hear what was going on in Riseborough (though she had been there herself only yesterday) that she positively had been unable to wait for his return, and had come to meet him. He was guileful.

'Nothing, my dear,' he said. 'only the ordinary Riseborough tittle-tattle. The sort of thing you used to find so uninteresting.'

She walked briskly by him.

'You are quite wrong, Henry,' she said, 'to think that I did not take an interest in the little affairs of dear old Riseborough. So tell me what you picked up.'

He produced a sort of salmi of the most delicious tit-bits; he had seen Mrs Ames coming out of a Methodist chapel; what did that mean?... he had been told that Mr Turner had actually got a French chef... there was a new house building in Queensgate Street, and positively nobody knew who was going into it.... General Fortescue was supposed to have had a stroke, but there was reason to believe...

'And our old house is still vacant,' he added.

She turned on him.

'Henry, I believe you want to go back to Riseborough,' she said. 'Be a man, instead of shilly-shallying, and confess it.'

'They had the sense to see at last,' said Mrs Ames, 'that there are certain things which it is better to be born to. Cousin James, who is so generous, has let them out of their lease, though, of course, they had to pay something. They put electric light in, I hear, and a new bathroom, so Cousin James has not done so badly.'

The Defeat of Lady Hartridge

THE *Celtic* was to sail in an hour's time from the pier of
the White Star Line in New York Harbour, and the huge
decks were dotted over with little groups of travellers and the
friends who had come to see them off. Out on the river, ferry-
boats splashed, churned and hooted, and the great sky-scraping
buildings so dear to the commercial sentiment of America that
it believes them, with a sort of mother's partiality for a child, to
be beautiful, stood up in the hard, clear atmosphere, typical and
characteristic.

Characteristic, too, was the unhurrying, unceasing bustle with
which the mail-bags were passed into the ship—everyone concerned with the operation was in exactly his right place, and did
swiftly and smoothly exactly what he had to do. And immensely,
blatantly characteristic was Mrs Cyrus S. Vane as she made her
hospitable farewell speeches to the Hartridges, who had been
her guests on her immense steam-yacht during the processions
of the *Defender* and the *Shamrock*, and for the last week up at
her 'cottage' in Newport. She spoke in a shrill, piercing voice,
audible without effort above the pounding of the donkey-engine.

'Well, Lady Hartridge,' she shrieked, 'I'm sorry, I'm real sorry
you're going. I guess you're the loveliest woman I ever saw; and
it's been just too sweet having you with us, and it's too bad of
you to go home so soon. Why, when we get hold of people like
you, we want you to stop as many months as you've stopped
minutes. It seems just yesterday that Cyrus and I came down to
meet you. And you'll come back. You promised that, and if
Cyrus and I are at San Francisco, we'll come to meet you.'

Lady Hartridge, to do her justice, had been extremely unwilling to come to America at all. But having gone, like the sensible
woman she undoubtedly was, she made the best of it. And there
was a good deal put at her disposal, for in her honour Mrs
Cyrus S. Vane had assembled day after day at the cottage absolutely all that was considered brightest and best in the Western

civilization. Dinner-parties, fêtes of the most extravagant and ingenious kind, balls, bridge parties had succeeded each other without intermission, and Lady Hartridge had eaten, drunk, danced, laughed, and won money with bewildering rapidity; and, being a woman of the world, she had made herself perfectly charming and immensely popular.

All the same, she inwardly vowed fifty times a day that never under any circumstances would she set foot in this continent again. She would throw herself from the top deck of the *Celtic* first, into the less objectionable depths of the Atlantic. And now, at the moment of their departure, she laid herself out for the last time to be pleasant.

'Dearest Elizabeth,' she said, 'I told you quite distinctly this morning that if you called me Lady Hartridge I should not answer you. Mabel, yes, that's it. Now you've been quite too charming and kind to us for words, and as I am an extremely greedy person, as you have probably found out by this time, I'm going to ask one thing more of you, and insist on getting it. Whenever you come to England, let me know; I insist on that. And wherever we are, you must come and stay with us; I insist on that too. Dear me, how I have enjoyed myself! Tell everybody that my heart is cut up into about three thousand separate little pieces and sent round, like wedding cake, to all their houses. I keep just one piece, the smallest of all, for Tit-bits. Where is Tit-bits? Come here at once. Elizabeth is going.'

Tit-bits was her husband, a huge, blond, contented man, who, by the side of his wife, looked like a big retriever taking care of a beribboned Yorkshire terrier. He was so called because of the amazing quantity of scrappy information with which his mind was stored. At this moment he was engaged in acquiring more concerning the construction of steel frames for houses, from an American architect who was crossing with them.

'Well, it is too sad, Mrs Vane,' he said. 'We've both enjoyed ourselves enormously. And Mrs Vane is coming to us—eh, Mabel? Quite so. Goodbye, and thank you a thousand times. Let me see you down. Over twenty-one thousand tons this ship. Marvellous, isn't it? And seven hundred and five feet long.'

The bell had already warned all but passengers ashore, and soon after the huge bulk of the ship began mysteriously and silently to slide out into the river, with solemn and raucous hoots and bellowings. Lady Hartridge, consistent to the last, waved a tiny handkerchief in the direction of Mrs Vane, and even made believe to mop her eyes with it, till the ship swung round. Then she turned to her husband.

'Tit-bits, I have survived,' she said. 'That is all, literally all, that can be said. I shall now go to my cabin—I beg its pardon, my stateroom—and sleep for three days. See the steward, or whoever it is, at once, please, and arrange that no American shall sit within six paces on either side of me at dinner.'

It was mid-May, some nine months after the shores of the West had faded from Mabel Hartridge's unappreciative eyes, and she was sitting in her drawing-room in Bruton Street, discussing a certain question with her husband, and disagreeing with him. She held a long, closely written letter in her hands, which she suddenly crumpled up and threw into the wastepaper basket.

'It is perfectly impossible,' she said, 'and I absolutely refuse to do it. If we take in her and her husband, it will only leave one spare bedroom in the house. Besides, nobody has people to stay with them in London. It isn't done. Think what a frightful nuisance it would be! People from elsewhere stay in hotels. That is what hotels are for.'

'Then what is the point of having even one spare room?' asked Tit-bits, rather pertinently. The question was so pertinent, in fact, that it seemed to his wife to be almost impertinent, extremes meeting. So she disregarded it and went on with what she was saying.

'*Ces gens-là* have no sense of moral geography,' she exclaimed, impatiently. 'Because we stay with them at their horrible Newport there is no reason why they should stay with us in London. One talks to, one is intimate with, people abroad one would cut dead here: Consuls, P & O captains, all sorts of people.'

The wholesome and honest retriever was perplexed at this yapping.

'But you asked them to come,' he said; 'you insisted on it.'

'In New York. That is exactly what I am saying. I used modes of expression suitable to foreign countries. Of course, I will be nice to them; ask them to luncheon or dinner. But stay here—no. They are coming to London on 15 June, they say.'

She took up her engagement book and turned the leaves rapidly over.

'We're not doing anything that night,' she said. 'Ah, yes; there's the ball at Hampshire House—Gladys' swan song, she calls it— for they simply can't afford to keep it open even for the rest of the season. I'm sure she will let me ask them; it doesn't matter who is at a ball. And they shall dine here first, and lunch the next day. That will be delightful for them, and it always looks so hospitable to ask people to two things—three, in fact—all in one note. I will write to them now. What is the address? O yes; Windermere Hotel. And they are going on to Stratford-upon-Avon, Boscastle and Stonehenge; all the places that nobody but an American would ever think of going to.'

Tit-bits walked up and down the room jingling the coins in his pockets.

'I don't like it, Mabel,' he said. 'You ought to ask them to stay. We were their guests for nearly a month. If not here, at any rate for a Saturday till Monday.'

'My dear, don't quarter-deck about the room like that. It gets on my nerves. We are engaged or have our own party made up for every Saturday to Monday till the end of July.'

'But they made all sorts of arrangements for us——'

'At Newport. Besides, if we had been Mr and Mrs Smith, do you think they would have?'

Tit-bits shook his head.

'That's rather beastly of you, Mabel,' he said.

'But true.'

'Well, Scotland then?'

Mabel looked up at him with renewed impatience.

'Mrs Cyrus S. Vane cast on my hands from morning to night on a wet day!' she said. 'Thank you very much. Besides, they will probably have left long before. Please go away; I have a hundred things to do.'

Mabel was an adept at finished insincerity, and the note was quotable.

Dearest Elizabeth,

How quite too unkind of you not to have let me know before that you were in England. I shall not forgive you till I see you, and then I shan't be able to help it. Tit-bits, too, is *furious* with you. My dear, what with country cousins, and all the silly fuss of a London season and this poky little house of ours, we haven't an inch. But you must, you literally must, dine with us on your first night, the fifteenth, come with me to the dance at Hampshire House—people are tearing each other's eyes out to get an invitation—and lunch with us next day to talk over all the frights of London.—Longing to see you, yours affectionately,

MABEL HARTRIDGE.

This letter reached the Vanes as they were breakfasting. 'Dearest Elizabeth' read it through twice.

'Well, I'm sure. She don't want us, and that's what it is, Cyrus.' Then she laughed.

'Ball at Hampshire House!' she said. 'Why, if that doesn't tickle me to death. She treated Bertie Vandercrup like that when he was over last fall.'

Cyrus read the note his wife passed him, and took a telegraph form.

'Many regrets otherwise engaged' he wrote on it. Thus the finish, though not the insincerity, of Lady Hartridge was lost on people of such brutal directness.

The season was by now at its height: it had warmed up and got thoroughly going, and had not as yet lost its freshness, and Mabel Hartridge went meteor-like and brilliant on her way. She was one of the real thorough-going Londoners, and hurried unceasingly from one house to another, never pausing to think, content merely to be present at, whether it amused her or not, every social function that could be crammed into the day. In spite of the 'pokiness' of her house, she entertained also largely herself, and probably no name in London occurred so frequently in the lists of parties, no costumes were so often described as being seen in the Park, as hers.

But by slow and gradual degrees, while the Vanes were engaged on their round of visits to wholly impossible places, misgivings began to cross her mind. Somehow the Vanes were in the air: people talked about them, about their amazing wealth; it was said that they were going to settle in London for the last six weeks of the season, and were negotiating for a house. And as the middle of June approached, these misgivings became less vague, but far more unpleasant. Two or three times it happened that people mentioned they were going to the Vanes' party at the Carlton on the 20th, and in a sort of defiance rather than defence, Mabel, who had received no personal intimation of any such party, began to allude to 'those dreadful friends of Tit-bits, whom we stayed with at Newport. My dear, quite impossible; I nearly died of them.'

Then they came.

They had taken, it appeared, nearly a floor at the Carlton, and without pause for survey or reconnoitring, Mrs Cyrus began the siege of London. Singers, dancers, actors, pianists, performing dogs, fortune-tellers, and acrobats, all that there was of entertaining talent in London was spread in bewildering profusion before her guests. And London, like a school of gulls over a shoal of herrings, fluttered, flocked, and was fed. More terrible than that, all sorts of people, even those in Mabel's immediate set, found Mrs Cyrus too delicious for words. They enjoyed her hospitality, and they genuinely liked her great good-nature and her evident and enormous power of enjoyment. And the cream of the thing almost was the situation as it concerned dearest Mabel. For dearest Mabel, according to her account, had refused to go near Tit-bits' awful friends, while Tit-bits' awful friends, according to their account, had not asked her. Already she had the worst of it, for while it was clear from what she herself said that there was war going on, Mrs Vane, it appeared, was quite unconscious of the war.

Things were in this state when one morning Gladys Hampshire descended on Mabel in a perfect hurricane of excitement and exultation.

'Darling, I had to rush and tell you,' she cried. 'At last we've let Hampshire House! Those dear, angelic people—O! I forgot, you don't like them—anyhow, they have taken it for a year, simply at our own price. Hampshire didn't breathe a word of it to anybody till it was all settled, for fear of disappointing me. So, instead of living like starving bluebottles in a palace, we shall have a dear little poky house, so much more sensible, and be able to have tinned meat for breakfast whenever we like, so to speak. And they are coming in absolutely next week, and are giving a huge fancy-dress ball the week after. Yes, the Vanes, of course. They find London so charming that they are seriously thinking of settling in England, or of being here, at any rate, every season. I delight in them, and she is going to send out two thousand invitations. You really must come whether you like them or not.'

Mabel Hartridge had not got that concentration or that

consecution of reasoning faculty which is necessary to anyone who has to 'sit down and think', and the longer she thought the less on the whole she liked it. This defection of Gladys, too, was a serious blow: her friends were laying down their arms and going over to the enemy in shoals. It was merely a waste of energy to go about abusing the Vanes, if abuse did not impede— as it certainly did not appear to do—their triumphal progress. Humiliating as it was, she came to the conclusion that she had better climb down.

So she called—in person. Mrs Vane was out, but two days afterwards a footman returned a polite pasteboard with 'Hampshire House' already printed in the bottom left-hand corner. Then she waited amid the growing clamour about costumes, but still her invitation did not come. Everyone, it appeared, was going: it was to be *the* event of the season. And she would not be there: the bitterness of that was inconceivable except to one whose sleeping and waking thoughts were wholly occupied with Society of the very largest S. She would almost as soon have been found cheating at bridge as absent from the party. At last she could bear it no longer, and she wrote humbly, imploringly, privately, begging for an invitation.

Mrs Vane was emphatically a good-natured woman; but this letter gave her a pleasure which it was impossible to acquit of malice. She showed it to her husband, who grinned.

'I guess she's had enough,' he remarked. 'Don't worry her any more, Lizzie. Write nicely.'

'Shan't I wait just one mail, Cyrus?' she asked.

His shrewd, sharp face relaxed.

'Well, one,' he said; 'but only one.'

This answer reached the 'poky little house' about lunch-time next day:

DEAREST MABEL,
I can't think how my secretary has been so stupid not mailing you an invitation. Of course you must come to my little dance: I shall be just mad if you don't. And won't you come and see us before? I know how busy you are, but you might spare an hour for your old friend
                                                        ELIZABETH VANE.

Lady Hartridge quite suddenly felt her eyes grow a little dim. 'Really, she is rather a dear,' she said to herself.

The Jamboree

CAROLINE LADY CAMBER took it almost as a personal insult when her nephew, who, on the death of her husband, had succeeded to the title and the house and the impoverished estates and the famous Camber pearls, succeeded to the pigs also by his marriage with Margaret Joicey, daughter and heiress of the Chicago millionaire. The fact that he and his wife were devoted to each other did not detract from the infamy of the alliance: it was like a buffet in the face to be forced to receive this odiously modern young woman.

Caroline had an apt and acid wit and a soft, dreamy, meditative way of saying the nastiest things, which made them doubly telling, and her murmuring enunciation when she realized that the pearls would no longer be worn by her was peculiarly venomous. 'So suitable,' she said, 'that Margaret should have the pearls, for "Margaret" means "pearls", does it not? And the pigs! Isn't there some text about pearls and swine?'

Of course this duly came to Margaret's knowledge, who screamed with laughter and said, 'Isn't she lovely?' and the next time when the two met the young bride came running up to her.

'Dear Aunt Caroline,' she said. 'I tell everybody that you're the wittiest woman in London. It's perfectly killing what you said about me and my pearls and my pigs. I wish Popper had been alive to hear it; it would have tickled him to death. But I've cabled it right along to the advertisement department at home, to see if they can't use it some way. A great poster, you know, with red headlines: 'What Lady Caroline Camber says . . .' And then a picture of me with a necklace of pearls and sausages. I think you're the loveliest woman I've ever seen. By the way, you must promise to come to my jamboree. Why, don't you know what a jamboree is? You sit on the floor and have a good time, and look at the Russian ballet or whatever's going on between whiles, and dance. Engaged? Why, that's too bad, particularly as you don't yet know what night I'm giving it.'

With beaming good nature Margaret had crammed into this effective little speech all that she stood for, and all that, in consequence, Aunt Caroline particularly detested; for while Margaret stood for the present in the society of today, Caroline Camber quite as typically stood for the past, and for the order of things that had vanished. Those days (so Caroline would have put it) were distinguished by decorum and stateliness and exclusiveness; Society consisted of a small compact phalanx of folk, mostly related to each other, and quite unaware of the meaning of jamborees. They met each other two or three times a day, they dined, they danced, they stayed with each other, they never alluded to money or the internal organs of the body, and if any scandal occurred within the sacred portals, though they talked it over in corners and discreet whispers, they never conducted screaming public discussion of it over the dinner-table.

It was for that order she stood, and it was with a sense of duty, positively pleasant, that she shut her doors and sharpened her tongue against the casual mannerless invaders who now had pushed their way into almost every house but hers, and in short skirts and braces (literally no more) jabbered and jazzed and jamboreed. Their very virtues were abhorrent to her, and Margaret's serene good-nature seemed insolent. Besides, one was so helpless against that careless indifference.

And the jamboree! The impertinence of Margaret asking her to this nameless orgy! Somehow or other the jamboree must be stopped, and as this determination rose hot within her, she cast aside her sense of helplessness and felt like a Crusader.

There was a great deal of mettle about Caroline Camber, and as the days went on, she began to be aware that she would need it all. London generally, including the thin line of heroines to which she belonged, who had previously stood pretty firm against modern invaders and encroachers, was getting culpably interested in the jamboree, and the thin line of heroines began sensibly to waver. There was an air of mystery about it, and the small hints that leaked out, and the large fabrications which were invented about it, added spice and pepper to London's curiosity.

Certainly a constellation of stars from the Russian ballet (lit at staggering expense) was going to shine there, for so much Margaret herself had told Aunt Caroline, and it was probably a fact that a very ingenuous young lady from the French stage was to recite something that had never been recited before. Then rumour got busy and said that one of the most advanced Bolshevists from Moscow would give a short lecture on murder, and Margaret, when approached on the subject, gave the further information that his lecture would be made more interesting by several practical illustrations of the subject.

The party, in any case, as was certain when the invitations were sent out, would be quite a small one, for only a hundred of these had been issued, and in consequence there was an agreement (gratifying to Aunt Caroline) among those who had not been asked that they would not have gone if they had been. Among such Aunt Caroline briskly and poisonously proselytized, and the fact that so many had called (in anticipation of the event) and so few been chosen gave her a great deal to do. All the elect, who had been invited, had feverishly accepted, and she had an occasional qualm that those who had not been invited would not have been so acid in their denunciation of jamborees if a chance of this jamboree had come in their way. The crusade, in fact, was not really prospering, and public feeling was not making headway.

And then, at the last moment, Providence intervened in the vulgar democratic manner characteristic of it. Aunt Caroline's aunt, who for years had led a sequestered and paralytic existence, died only a couple of days before the date for the party, and she, who in expectation of a handsome legacy, had long said that it would be a blessing for all concerned when this event occurred, thought that she had never spoken a truer word. For of all the proprieties that had the sanctity of Mosaic law to her family, that of showing due respect for the departure of the most distant relatives was perhaps the most scrupulously honoured, and it was with something approaching hilarity that Aunt Caroline went to Camber House as soon as ever she had put on her habiliments of woe to announce the calamity, and indicate, if that was necessary, the propriety of cancelling the jamboree.

Such indication seemed to be needful, and even then Margaret looked puzzled.

'But why,' she asked, 'must I put off my party because your aunt is dead? I guess she isn't any relation of mine, nor of Tony's either. Of course you won't come, Aunt Caroline, for you told me that before, and I'm ever so sorry for you if you feel stricken, but how Tony and I come into it beats me. And then there's the Russian ballet, engaged and paid for, too, which I understand isn't always the case. And then there's Mademoiselle—oh, I nearly let that out——.'

Aunt Caroline gave her wide wan smile, so suitable for bereavements.

'Dear Margaret,' she said, 'how sympathetic you are! And it's quite natural that you shouldn't understand our old-fashioned ways. You see—you are one of the family now, and the family is in mourning. If your aunt died, dear——.'

'You would go into mourning?' asked Margaret with that childlike smile which it was difficult to interpret.

Aunt Caroline had not meant to put quite so preposterous a case, for the idea of Margaret having any relations at all was alien to her. With another wan smile she slid off the topic.

'We needn't go into that,' she said, 'and, indeed, I have not come here to argue with you, but just to tell you. You have to conform to our ways. If I ever went to America I should conform to yours. That is a mere matter of good breeding.'

'Ah, do come to America,' said Margaret. 'Come with me when I go over in the fall—I mean the autumn. But about my jamboree. What will happen, Aunt Caroline, if I do give it? What will *happen*? Try to imagine!'

It was useless to continue talking to anybody who seemed really to have no grasp of what was being said, and Aunt Caroline rose.

'I will see your husband, dear,' she said, 'and get him to explain to you.'

'Yes, that will be the best plan,' said Margaret.

Margaret had a very fair notion of how things stood when her husband had explained them to her. It was not that she was supposed to be so overwhelmed with grief at the death of an old lady whom she had never seen, and was not related to either of them, that she could not summon up spirit for her jamboree, but simply that when a death of someone, however collaterally remote, occurred in families like the Cambers, they had a habit of not advertising their gaieties for a little while, and the jamboree had been very much advertised. Tony agreed with her that this was a perfectly empty form, and with her to lead and him rather timorously to acquiesce, Margaret concocted a scheme which would satisfy Aunt Caroline and the proprieties without the sacrifice of the jamboree.

Next morning, so ran the plot, there would appear in all the leading journals a short paragraph to state that, owing to a family bereavement, Lady Camber's party would not take place, and in order to ensure that the announcement should reach all the friends who had accepted her invitation, she had a small slip printed to be sent to each, containing the same information. But at the bottom of each slip she scribbled in her own hand: '*Private. We had to put the party off, but come quietly just the same.*' Her secretary meantime was busy addressing envelopes, and Tony giggled and made little cowardly objections to what he was sanctioning, as is the way of a man.

'Aunt Caroline will be sure to hear about it,' he said. 'If you tell a thing privately to a hundred and twenty people, it will leak out.'

'No, dear,' said Margaret. 'If you tell a thing privately to one person, I agree you might as well shout it out in the square. But if you tell a thing to a great many, they don't care to talk about it; everybody knows.'

She went on swiftly scribbling.

'Besides, even if she does,' she asked, 'what will Aunt Caroline do? What will happen, as I said to her? If it hadn't been for you, I should have defied her; it's only for the sake of your peace of mind, Tony, that I stoop to deceit. There! I guess that's all. Oh, and I shall write a little sweet note to Aunt Caroline, telling her I've put off my jamboree, just in case she misses it in the papers.'

This note was soon finished, and she rose from the table, where the pile of envelopes which her secretary was addressing was already rising high.

'And you'll put a slip in each envelope please, Miss Rivington,' she said, 'and get them off by the early post. I must go out, Tony; shall I drop you? It's the dentist for me. Or is that forbidden after a family bereavement?'

So Miss Rivington was left to finish directing envelopes and putting into each one of the slips which Margaret had scribbled on. She worked in rather a hurry, for there was a good deal to be done before post time, and thus it happened in the most natural manner that when she came to the envelope which Margaret had addressed to Aunt Caroline, but had omitted to fasten up, she thought it was one of her own, and inserted under its flap one of those slips which begged the recipient to come to the jamboree in spite of the official cancellation . . .

Now, among her more Victorian passions, old Lady Camber had that of curiosity. She had seen with approval the notice in the papers that the jamboree was abandoned, and not knowing the history of Miss Rivington's mistake, was completely baffled to guess why Margaret should not only write to her to remind her of what was public news, but insert a further statement of that, and scribble at the bottom her hopes that Aunt Caroline would come just the same.

There was clearly something at the bottom of this, and faintly suspecting the worst, Lady Camber felt that uncertainty as to what was going on was intolerable, and made up her mind to go. Jamborees, she understood, were evening parties, and she supposed that whatever was happening would be happening about eleven o'clock.

As a matter of fact, the jamboree had begun an hour before, and at this fell hour of eleven there happened to be a moment of complete silence in the ballroom where Margaret's party was assembled, for Mlle Baltôt was on the point of beginning the recitation which nobody had ever heard before, and the audience were anxious not to miss one single word. There they all were sitting casually on cushions on the floor or perched on the arms of chairs, with a buffet in the corner of the room, and a keg of beer decked in gardenias standing by it, and most of them were smoking and more of them were in the costume of braces and skirts (so detestable to the soul of Lady Camber) with bobbed hair and tiaras, and members of the Russian ballet mingled with them, and all was steeped in that atmosphere of modernity which stank in her Victorian nostrils. Wide was flung the door, and a footman (selected for his sonorous voice) called out, 'Lady Camber.'

Margaret, sitting near the door, had one wild, bewildered moment in which she thought that her footman, having gone mad, was calling her, for really there seemed no other explanation less outrageous, and, turning, she saw Aunt Caroline!

At that moment Mlle Baltôt began to speak, and Aunt Caroline's face (she knew French perfectly) became the visage of the Gorgon. Stonier and stonier she grew, while roars of laughter greeted what Mlle Baltôt, with her singularly pure enunciation, made so transparently clear. While this was in progress Margaret found herself acutely wondering what would happen at the end of the recitation. She made up her mind what initiative she would take; the rest depended wholly on Aunt Caroline.

The end came, and, wreathed in smiles and pearls, Margaret bewitchingly advanced.

'Dear Aunt Caroline,' she said. 'How nice of you to look in. We——'

Aunt Caroline had to raise her voice from its usual soft dreaminess in order to make herself heard through the din of applause and laughter. She was determined to be audible.

'I beg that you won't speak to me,' she said. 'You tried to deceive me into thinking you had abandoned your party, instead of which——'

For a moment words failed her.

'Instead of which,' she said, 'I find an indecent Frenchwoman amusing your indecent guests. I am now going away.'

Margaret stared at her, and immediately found herself staring at her back. She followed her out into the hall. Then she spoke with a pleasant smile.

'But now you've got to apologize to me,' she said.

'My cloak,' said Aunt Caroline.

Margaret made a gesture of dismissal to the footman.

'I don't want to threaten you, Aunt Caroline,' she observed.

Aunt Caroline made a curious noise like a grasshopper whirring. It indicated scornful laughter.

'Threaten me?' she said. 'Threaten? Me?'

'Yes. For instance, you would not like me to send a list of my guests to the press—would you?—and include your name among them——'

Suddenly a sense of outrage seized Margaret. She still spoke in her ordinary voice, but as she thought over what she had suffered from Aunt Caroline she felt a difficulty in controlling it.

'The world would laugh at you, Aunt Caroline,' she said. 'It would say you were an old hypocrite for pretending to be in mourning and coming to my jamboree on the sly. And you weren't asked either. It's true I gave you a sort of verbal invitation, but you weren't polite to me, and so I didn't send you a real invitation. If you come out with me to America in the fall you must learn not to go to houses where you're not asked. No well-bred American does that. We consider it a matter of good breeding not to go where we're not asked. Upon my word, I won't threaten you, I'll send the list of my guests to the paper right now. And there's a very bright young friend of mine in there who'll write something snappy about your entrance at the beginning of Mlle Baltôt's recitation!'

Margaret paused, and again all her good nature came bubbling up, aerated, so to speak, by sheer amusement at Aunt Caroline's face. In all her blameless years she had never looked so blankly and helplessly surprised.

'Why, it's only my fun, Aunt Caroline,' she said. 'Must you be going? Well, I must get back to my guests. But don't be rude to me again; it makes me mad—angers me I should say.'

Complementary Souls

IT was not in the least because Walter Steeples and his wife disliked each other that they decided after three years of married life to obtain their divorce, nor did either of them desire to be married to anybody else, and when they parted their farewells were made with much emotion and real regret on both sides. But they were far too sensible to let sentiment override the conclusions which their rational minds told them were well-founded, and they kissed each other for the last time with great affection but with Spartan firmness. Belonging as they did to the free republic of the West, the matter was arranged with the minimum of irksome formalities, and neither of them was obliged to go and stay under an assumed name at any dingy hotel, while a detective watched outside.

This would have been a great trial to them, not only because they both disliked dingy places, but chiefly because their fine sense of honour would have revolted at so insincere a proceeding.

Their superb mansion in Fifth Avenue, which for these three years had been so conspicuous a centre of fads and fashion, and art and athletics, and soul-culture, was sold by auction, for they had both determined to settle in England, and it was by a pure coincidence, though a pleasant one, that they had both booked passages on the same sailing of the *Majestic*. They saw a good deal of each other on the voyage, and parted at Liverpool with renewed regret. They had both of them, of course, ordered special trains to convey them and their suites to London, and though Walter's special was due to start ten minutes before Amelie's, he insisted on her taking the priority, and waved his hat to her as she steamed away in great dejection, for this was their final adieu; henceforth their ways would be apart.

As he waited on the platform he let the memory-pictures of the three past years present themselves, like the exhibition of some super-film, in swift procession before his mind.

The two had from childhood been earmarked for each other

by their respective parents, for Amelie was the only child of her mother, who was the Tinned Salmon Queen, and Walter the sole heir of his father, the Green Corn King, and the fitness of an alliance between the future owners of so much edible property was obvious. The two children had been brought up in the faith of this destiny, and no idea of propping up any decaying English dukedom with tinned salmon had ever entered Amelie's head, nor had Walter ever contemplated a marriage into any effete though royal house.

As they developed, their fitness for each other became even more marked, for their tastes were utterly dissimilar, and thus each was the complement of the other. Amelie was of extremely serious and studious bent: she doted on 'isms', and the housing of the poor; psychoanalysis, the New Thought, the Girl Guide movement, architecture, and ecclesiastical history were her dearly loved hobbies; while Walter was passionately devoted to dancing, athletic exercises, and all that was redolent of youth, gaiety and laughter.

To be sure, there were pessimistic persons among their parents' friends, who abounded in gloomy prophecies as to the improbability of the union of such diversely minded young people proving a success, but the engaging doctrine of complementary souls was just now very popular in the high, intellectual circles in which their parents moved, and the two who were to be experimented on were perfectly willing to be formally engaged, with a view to marriage after six months' probation.

But hardly had half that period elapsed when a terrible calamity overtook their parents. The Tinned Salmon Queen, partaking too freely of green corn, died of galloping colic, while the Green Corn King contracted ptomaine (or possibly botulistic) poisoning from eating a kedgeree made of tinned salmon, and expired within a few hours of the other. The bereaved children therefore felt themselves more than ever bound to execute their parents' wishes.

Not only did beloved voices, now for ever mute, seem to lay the marriage upon them as a sacred duty, but this seemed the best way of restoring public confidence in the delicacies in question. Tinned salmon and green corn formed the staple of the wedding breakfast, and, freely indulged in by over five hundred heroic guests, vindicated their entire wholesomeness.

For a few months after the conclusion of an uneclipsed honeymoon it looked as if the theory of complementary souls would vindicate itself as thoroughly as the tinned salmon and green corn had done. Bride and bridegroom grew daily in affection for each other, and while Walter esteemed the fine intellectual fibre and noble aspirations of his wife, Amelie, descending from the rarefied atmosphere of her serious studies, refreshed and relaxed herself in the gaiety and vigour of her husband. She even found herself in her less lofty moments remotely envying the exuberance of his youth, and he, in some occasional weariness from one of the physical exercises at which he so superbly excelled, or returning very late after some uproarious supper party to find her pure profile bent over her Plato, was victim of certain vague qualms and spiritual twinges at the thought of the remote years to come when he would be able no longer to play polo, and when his ears would be deaf to the entrancing syncopations of ragtime.

Such moments confirmed the complementary soul theory, and drew them closer together.

Primarily, then, it was not any incompatibility of tastes or temper that caused the rift to widen in their married lute. They liked and appreciated each other; but what neither of them could stand, and what daily became more intolerable was the continual presence of each other's friends.

As befitted their dazzling pre-eminence in New York society, their great house in Fifth Avenue must continually blaze with magnificent hospitalities, and these feasts and festivals were of the deadliest description to them both. For a while they tried to mix their respective friends and affinities in a delirious *macédoine*, and haggard females (allies of Amelie's) with missions and earnest faces and serge dresses found themselves taken into dinner by polo players; and gay young music-hall artistes like Garnet Grosvenor and Liza Lambeth were paired off with Professors of Palæontology and exponents of Right Thought, Disciples of the Simple Life who ate no cooked food, but chewed raw carrots and Brazil nuts, starved in the opulence of truffles and ortolans, and the New Rechabites recoiled from the winking bubbles of illicit champagne.

After dinner the earnest clustered round a black bishop who told them of the wonderful vegetarian movement among cannibal tribes, and pointing to his wooden gaiter recounted how, in their less regenerate days, he had nearly suffered a completer martyrdom, while his thrilling sentences were punctuated by melodies from the jazz band in the ballroom. Sometimes Amelie held a spiritualistic séance before dinner, and to the mediumship of Miss Venetia Trench they sat in the dark and gently warbled hymns as they waited for Lotus and Bluebell (those elevated disembodied spirits) to give them glimpses into the Unseen.

And when Lotus was in the middle of her most encouraging information about the Other Side the door opened, and a footman stumbled into the pious dark with a tray of cocktails.

Some adjustment in the pursuit of their respective aspirations was clearly advisable, and Amelie suggested this one morning after the first of a series of breakfast parties, at which the Dean of Abbotsville who went into trances and amazed everyone by his inspired utterances, distinctly addressed Garnet Grosvenor as Jezebel, which was not her name at all.

'My darling,' said Amelie to her husband, when the painful scene was over and they were alone. 'We must not try to make discordant elements mix. It seemed to be very rude of the dean——'

'It was,' said Walter.

'I hadn't finished. But it wasn't the dean who was rude: it was the high spirit who was inspiring him. Also, Miss Grosvenor should have kept calmer.'

'She had considerable provocation,' said Walter. 'You wouldn't like to be called Jezebel before ever so many people.'

Amelie wanted to be fair.

'No,' she said, 'I should not. So we must avoid the possibility of such scenes. Our position demands that we should take the lead in social entertainment, but we must select, we must classify. We might give three dinner parties a week for your friends with dancing, and three for mine with lectures. I am mortified, I confess, about the failure of our first breakfast party: people are savage in the morning. But whatever the provocation Miss Grosvenor should not have thrown her sausage at the dean.'

Her fine eyes filled with tears.

'I am mortified, dear,' she said, 'as much on your account as on mine.'

Walter patted her hand.

'Well, don't take it to heart, Amelie,' he said. 'You shall have parties for your friends, and I for mine. I don't want you to give up your friends: I don't ask that.'

Amelie's charming little head gave a most determined jerk.

'Naturally you do not,' she said. 'I guess you've got enough sense to see that it wouldn't be a particle of good if you did. And I don't ask you to give up yours. But after this experience we must clearly keep them separate. I won't have good food thrown about.'

'And I won't have my friends called Jezebel when they're not,' he retorted.

But this policy of the isolation of warring elements proved no better than the mixed parties. There were, it is true, no hurtlings of sausages and opprobrious names across the table, but the gatherings became even more awfully intolerable to one or the other of them.

Hitherto, Walter had been able to seek refuge from Amelie's highbrowed guests among his own, and she to disinfect the vapid conversation of athletes and actresses with lofty talk; but now one or other of them was always marooned on a desert island. The inherited courage and perseverance which in past years had amassed their immense fortunes gave them the grit to endure, and for a couple of years more they persevered in this nightmare life, preserving for each other regard and affection, but choking and strangling among each other's friends.

Finally, the breaking-point came, and following the inexorable conclusions of good sense and reason, they freed themselves.

Walter was roused from his retrospective reverie by the stationmaster who told him, firmly but politely, that his special should go without him, if he did not hurry. Though he was unaccustomed to be spoken to like this, he hurried.

The reason why Amelie had determined to settle in England was worthy of her good sense. After the splendour and brilliance of New York, London envisaged itself as a leisurely tranquil backwater well out of mid-stream. It promised the fragrant seclusion of a country town with a cathedral (St Paul's), and the mouldering mellow beauty of ancient places.

There were old residential squares to be found there, as she knew from photographs, where electric trams and elevated railways never whirled and whistled. They had shady gardens with velvet lawns, and she had pictured herself sitting under a sumac tree, with her notebooks and papers round her, listening to some venerable professor from London University, whom she would hire by the hour to give her instruction in New Thought and ancient history. She would devote all the energies of her indefatigable nervous system to acquiring the treasures of learning and research, while she devoted the more material treasures derived from tinned salmon to the furtherance of these pursuits.

She did not definitely discard all thought of matrimony and maternity, but her immediate business was to improve herself and benefit others. It was with a sense of conventual peace that she bought two adjoining and (to her mind) old-fashioned houses in Grosvenor Square, and unleashing three different firms into them, in order to get the bare essential improvements made before she was too old to enjoy the amenities of a habitable house, installed bathrooms and telephones and heating apparatus up to the level of decency. She picnicked in corners of these hovels till a tolerable house emerged.

It was in quest of a somewhat similar simplicity and amateurishness that her late husband also crossed the Atlantic. America, for all his physical energy, was a bustle of professionalism. In England people took things more quietly, and in the intervals of playing games and shooting and hunting lived a soft, slug-like life in London.

A house on the river (if you could call the Thames a river) would be pleasant for a London residence, but finding that Lambeth Palace would not be leased to him at any known figure, he postponed the selection of a town house and went down to Sandwich to play golf. He liked the links so much that he offered to buy them straight away, but again there was nothing doing; and, as it was now mid-August, he took the grouse-shooting and deerstalking over a greater part of Ross-shire, and a slice of Norfolk for subsequent partridges. The fame of him soon went abroad, and he woke to find himself extremely popular.

Any amount of amiable young men were delighted to shoot his birds and ride his horses when hunting began, and they brought down to the little castle he had taken in Leicestershire a corresponding number of charming young women. They all treated him nearly as one of themselves, and before long a migration of mothers, quite as young as their daughters, followed them.

But though Walter appreciated the charm of mature and youthful sirens alike, he began to sweat with chilly qualms and misgivings. Daughters and mothers (if widowhood rendered the latter eligible) seemed to have designs upon him which were not confined to eating and drinking and hunting at his expense. Ladies of title in want of pearls, who admired the moon, made it quite clear that they wished to admire it with him, and impecunious adventuresses tried to cut out their daughters, when he had only shuddered at the advances of these maidens. A young earl, resembling a canary in voice and colouring, called equal attention to the charms of his mother and of his sister, and in a word Walter, who had theoretically rejected all notion of marrying into even a royal house, found himself expected to marry any nameless nobody.

But Providence intervened on his behalf, and the little castle in Leicestershire was burned to the ground in a single night. That ensured the dispersal of his party and gave him breathing space to think.

During these hectic weeks he had occasionally obtained news through the public Press of Amelie's movements. Under her maiden name she was making a prolonged tour through the cathedral cities of England, and Walter brooded over the Gothic tranquillity of her life. She travelled from fane to fane in a procession of sumptuously fitted motor-vans, and encamped in the bishop's garden in the close. She requited this delightful hospitality with enormous cheques for the fabric funds, and was justly popular. Walter perused the illustrated accounts of her progress with heart-felt sympathy, and rejoiced that she at least had found her *métier*. A bevy of archaeologists, architects and archdeacons accompanied her, and the tour was a debauch of lectures. The cause of mental improvement was not confined to ecclesiastical interests, for he noticed that the Regius Professor of Astronomy had joined the party on the eve of an eclipse of the moon, and several noted spiritualists had enlivened the ruins of Glastonbury with astounding manifestations. At intervals she inspected regiments of Girl Guides and elementary schools.

Sometimes as he read about the brilliant tranquillity of her progress he felt terribly envious of her, for not only had she found the elevating life she loved, but this unceasing pursuit of pleasure on his own part was beginning to weary him, mixed up, as it was, with the perils of menaced matrimony.

Again and again, in moments of depression, he asked himself what his ultimate goal was, for some stern fibre of puritanism was entwined with his frivolity. Before many years his eye would grow dim and his nimble muscles slack, and, unable to pursue his various veneries, he would have no store of appropriate pursuits to divert the long leisure of old age.

He bought a lucid architectural manual and tried to grasp the difference between the Decorated and Perpendicular styles, but, unused as he was to reading, he found it dry and difficult work. Yet to Amelie it seemed absorbing, and probably some seeds of interest lurked there. Meantime hunting was over and his castle burnt, and in the early spring he came back to London to while away a few months there.

He could not abide hotel life, and being rather charmed, one bright morning of March, with the cheerful aspect of Grosvenor Square, he selected a couple of houses on the north side of it, evicted the inhabitants with a colossal cheque, and turned his purchase over to builders and decorators to convert into a tolerable dwelling-house.

Amelie having finished the English cathedrals a fortnight ago, had shipped her caravan over to France, and was pursuing the primrose path of mental culture on the Continent. One van was equipped as a travelling library, and after a day of lectures and sightseeing, she was accustomed to spend her evenings there with her ever-increasing notebooks. She had gone first to the Basque country, avoiding garish Biarritz, and, moving by stages northwards, came in a week of most inclement weather to the interesting town of Rouen.

The incessant rain no doubt depressed her spirits and made the lamp of culture burn low, and one evening she abandoned her studies and visited the theatre where *La fille de Mme Angot* was being played. She was ashamed at the thought of how immensely she enjoyed it, and it woke in her certain obstinate questionings, which, on her return for an hour's study before going to bed, seemed to get between her and the pages of her book.

Her own youth stood beside her and entreated her. It told her that she was starving and imprisoning it; it begged to be allowed to come out (as it had done that evening) for longer and regular periods. It would not always be with her; it would soon drop from her side into the dark well of Time. . . .

She tried to stop her ears to the insidious importunate voice, to seize and eject the intruding presence, but it slipped from her grasp and mocked her efforts to capture and evict it. It was as elusive as the play of sunlight on water; it danced to the gay little melodies she had heard at the theatre, and rustled to their rhythm; it would not allow her to fix her attention on her interesting studies. Then suddenly grown strong, it plucked her from her seat and made her look northward from the window to where in England Walter was gloriously fulfilling the call of his youth. She felt a pang of envy at the thought of him; he was living appropriately to his age, while she was anticipating the years of curtailed activity which she might never reach. Meantime the days of her youth were slipping from her like bright beads spilt.

This would never do; she told herself that she was pandering in thought to frivolous appetites. This lazy caravan life was corrupting her more earnest purposes; with a cathedral here and a lecture there it was a mere concession to idleness and trifling, and she resolved to cut it short, return to London, and plunge herself in the seas of more strenuous mental activity.

The seas, on her arrival, seemed quite prepared for her plunge, for she found in Grosvenor Square a vast accumulation of prospectuses and agenda. Directly she had dined she sent for her shorthand secretary and her typist, and took a resolute header into the waiting waves. . . .

She sat in the magnificent library which stretched its studious length along the west wall of her house. Usually it had enjoyed the quiet of annihilation, for there were double windows on to the square: at the back it looked out on a secluded garden, and when she left it for her tour in France the house next door had belonged to some recluse Dowager. But now there came through the wall the intimation of a livelier occupant; there was the blurred squealing of a band and the dim beat of rhythmical feet.

She tried to tie down her mind to her studious tasks, but it seemed as if the adjacent festiveness was throbbing in her very pulses. Part of her passionately resented these intrusive cadences;

but there was some unchained rebel within her which delighted in them. Strenuously she tried to smother that light-minded imp, and for two hours she grimly dealt with her edifying correspondence. Then she dismissed her secretaries, and, making sure that the door was shut, she pirouetted partnerless over the polished parquet of the floor. The guilt and the rapture of rebellion was hers, and she wished that Walter was here to dance with her.

She had a very early engagement next morning, for a regiment of Girl Guides, of whom she was honorary colonel, were leaving Victoria Station at five-thirty on a sisterly tour to the Argentine Republic, and she had promised to see them off. At a quarter to five, therefore, to give time for a treat of buns and chocolate, she was on her doorstep, and even as she walked across the pavement to her Rolls-Royce, the door of the house next door flew open and emitted a bubbling stream of young men and maidens in fancy-dress.

As her day's earnest work was beginning, the nocturnal enjoyment of these bright creatures was only just drawing to its reluctant close, and with a leap of the heart she realized that she was no older than they. They fluttered with laughter and gay conversation towards the waiting vehicles, Cleopatras and Apaches, and, apparently, Adams and Eves. Even as she watched, fascinated by their brightness, a splendid Bacchus or something similar appeared on the threshold. He was quite unmistakable.

'It's real rotten of you old things not to stop to breakfast!' he cried; 'but if you will all go.... Half-past one then, Evie ... yes, you dine with me, Clara, after our tennis.'

There were cries of 'Good-night, Walter darling' and flutterings of kissed hands. As, slightly shivering, and no wonder, he turned to go back into the house, he saw her.

'Why, Amelie!' he cried.

She tried to induce her feet to carry her to her motor. They refused.

'Walter!' she said. 'Why, is it good-morning or good-night? I wish you them both, my dear, and don't wait, for you'll catch cold. I'm just going to see a party off!'

'And that's what I'm doing now,' he said. 'Lord! how fresh and charming you look, Amelie—and I—I've been up all night. I feel like nothing at all.'

'I heard revelling going on,' she said. 'And to think that it was you! I was dictating letters.'

'I must apologize if we disturbed you,' said he.

She remembered her solitary pirouetting and was fair.

'You didn't,' she said, 'I joined in for a minute, before I went to bed. It sounded lovely. But I must go now; I've got to be at Victoria in ten minutes.'

'Mayn't I come with you?' he asked. 'I should love to have a talk after all this time. If I put on a fur coat and buttoned it up. . . .'

She threw back her head, laughing.

'Certainly you may not!' she said. 'The Girl Guides would have fits. Besides it's yesterday with you still: I'm today.'

'But I'm today,' he protested. 'I can't go to bed now. Come, anyhow, and have breakfast with me when you get back. Yes? Why, I'll go and order it at once. Coffee, isn't it, for you?'

The builders and decorators had to return once more. The four houses, now thrown into one, made a tolerable residence.

Dodo and the Brick

UNLIKE most women who are old enough to know better, Dodo had a birthday every year and called special attention to it by giving a dance and a dinner party at which there figured a sumptuous ceremonial cake with an ever-increasing galaxy of candles burning round it, the number of which accurately corresponded to that of her years.

'I always cut it myself,' she explained to Edith Arbuthnot who was having tea with her, and David up on leave from Eton, 'and with all those candles the scene resembles more and more some highly popular shrine with the figure of the saint (that's me) as large as life and beautifully dressed, beaming down on the devout. I think that's rather profane; you needn't listen, David.'

'I say, mummy, what particular saint do you think you——' began David.

'Jessie, the mother of David, darling,' said Dodo hopefully.

'But Jesse was his father,' said David.

'David, don't argue. Jessie was his mother, too. Master Jesse married Miss Jessie, and they lived happily ever afterwards. Nowadays every boy knows so much better than his parents.'

David put five lumps of sugar in his tea, one after the other. The last stuck up above the surface.

'I know better than that,' he said. 'Jessie isn't a woman's name in the Bible. There's Jezebel. She looked out of the window.'

Dodo found herself in the usual dilemma of those who talk nonsense, and changed the subject.

'David, is that tea or syrup?' she asked hastily.

'Syrup,' said David. 'Have some?'

Dodo declined this magnanimous offer, and as David's pony and his father (who seemed to matter less) were waiting for him, he drank his syrup and went off for his ride.

The season was just beginning to break forth like the sheaf of leaf-buds on bare twigs, and Dodo had been jotting down some dates for her own functions. These now included a musical evening party entirely consisting of Edith's compositions.

'But I'm an anachronism,' she said. 'You had better get somebody else. I would much sooner wrap my worsted shawl about me, and, what they call, "give over".'

'No, you wouldn't,' said Edith. When she did not agree, she usually stated that fact quite shortly.

'So much the worse for me if I wouldn't; it would really be more suitable if I did. I've had a splendid innings, and I ought to retire, sixty not out, like the whisky, and sit in the pavilion. But who's to go in next I should like to know? There's nobody who's doing my stunt any more. There's no one with a sense of splendour. I daresay it's out of date; probably a good thing.'

'Excellent,' said Edith very ungratefully. But she was standing for Parliament as a Labour candidate.

'Oh, you've got to say "excellent",' said Dodo. 'That's part of *your* stunt. But you don't really think it any more than I do. You like splendour and distinction and the right sort of extravagance. Dear me, what a long way I've travelled. When I was young I put my foot through every convention there was within ten miles of me—it would be more now because of motors—and now I've begun to believe in quite a quantity of them, just when everybody else regards them as obsolete. Manners, behaviour, reasonableness, for instance. But I never could take things for granted: I always had to see what would happen if one didn't. But on the whole that leads to reality. We may not be edifying, darling, but we're real!'

Edith laughed.

'Oh, let's cling to it,' she said. 'It's getting rather rare. The young generation are phantasmal. They're so much occupied in proclaiming how real they are, that they have no time left for being it. I suppose the war exhausted their capacity.'

'They still carry on the tradition of the war,' said Dodo. 'Young men who were then being firmly spanked at school behave still as if they were on three days' leave from France, and girls who were then in pigtails as if they had an evening off from hospitals or munition work.'

'And they all recite the creed that anybody over thirty is *gaga*!' said Edith.

'After all our elders said much the same about us, if I recollect rightly,' said Dodo. 'And we thought, as you know quite well, that our elders and betters were back numbers, and how right we were! We shouldn't get on if everyone behaved as others had always done. What's good enough for our fathers should never be good enough for us!'

'But the mistake they make is in thinking that nobody was ever so marvellous as they,' said Edith. 'You and I were much more marvellous. In fact we are still. We've got an individuality, which I totally deny most of the young generation have. They are only interested in themselves, and that's a very shoddy sort of individualism.'

'Darling, are you sure you don't mean that they're not interested in you?' asked Dodo.

'I'm quite certain of that, but you needn't be personal,' remarked Edith. 'Anyhow, you don't arrive at individualism, which is the only thing worth living for, by being absorbed in yourself. You've got to be absorbed in other interests, and to get rid of yourself before you begin to have a real existence. You have to immerse yourself in other people, and wipe out all sense of your own identity, before you arrive at it. And then some morning, when you have a moment to spare, you turn your attention to yourself, and with a sense of discovery you exclaim, "Hallo, there's someone here!" And you find it's you.'

'Aged sixty,' said Dodo.

'There you are, thinking of yourself again,' said Edith.

'Not at all, I was thinking of you that moment,' said Dodo. 'Of course, age doesn't matter so long as you keep yourself somewhere about twenty-eight in outlook and elasticity.'

'Why twenty-eight?' asked Edith.

'Because my Nadine and her Hughie are twenty-eight,' said Dodo, 'and they are having rather a jumpy time. So if I am to be of the slightest use I must cling firmly to their age and see with their eyes.'

'I can't be too thankful I never had a daughter,' said Edith parenthetically. 'I couldn't bear to be hated as much as a daughter would be bound to hate me. Just imagine yourself, Dodo, at Nadine's age with me for a mother.'

'Awful,' said Dodo. 'But do regain your individuality, and

think about me. I want to know what I ought to do if I was
Nadine's age. I should know what to do if I was my own. But
the wisdom of twenty-eight is different from the wisdom of
sixty. Make yourself twenty-eight, Edith, and tell me what line
to take.'

'I haven't the slightest idea yet where you want your line to
take you! I know nothing about anything.'

'Don't interrupt me, then. There's a dreadful woman whom I
won't know, beyond being on grinning terms, called Delicia Brick.
It sounds like a racehorse running into a stone wall. She has
taken the Ritz as a *pied-à-terre*, and asks everyone to dinner every
day. I believe you find a string of pearls in your napkin, only she
calls it a serviette. That kind of woman. She collects pearls and
other women's husbands, and walks about with them on a leash
like—like Pekinese. She doesn't want to take them off the leash
singly, so I understand; she only wants everybody to see them
there. She carts them into the country from Saturday till Monday and they all jump through hoops, and she pats them on the
head and they wag their silly tails. That's who the Brick is.'

'And Hughie's among them?'

'Yes. Aren't men odd? If a woman is pretty and pets them,
they often can't see what a bounder she is. We're rather the same
about men, by the way. And Nadine hates it.'

'Why doesn't she intimate that to her Hughie in the usual
manner?' asked Edith.

'From sheer stiff-necked pride. Where she got it from I don't
know; it certainly wasn't from me. She would die sooner than
tell Hughie to come off the leash. Besides, they're having their
difficult time, which always comes to young married couples,
and have to be so carefully handled. If they are wise and patient
and don't attempt to use the curb, the difficult time ends in
devotion and happiness, but if they're impatient and fidget each
other it may end in divorce.'

Dodo's gay brown eyes smouldered with tenderness.

'Everyone has had that difficult time,' she said, 'when the divine madness of passion grows sanc, and people find that they're
locked out of that wonderful asylum; when they see that they're
just ordinary husband and wife, and that their little tricks and
failings aren't lovely any more, but only irritating. They've each
got used to the perfections they once adored, and now they've

got to get used to their imperfections as well, and love each other
for them, if they are to float safely into the waters of middle-age
and old age. Nadine and Hughie will do it if they're careful, and,
above all, if no busybody like me hustles them. My inclination
is to take them by the scruffs of their necks and lock them into
a small bare room, and call through the keyhole: "You shan't
come out till you adore each other," which at heart they do. But
if there is one way to make disaster, it's just precisely that.'

'And the immediate trouble is the Brick?' asked Edith.

'Yes. I daresay they'll find others before they're through with
it, but she is the trouble just now. Darling Nadine turns quite
cataleptic with hatred when she sees Hughie dangling on the
Brick's leash and being patted on the head, and she puts her
delicious little nose in the air, as if the Brick was a faint bad
smell, and is more polite than anything you've ever seen. Nadine
polite, poor lamb! That shows you how she hates her. Hughie's
not the least in love with the Brick, and the Brick's far too busy
climbing to be in love with anybody. Nadine's delighted with
me because I won't have the Brick in my house, but part of her
delight is that it vexes Hughie. If only the woman would do
something really quite awful which would open Hughie's eyes!
It's no use my telling him that he ought to drop the Brick because Nadine hates her, for that would only make him think
Nadine hopelessly unreasonable.'

'Which she is,' said Edith.

'Certainly she is; but who in the world is reasonable? If she
was she would shrug her shoulders. And if she was awfully and
wonderfully wise she would cram the Brick down Hughie's throat
and ask her to lunch, dinner and tea every day till he vomited.
That's what I should do if Jack took up with some mature old
siren. But you can't do that at twenty-eight; you've got to be
sixty next birthday.'

Dodo, more than ever this year, was on some amazing social
pinnacle in the world that had begun to glitter again after the
war and the two years that immediately succeeded it. Without
being obsolete, she still triumphantly stood for an age that had
passed away, and hers was practically the last great house in
London that flung broadcast the hospitalities of ten years ago in
the old manner.

Many houses had been sold and had passed into the hands of even wealthier owners, but the personality of them had not somehow been included in the sale, and the difference, though vague, was immense. Others had been half shut up, and there, though the personality was still in possession, it sat quietly in a corner.

Comparative poverty as contrasted with the careless pre-war prosperity partly, but only partly, accounted for the eclipse, for the old entertainers of the dignified magnificent sort felt that the day for that was over. It had once been their very enjoyable duty with all its exertion and expense, but it was clearly a duty no longer. The younger generation really preferred to dine at a restaurant with cocktails and cigarettes in the bar, and dance in the hotel ballroom, still with cigarettes, afterwards; and since there were many Mrs Bricks tumultuously eager to be their entertainers, it was only reasonable to let them have their way. The guests who had been invited brought any friends they chose, introduced them to the Brick of the evening if they knew her by sight, and the whole affair had for them the advantageous liberties of a night club without the disadvantages of having to pay for the entertainment.

Dodo was quite in sympathy with all this; the point was that people should enjoy the particular brand of gaiety which they desired. She gave quantities of little dances for which she sent out a hundred messages through the telephone, and boys and girls romped and ragged, and smoked and sat on the floor, but when she gave a 'ball' it was otherwise, and she reserved the right to call the tune.

'A ball isn't a dance,' she explained to her husband. 'A ball is a pleasant old-fashioned function, where there happens to be dancing. At a ball people dance in the ballroom and smoke somewhere else; they sit up and behave, and if they find it dull they can go away. I shall give a ball on my birthday, Jack, and we'll have a dinner party first with two, if not three, large round tables decorated with sprays of pink Aurora Borealis as you'll read in the paper next morning, and you shall wear my tiara, and I shall wear your Garter, and there won't be a single soul there whom we don't know by sight, or whom we haven't asked. Won't that be odd? Of course, it will all be terribly old-fashioned, but I tell you that everybody will come, and nobody will think of going away till well on in the following morning. It will also cost an extraordinary lot of money, so you mustn't complain afterwards that I didn't tell you. But it is such fun being an interesting survival.'

Dodo had certainly survived. She seemed this year to have drunk of the fountain of perpetual youth, and during these early weeks of the season she converted the rather creaking progress of social gaiety into a chariot-race of flying steeds and whirling axles.

The somewhat remarkable exploits of her youth were already growing legendary; she had had her heyday before the golden girls and boys of the present generation were born, but she had stepped down, as it were, from the fading fresco, and took the floor with incomparable zest. She was not, heaven forbid, of grizzly kittenness: it was a genuine youth that infused and inspired her activities. She combined somehow the wisdom of experience with the dash of the adventuring pilgrim, and the golden youth flocked round her.

The Brick meantime was pursuing with adamantine firmness the path of her ambitious hospitalities. She was certainly very pretty (old enough, as Dodo said, to be her daughter), she had an audacious and amusing tongue, and about as much wisdom and breeding as a house-fly. But she had a fly's pertinacity, and already many of the more old-fashioned regime in London, who a year ago had said to those who had succumbed to her pertinacity: 'How can you?' were now capable of doing the same themselves.

She continued her collection of husbands with striking success, and their wives were beginning to find out that she meant no harm whatever, but only aimed at publicity. In consequence many of them (Nadine being a firm exception) accompanied their collected husbands, and the welcome they received further convinced them of the Brick's harmlessness. The Brick only wanted to be completely 'in it', and now no end of fine folk went to her gatherings and ate her food and danced to her fiddles, and good-naturedly laughed at her, and said: 'Fancy finding you here,' to the latest proselyte.

She had a pleasing and peremptory device of sitting at her telephone and asking the selected victim to dine on Tuesday. If he refused, she offered him in turn Wednesday, Thursday, and

Friday. If he was still firm she told him to get his engagement book and see which his first free evening was. Thus the only alternative to going to dine with her was to say: 'I am engaged until the end of the world.'

When all her efforts to capture Dodo had failed, she rather mistakenly tried this manoeuvre, and Dodo alone, out of all London, countered it successfully, for, without a moment's pause, she said she had so few engagements that she didn't keep a book, apologized for her deficiency, and replaced the receiver. Jack was finishing breakfast, and the indignant Dodo turned to him.

'Did you ever hear such impertinence?' she asked. 'The Brick telling me to get my engagement book! The Brick! *Me!*'

'Who's the Brick?' asked Jack.

Dodo laughed.

'You are the most refreshing person,' she said. 'I wish I had added: "My husband desires me to say that he's never heard of you." She's one of our conquerors, darling, from Africa or Australia, and she's marching across London exactly as the Germans marched across Belgium. But she doesn't march across me. She will have to go round. Oh, Jack, I do like your never having heard of her! "Pleased not to have met you."'

Jack finished his breakfast and settled himself by Dodo in the window-seat.

'That's slightly unlike you,' he remarked. 'You show animus, though I've often heard you say: "Everyone goes everywhere now, and what does it matter?" Why not go Bricking? I'm pleased that somebody is called Brick.'

'I daresay you are, and her Christian name is Delicia. But I won't go to her house, which is the Ritz, by the way, and she shan't come to mine. Not while I'm alive, at least. You shall do as you like afterwards, but she's too old for David.'

'Why all this?' he asked. 'There's some reason.'

'Of course there is. She makes trouble; she's made it between Nadine and Hughie. Oh, it's all right; there's nothing wrong, but Hughie likes her, and lets himself be led about. She whistles to him and pats him, and says: "See what a fine young man!" and when two people are a little on each other's nerves as he and Nadine are, it all makes friction.'

Dodo paused.

'It's been bothering me a little,' she said. 'Hughie's rather an owl, and Nadine's another with a stiff neck. If only the Brick would do something revolting, as I said to Edith. Anyhow, I'll tell Hughie and Nadine about the engagement book. I must poison his young mind somehow.'

Dodo told the tale of the engagement book in all its sweet simplicity to Nadine, who gurgled with laughter and looked pointedly away from Hugh. He, with slight avidity, said he was sure that Dodo had an engagement book.

'I've seen it,' he said.

Somehow this rather stringent attitude seemed hopeful to the astute Dodo. It looked as if he felt he ought to stick up for the Brick rather than that he did it instinctively.

'Dear Hughie,' she said, 'I know you've seen it. That's part of the joke, which you seem to have missed. If I hadn't got an engagement book it wouldn't be funny. How shall I explain? You see, your nice Mrs Brick wanted to get her name in my engagement book. Shall I go on?'

Hugh's mouth relented.

'But why have you got a down on her?' he asked. 'You said you didn't know her.'

'Oh, but I do now,' said Dodo. 'I know all that's necessary about anybody who tells me to get my engagement book. But don't let's discuss anything. Discussion is the first infirmity of feeble minds. Now what are you doing next Saturday? Come down with Jack and me to Winston, and on Monday we will return, grin like a dog, and have a birthday party.'

'Already engaged, I'm afraid,' said Hugh.

Dodo had sufficient sense not to ask what his engagement was. Besides, the angle of Nadine's nose showed it her.

'Well, I expect you'll have a far livelier Sunday,' she said. 'What about you, Nadine?'

'Love to come,' said Nadine.

Now the affair of the engagement book, which at once became common property, caused London to grow wildly excited about the Brick's power of penetration, and the impregnableness of Dodo's defence.

So many had yielded who said they would never yield, but the Brick had continued; she just continued shining like some hard, unwavering luminary which, sooner or later, melted the ice on

which her beam directed itself. She blinded people with her intolerable effulgence, and led them still dazed and groping into
the Ritz, where she made them comfortable and gave them
something nice to eat. But still no invitation came to her for
Dodo's birthday party, about which now the whole world was
talking, and her repeated application to Dodo's intimate friends
(Hughie among them) to procure her a permit, or take her under
their wing from one of the numerous dinners which were to be
given 'for' the ball, had produced no result, except to cause a
distant and delightful possibility to flicker through Dodo's brain.
There were plenty of pro-Dodos who held that an English-
woman's house is her castle, and that she had every right to
exclude anyone she chose; but there were plenty of pro-Bricks
as well, who argued that castles and drawbridges were medievally
obsolete in these democratic days, and that it was unkind and
obstinate of Dodo to make a pariah of that good-natured crea-
ture who only wanted to 'come and look'. She wasn't going to
steal the silver. To which Dodo, nursing her wonderful notion
said, 'She may take my tiara too, if she gets to the top of
the stairs.'

And then the Brick, swollen with the season's success, and
rendered desperate by present failure showed her true quality,
and did exactly what Dodo had regarded as a distant possibility.
As she drove Hughie up from the country on Monday morning,
she told him quite casually, to look out for her at Dodo's ball;
she would not be able to arrive till rather late. Naturally it did
not occur to him to enquire whether Dodo had asked her, so he
merely said, 'Oh, hurrah! That's splendid,' and on arrival at his
house told Nadine, with a spice of malice, that her mother had
done the sensible thing. Nadine was dining with Dodo before
the ball, and, by request, came early to help in receiving.

'So you have asked the Brick, after all!' was her slightly re-
proachful greeting, and she learned that Dodo had done nothing
of the kind. Dodo stared for one moment at these great tidings,
and then began to laugh.

'Oh, my dear, how delicious of her,' she said. 'I just wondered, I just hoped that she would come out strong like that.
Now you might let it be gently dropped about like dew that I
never asked her. Jack, the Brick's coming to our ball; Nadine has
just told me. Darling, don't look anxious like that, as if you

thought I should be rude to her. I think it's charming of her to come—just what I wanted. What a fool!'

Dodo guessed that the Brick would inflict a rather dire injury on herself, for communistic as London was, it would not quite approve of so piratical a proceeding; but what really mattered was not what London would think of it, but what Hughie would think of it.

She stood to receive her guests at the top of the great staircase, just inside the entrance to the suite of rooms which led to the ballroom. These stairs ascended in two flights to right and left of the hall, joining at the top in a broad landing. By eleven o'clock the full gleaming tide of folk was pouring up on both sides and pressing through the thronged landing, where many waited to watch the crowd, to where their hostess stood.

Hughie was hovering about there, and Dodo, though busy with her welcomings, told him to remain firmly and solidly anchored immediately behind her, for she must have an aide-de-camp whom she could send flying on any urgent errand of the moment. Up came the seemingly endless stream, glittering with jewels and ablaze with Orders; not since Dodo's last great ball, on the eve of the war, had such a splendour shown itself.

No other house had quite such a staircase, such vista of noble rooms, such an air of natural magnificence, and none had a hostess quite so superbly in her element. Yet all the time she had an eye to see that Hugh was quite close at hand, and she glanced every now and then to where Nadine, by her directions, stood on the landing above the stairs to signal the particular advent for which she waited.

By half-past eleven the tide had slackened, and the two footmen who stood just inside the door to shout out the names of new-comers audibly above the din of laughter and talk, were no longer continuously vocal. A dance had just come to an end, and the room behind Dodo's back was filled with folk, most of whom, by now, were aware that the Brick was uninvited and expected.

Just then Dodo saw the signal of a waved fan from Nadine, and one of the footmen shouted out the name. No one had the smallest idea how Dodo would take it, and a complete hush fell. She glanced at Hughie; he was at her elbow, and advanced half a step with outstretched hand.

'Dear Mrs Brick,' she said. 'How perfectly delightful of you to dispense with the formality of an invitation and look in on us. I began to be afraid you were not coming. You will find ever so many of your friends here. Do you know my husband? I think he told me you had not met. Jack, this is Mrs Brick.'

Dodo turned to Hugh.

'Hughie, I must begin to enjoy myself,' she said, 'now that I've done my duty. I think everyone has come who is coming, unless there are any more surprises. My dear, Mrs Brick! What a pretty woman! What pearls! What a cad! Take me to the ball-room and let me have one turn and then you can dance with Mrs Brick all night.'

Hugh made one charitable attempt.

'But perhaps somebody did ask her,' he suggested.

'Not a bit of it. No one would have had the cheek. Now let's enjoy ourselves and not think about her.'

About four in the morning Dodo had a word with Nadine.

'Be very wise, dear,' she said, 'and never, never mention the Brick's howler to Hughie. Don't gloat. Gloating will spoil every-thing. You didn't see his face when he realized that she hadn't been asked, and I did. After all, I hope she's enjoying herself, for she's done a good work. At least, I think she has. Here comes Hughie.'

Nadine looked at Dodo in silence.

'I think you're rather a wonderful mother,' she said.

'Aren't I? Well, Hughie, has it been fun? And are you coming to ask Nadine to dance, or me?'

'Nadine,' said Hugh.

'That's right. We'll have breakfast by and by, shall we? The ball is over, by the way; anyone may do anything. Let's smoke—let's change hats. . . .'

A Comedy of Styles

THE blaze of the January sun was pouring down on to the huge rink at Frédon, hot and invigorating, and yet by that inimitable conjuring trick which the sun so deftly performs all day in the high thin air of Alpine eyries, not melting one fragment of the ice, nor making the surface of it even soft. Above stretched steep pastures covered with fresh-fallen snow, and dotted with chalets fit to be hung on some immense Christmas tree, complete and toy-like with their little green-shuttered windows and their icicles depending from the snow-smothered eaves of the shingled roofs. Above, again, stretched the forest of pines, looking raven-black, where the snow had melted from off their tassels, against the shining dazzle of the white fields, while behind and beyond, remote and austere, rose the horns and precipices of the greater peaks.

Below, the ground declined sharply away: a few outlying chalets of the village stood in the foreground: beyond them the hillside leaped like a waterfall into the cloud-smothered valley of the Rhône, a couple of thousand feet below. Like a solid floor of grey mottled marble, this platform of cloudland, as seen from above, stretched right across to the slopes on the far side of the valley, a floor level and motionless, fitted in with the cunning of some neat-jointed puzzle to the promontories and bays of the hills opposite. These, as they climbed upwards, rose again into the blaze of the midwinter sun, and guarding it all, like some great beast with head thrown back and paws outstretched, rose the shining snows of the Dent du Midi.

The rink, which had been crowded all morning, was emptying fast, for from the various hotels the bells had announced lunch-time, and there were but half-a-dozen enthusiasts left. Among those, enthusiastic to the point of mania, was Agnes Cartright, who, recuperating for a few minutes on a bench at the side of the ice, was utterly oblivious to the view and glory of the sun, and was entirely intent on a small and ragged pamphlet which she held in her hand, and which contained the list of the greedy requirements demanded of any who offered themselves as candidates for the first-class English test of skating.

For the last three weeks she had lived, breathed, and dreamed skating; nothing else in the world seemed to her to matter at all, and if she had been awakened in the night by an armed inquisitor, who, with pistol to her head, had told her instantly to name the three greatest men in the world, she would have unhesitatingly have told him the names of three very fine skaters who were spending a month here. Two were to be her judges in the approaching test, the third was her brother, who, sitting beside her now with his mouth full of ham sandwich, was trying to explain to her the placing of one of those horrible and adored figures.

'Hold on to your back outside edge,' he said, 'till you get quite close to the centre, and change it at the centre. When you change it, don't wobble like a Channel boat in a cross-sea. Just change it. Hold on to your inside edge till you get half round the circle, then make your three, and—and stand still and go to sleep till you come back again to the centre. I don't see what bothers you in it.'

'Skate it for me, Ted,' she asked.

'Just when I'm lunching! You are the most selfish and inconsiderate——'

'I know. But I do want to see it done. It helps so enormously.'

He stood up, with half-eaten sandwich in one hand, a tall, satisfactory sort of young man, snub-nosed and sandy-haired, a sort of parody of the tip-tilted golden-haired girl who stood beside him. It was easy to see their relationship; the parody was unmistakable.

'I'll skate the whole set with you if you like,' he said. 'We've got the ice to ourselves.'

'You *are* a darling. If I can get through this thing at all, it will be entirely your doing, Ted.'

'Well, yes, mainly. All the same, you have got a certain natural aptitude.'

Then followed a quarter of an hour of strenuous performance, as they wove the mystic dance, with its swift long edges and flicked turns, which is known as English combined skating. Whatever Agnes's power of execution might be, there was no question about the excellence of her style, as standing erect, yet not stiff, she swooped like a swallow into the centre, and sped out again to the circumference of the figure twenty yards away.

It was impossible to see where the impetus for these bird-flights came from; they were as inexplicable as the movement of a soaring eagle, and her brother's speed was even more incomprehensible. He but seemed to lay his skate-blade on the ice and shot off with ever-increasing velocity. Their timing, too, from long-repeated practice together, was perfect; they passed each other at the centre with hardly a foot to spare between them, and soared away again. Occasionally he called a critical word to her, or made her repeat some evolution; but when, a quarter of an hour later, the practice was over, his praise was almost unfraternal.

'Yes, that will quite do,' he said. 'If you skate no worse than that, you will get through. Now, for, Heaven's sake, let us finish lunch in peace.'

She beamed appreciation of these high compliments.

'I'll just have ten minutes more alone,' she said. 'You might be an angel, Ted, and shout curses at me if I'm not up to the mark.'

A young man, who had been watching this really charming performance, skated up to the bench where Ted was sitting, with arms and unemployed leg outstretched, in the approved and graceful International style. He really did rather resemble some flying Mercury, a pose which all skaters of his school do not attain with any marked degree of success. He had arrived here only the evening before, and nodded kindly to Ted, unaware of his immensity. In Agnes's opinion, this would be about equivalent to some criminal in the dock—skaters in the International style were all criminals in her eyes—negligently saluting the Lord Chief Justice on the bench.

'It really makes one doubt whether English skating is such a ramrod sort of performance as we think it,' he said, 'when you see a girl like that doing it. Isn't she at the Royal Hotel? I think I saw her there at the dance last night. You were skating with her, weren't you? What is her name?'

Ted Cartright looked at him with a rather pleasant mixture of amusement and resentment. The resentment was for this infernal patronage of the only real form of skating.

'Her name is Cartright,' he said. 'Miss Agnes Cartright. Perhaps I had better mention that my name is Cartright, too.'

He paused a moment.

'In fact, I'm her brother,' he said.

The flying Mercury laughed.

'Do you know, that's rather funny,' he said. 'Then, of course, you are *the* Mr Cartright who skates. I assure you that the people I came up in the train with mentioned you with a sort of holy awe. And here am I telling you that perhaps English skating is not entirely a ramrod performance. But, really, I couldn't tell. I hope you don't mind. My name is Turner, if it's the slightest interest to you.'

Ted Cartright laughed also.

'Then, of course, you are *the* Mr Turner, if it comes to that,' he said. 'And your arrival has been spoken of with holy awe. You won all the cups and things last year, didn't you, in—in your style?'

'I suppose I did. It looks awful to you, doesn't it? A silly, showing-off, posing kind of game?'

'Well, I don't want to do it myself. But I expect——'

Further attempts at compliments were interrupted by Agnes.

'That was better, wasn't it, Ted?' she asked.

'I don't know; I wasn't looking. Agnes, may I introduce Mr Turner to you?'

Mr Turner, apparently, had already lunched, and soon left them. He skated off to the other side of the rink, and there took advantage of the empty ice. With flying, outstretched arms, he glided and poised and turned, launching himself at full speed on his hard, curved edges. He whirled in entrancing spirals, every inch and muscle of him was plastically part of woven loops and brackets. Anyone could see how masterly was his control, how vehement his force.

Agnes turned to her brother.

'It's really rather nice when it is done like that,' she said. 'You can see he is a—man.'

'He doesn't in the least degree resemble a girl,' said her brother. 'Nor does he look like a cross between a hairdresser and a dancing-master, if that is what you mean.'

'Yes, just that,' she said. 'But, of course, we can't call it skating. All the same——'

And she drank the remainder of Ted's beer.

Two days afterwards Agnes went up for her supreme trial. She was horribly nervous, and the sight of the reserved end of the rink, entirely emptied of skaters on her behalf, who lined the edges of it instead, made her think with bitter envy of Korah, Dathan, and Abiram, those happy victims of the opening earth. But the moment she got under way, as soon as she felt her skate really bite the smooth, satin-like ice, she was conscious of nothing else but extreme exhilaration. Mr Turner had left his International followers, who were standing about on one leg, in attitudes of extreme dejection, like hens on a wet day, and established himself on a seat in the sun, and the sight of him following her with perfectly undisguised admiration, made her not nervous, but immensely self-confident. Even the approving grunts of her brother, when in pauses she went and sat by him, did not lend her such solid encouragement. She had begged Mr Turner not to come and watch her, when she danced—rather frequently—with him the night before at one of the hotel balls, and it may be added that she would have been extremely vexed if he had been so untrustworthy as to dream of keeping this promise she had extorted from him. In fact, as far as he was concerned, her state of mind is thus sufficiently indicated. Once or twice she made mistakes, which caused him much greater anxiety than they caused her. So his state of mind, as far as she was concerned, is also adequately outlined.

Ted skated excitedly up to her, after her judges had held but a brief conference.

'So that's floored,' he said; 'and now you can begin to learn to skate properly.'

'Oh, Ted,' she said, 'do you mean I have passed?'

'Yes, of course. Let's have lunch.'

Now, a certain proportion of the immigrant English at Frédon during the winter months think of practically nothing else all day, and a certain amount of the night, but skiing; to others, curling is a similar obsession; to others, tobogganing. But the greater number of the obsessed have no thoughts, day or night—except when they are actually engaged on some such frivolity as dancing, or dining, or bridge—but for skating.

And the skaters, divided into two camps, as has been seen, the English style and the International, abstain, if polite, from passing the smallest criticism or taking the slightest notice of the other's doings; if impolite, they use such words as 'ramrod' or 'dancing-master'. They have even been known to attempt to parody—with marked unsuccess—each other's styles. Consequently, rumours that began to creep about, some few days after Agnes Cartright had passed her first-class English test, thrilled these obsessed people to the core.

Very early in the morning Miss Cartright had been seen on a sequestered corner of the rink with her unemployed leg wildly waving. With her arms she appeared to be swimming in short, ungainly strokes. An examination of the ice where these contortions had taken place showed beyond doubt that somebody had been trying to skate loops there—those dreadful, wicked, horrible loops which violated every rule of correct English style, to practise which laid the foundations for every immoral habit. It was true that, when observed, she made herself into a ramrod again and jerked her shoulders about in that distressing English manner, but later on, when the rink had cleared for lunch, she was seen again trying to do a spiral.

Then she had been seen watching Mr Turner for quite a long time that afternoon. This, of course, might be for other reasons, and the speaker—who had been doing just the same—wreathed her withered lips into what must have been a sarcastic smile. Such was the thrilling news brought into the International camp.

Later in the evening a spy came into the English camp. He had been on the rink that afternoon when dusk fell, and with his own eyes had seen a solitary figure in a withdrawn situation at the further end, practising (apparently) in the English style. The speaker, at any rate, thought that these stiff, rigid attitudes, these jerked turns, were meant to be in distant emulation of it. With the amiable intention of assisting this ungainly struggler, and with a certain incredible conjecture in his mind, he skated up to him. The ungainly struggler, on seeing him approach, instantly began whirling his arms and legs again. It was Turner.

And that night, after dinner, Turner had been seen again in the lounge of the hotel, absorbed in a book which was easily recognizable as one of the textbooks of English skating. Being observed, he hurriedly covered it up with a week-old copy of a daily paper, upside down, and pretended to be immersed in it. A little later he and Miss Cartright played bridge together, and it was credibly ascertained that neither of them had mentioned the word 'skating' throughout the course of three long rubbers.

A week later all concealment was at an end. Agnes Cartright had openly joined the ranks of the Internationalists, while the star and mainstay of International skating was busy practising the English style, and hoped before the end of the season, if he was very industrious, to pass the third and most elementary of the English tests. What added to the comedy of the situation was that each went to the other for tuition, and each was at present hopelessly at sea. They, the pillars and ornaments of their schools, floundered and bungled, and were a source of the most blissful encouragement to other beginners. Occasionally a brief spell of apostasy would seize one or other of them, and Turner would giddily trace out a perfect back loop eight, or Miss Cartright, tall and swift and stable, would skim up to a centre from the distance of sixty yards, flick out a dream of a rocker, and hold the back edge for another sixty yards. But these were but infrequent weaknesses; for the most part, from morning till night, they were diligent with the alphabets of their respective studies.

In the evening they often sat near each other, strenuously reading. Turner's book was a volume on the English style, with Agnes's name at the beginning; she read the textbook he had written himself.

A further thrill awaited Frédon, ten days later, when their engagement was made known. As for them, they had a great deal to say to each other on other subjects; but one sunny day, as they sat on the edge of the rink, in the lunch interval, the question which had really been a good deal in their minds found utterance. Agnes broached it.

'There's another thing we must talk about,' she began.

'I know,' he interrupted. 'Skating, you mean. It's quite ridiculous to go on as we are. You see, I *had* to take to English skating when I saw you do it. I couldn't help myself. There was never anything so divine.'

She laughed.

'Oh, Jack, that's just what happened to me. And here we are, dear, both making the most dreadful fools of ourselves. I shall never be able to do it! I should be utterly miserable about it if I wasn't so happy. What is to be done?'

'We might toss up,' he suggested. 'The point is, that we should both skate in the same style, isn't it?'

'Of course.'

He took an Italian five-franc piece from his pocket.

'Heads, English style; tails, International,' he suggested.

'Yes,' said Agnes tremulously, and he spun the coin, caught it, and opened his hand.

And anyone who happens to be at Frédon this winter will see whether it was heads or tails.

Noblesse Oblige

M RS COPLESTONE was chiefly remarkable for her large
stores of opulent reminiscences, which bore no very close
resemblance to the facts on which they were so insecurely
founded.

She lacked the fearless irresponsibility of the more magnificent sort of liar, and when you blew off the copious froth of her
memories, there was always some minute sediment of truth at
the bottom of the glass, which did not fly into the air like the
rainbowed bubbles which overlay it. She did not lie for material
profit; she never reaped one pennyworth's pecuniary advantage
from her great histories, nor did she hurt anyone by them, for
she was as good-natured as she was inventive. She just wanted to
be grand, to present a noble and enviable appearance to the world
in general, and in pursuit of this innocent desire she often talked
very richly in trains, offering a sandwich or a morning paper to
break the ice, so that she might shine forth to strangers who
would be duly impressed with her splendours.

Today, as she travelled down, after a fortnight in London, to
Hatchings, that quaint, huddled, red-roofed little city where her
husband, a retired solicitor, lived out the contented afternoon of
his blameless days, she was in excellent form, for she had exactly
the audience she liked. She was in a second-class compartment,
and her companion was a poor and meek relative of Mr
Coplestone's, whom with the utmost tenderness of heart she had
asked to spend a fortnight's holiday in her comfortable home.
Opposite, the only other occupant of the carriage was a remarkably distinguished-looking woman, with marvellous red hair and
that cream-pale complexion which unaided Nature often bestows
on those whom she has already gifted with the Titian hue.

The train moved smoothly and softly, Mrs Coplestone's voice
was of carrying quality, and she had no doubt that the stranger opposite, who exhibited a studied attention to the book of which the
page remained so long unturned, was drinking in with reverence

and awe the grand things which Mrs Coplestone so much enjoyed saying to her husband's poor relation. All further information as to the exact social station to which she belonged
may be summed up in the fact that she invariably alluded to
her husband as Mr Coplestone. When, on rare occasions, Mr
Coplestone annoyed her, she addressed him personally as such.

'And here we are, quite close to our dear old Hatchings again,'
she said. 'We shall be there in ten minutes. Oh, look, my dear
Blanche, look quickly out of the window! You will see the
towers of Hatchings Castle quite plainly over the river. Dear old
Castle! What a lot of delightful memories swarm into my mind
when I see it!'

She pointed a finger to guide Blanche's reverential eye.

'Yes, and there is the lake,' she said. 'Such a delicious lake, and
it is even older than the Castle itself, which is of immense antiquity. How much Mr Coplestone and I miss our visits there! I
cannot remember the time when I did not remember Hatchings
Castle.'

'And don't you go there now?' asked Blanche.

Mrs Coplestone kissed her hand in the direction of the lake.

'No, it has been shut up for the last ten years,' she said, 'ever
since the late Lord Hatchings' death. What fun we used to have
there—picnics, luncheon parties, dinner parties, fishing parties
on the lake! It was a perpetual round of delightful hospitalities.
We were such friends. Yes, I shall never again have such a friend
as dear Lady Hatchings.'

'And won't it ever be opened again?' asked Blanche, straining
her pale eyes to catch the last glimpse of the lake and castle of
many memories.

'It is odd you should ask that, for Mr Coplestone wrote to me
only last week to say that the new Lord Hatchings had just
come down there, and intends to stay the summer. I am afraid
I shall feel him to be a sad parvenu. The Death Duties were
enormous—quite colossal, in fact—for the succession passed to
a distant cousin. The College of Heralds, or whoever manage
those things, had to go all the way up to Queen Elizabeth, and
all the way down again, till they found out who it was. I dare say
he is a most agreeable man, but it will never be dear old Hatchings
Castle to me again. My dear Lady Hatchings is still alive, but I
despair of seeing her any more in the old home. *Tempora*

mutantur, as Mr Coplestone says in his Latin. Yes, and here is the station for the Castle—Castle Halt, as it is called. We seldom went by train. You may be sure there was always a carriage to take us in and out.'

As the train slowed up, the Titian-haired stranger took a rather old mackintosh from the rack above her head. Outside the bleak little station there was standing a dog-cart, and Mrs Coplestone's quick eye caught sight of a coronet on the pony's blinkers.

'Ah, there is a dog-cart for the Castle,' she said, 'and I should not in the least wonder if that lady who has just got out is the governess of Lord Hatchings' children. There she is again, with a porter wheeling her bicycle. Now she is talking to another lady. What a foreign-looking person! I should say she was French. She is getting into the dog-cart, and our travelling companion is mounting her bicycle. Probably the foreign-looking lady is a guest at the Castle, and the other is her maid. That must be it. Mr Coplestone always tells me that I am quite a Sherlock Holmes, and that I know who everybody is, and what he has done, the moment I set eyes on him. I am convinced that our travelling companion was the French lady's maid. That is why she travelled second-class. Those maids are so high in their notions. But second-class is quite good enough for me, and if a lady's maid does sit opposite me, she is quite well behaved, and I have no quarrel with her. My dear Lady Hatchings always had a carriage reserved for her, and no wonder, even on the shortest journeys. My sweet Mabel!'

About half an hour after, the red-haired lady was sitting at lunch with a grey-haired lady at the Castle.

'It was really rather embarrassing, Cousin Mabel,' she said. 'I didn't know what to do. I couldn't have interrupted her and told her I was Charlie's wife. I wish you could guess who it was. Can't you remember a great, pompous woman who used to be so intimate with you? She talked about Mr Coplestone, too, in the sort of way that suggested that he was her husband.'

'My dear, why didn't you say that sooner, and save me the trouble of thinking?' asked Cousin Mabel. 'Now I do remember. We had a fishing competition once on a Bank Holiday, and there was a Mrs Coplestone who caught a pike. We shall soon know, for Charlie has sent out garden-party cards to absolutely every inhabitant of Hatchings, for the day after tomorrow, to celebrate the opening of the house. My bosom friend will be sure to come, and we will identify her.'

'Charlie told me he was going to. But Mrs Coplestone—what are we to do about Mrs Coplestone? She will see me here, receiving our guests. She will have an awful shock.'

'Serve her right!' said Mrs Coplestone's 'sweet Mabel'.

'I know. But she will be our guest. You can't let your guest have an uncomfortable moment if you can help it. She will see you, too. Really, it will be horrid for her. What can we do?'

'My dear Daisy, you are too amiable to live. You make me anxious.'

Daisy Hatchings laughed.

'Don't be anxious,' she said; 'I don't propose to die. But we must save the poor thing's feelings somehow. I think you will have to be tremendously cordial, and say what ages it seems since you and she met.'

'I couldn't—I should choke,' said the other.

'Oh, don't! You see, she can't fail to remember all she said in the train this morning. She was talking *at* me all the time, impressing me, showing me how great and good she was. It would be awful for her if in front of my very face you gave her a vacant look.'

'It's all your fault for travelling second-class,' said Mabel Hatchings. 'And I won't promise to be cordial. She's a pushing, swaggering thing, this Mrs Coplestone of yours. She deserves a vacant look. A carriage to meet her, indeed, for her picnics and luncheon parties and dinner parties!'

'Oh, Cousin Mabel, do be amiable! Besides, if you will be cordial and affectionate, and talk about old times, she will understand very well. There will be an irony about it. You will have done all that could be done to make her comfortable, and yet afterwards she will wonder.'

Mabel Hatchings sighed.

'That's true,' she said. 'If I can remember to think of that, I may be able to manage it.'

Mrs Coplestone duly found the card inviting her husband and herself to the garden-party, and was rather grand about whether she should go or not, for it would mean—for Blanche's edification—the tearing open of an old wound. But as she had no reason to suppose that her 'sweet Mabel' would be there, and she was devoured by curiosity to see the new Lady Hatchings, she consented to have the old wound torn open, and drove out rather magnificently with her husband in a hired motor-landau.

Guests were already assembled in large numbers, and they were conducted along the terrace to where, just within the great yew hedge that separated it from the lawn, their hostess stood with her husband and Cousin Mabel to receive them. Thus Mrs Coplestone heard her name sonorously announced before she saw her hosts at all.

Then she came round the corner of the yew hedge, and lo, one yard from her, was the lady of the Titian hair! Worse than that, there was standing quite close to her her 'sweet Mabel'. Mrs Coplestone was sure it was she. Her 'sweet Mabel' had given her a prize long ago for catching a pike.

Lady Hatchings moved a step forward as the name was announced, and gave her a delicious smile of welcome.

'How nice of you to come, Mrs Coplestone!' she said. 'And my cousin will be so charmed to see you. Cousin Mabel, here is a very old friend of yours. How-de-do, Mr Coplestone? Yes, are we not lucky to have such a fine day?'

'You were admirable, Cousin Mabel,' said Daisy Hatchings, a moment afterwards. 'But I knew you would be a dear.'

Mrs Coplestone was so staggered by her welcome that she began to think that she must have been very intimate, after all. But she was a little shy about saying so, which was exactly what Daisy Hatchings had intended.

An Entire Mistake

'OH, my dear, what on earth is the use of being beautiful?' said Lady Nugent, rather impatiently. 'Beauty and cleverness, those are the two gifts which an ignorant world has chosen as the enviable ideal. But in this rough-and-tumble of a life, I assure you they are no use at all. We are all of us hopelessly, ridiculously clever, we all know much more than the last generation, and can use our knowledge, which is the same thing as cleverness.'

'Oh, I don't agree,' said Millicent, in her low, soft voice.

'Perhaps not, but I am right. Take tact, for instance, the supreme exhibition of cleverness; it only consists in knowing human nature, its strengths, which are few, and its weaknesses, which are many, and using one's knowledge to the best advantage. Why, even beauty is a better gift than cleverness. People talk about beauty as being only skin-deep; plain people I notice talk most on those lines—but what, after all, are wits, genius even? Half the diameter of one's head at the utmost. If "skin-deep" means anything, six inches deep means very little now.'

'Ah, but it so happens that beauty is a merely physical gift; cleverness, genius, what you will, is a mental or even a spiritual possession.'

Lady Nugent, with one of the quick, decisive movements characteristic of her, set down on a table near her her empty cup.

'I never argue,' she said, somewhat inconsistently, 'because to argue goes far to prove that one thinks one is wrong. Anyhow, one has to produce reasons for what one says. Now, if one has said anything the least true, it is superfluous to adduce reasons for it: a true remark, a just conclusion, is so palpable. "What is truth?" said Pilate. Of course, he didn't wait for an answer. There was no need: twice one is two.'

'And truth?' asked Millicent Fane.

Lady Nugent laughed.

'Is probably a mistaken or distorted view. Anyhow, one

arrives at truth through exaggeration. You cannot possibly pitch into it. You have to go too far and come back, or else you find you have not gone far enough, and have to hurry forward.'

'Hurry forward, then. Beauty and cleverness are of no use. What is?'

'That which you with your green eyes and broken front tooth have—charm. And what that is, heaven knows. But seriously, what do you propose to do with my unfortunate husband?'

Millicent—with her green eyes—stared.

'Do with him?' she repeated.

'Yes, do with him. In other words, am I to elope with your husband, or are you to elope with mine? We are friends, that is so convenient, and we can talk it out. Harold Fane, being a fool, admires what he thinks to be my cleverness, which as far as concerns him only means that I know he is a fool and treat him accordingly. But Nugent, who is not a fool, is in love with your charm.'

Millicent made a soft movement in her chair.

'Have I really charm?' she asked.

'Yes, you darling fool. You may take it from me that you really have. Oh, Milly, why weren't you a man. I should have insisted on marrying you. As it is, we only quarrel about our respective and respectable husbands.'

'Have I been quarrelling?' asked she.

'Yes, in the most aggravating way—namely, by refusing to quarrel. There is nothing so wildly exasperating. Really, I believe that if I eloped with Harold tomorrow you would not care. You would only say, "Poor dear, how bitterly she will be disillusioned."'

'Are you illusioned then at present?'

'No, but he is. One illusionment is enough for two people.'

'Elope with him then. You will leave me in the rather anomalous position of being alone in the hotel with your husband. But Clarice would play chaperon, no doubt.'

Lady Nugent flew off at a tangent.

'What a treasure!' she said. 'You go up to dress at a quarter to eight, and come down dressed at eight. What a maid to have! What happens?'

'I don't know,' said Millicent. 'I think I sit down—no, I stand in the middle of the room, and she buzzes about like a bee. Then I come downstairs again.'

'How lucky you are. Now, Angelique, *mon Dieu*! Angelique! A scream. French assails me when I go up to dress; I give her the keys of my jewel-case, and pearls fly about the carpet. I pick them up. I sit down, and she pulls my hair off. I make the most of what remains, and plunge my hands into boiling water, which she has put in my basin. I scream; she gives notice. Then I say, "*Quel rot*", and she bursts into tears. I dry her tears, and give her smelling salts. And I appear at three minutes to nine. But she can make haste.'

'She is an extraordinarily handsome girl,' remarked Millicent.

'Oh, certainly. But Clarice is clever.'

'God send some fools along for them,' said Millicent piously.

Lady Nugent got up and strolled to the edge of the verandah; the brilliant blue of an August day filled the valley with a luminous haze of light, and down the white riband of the road below their hotel bobbed the gay parasols of the women and the white umbrellas of the men who had begun to stroll down again to take their afternoon dose of the very pungent water of Aix-les-Bains.

'Really, men are pigs,' remarked she, after a short depreciative contemplation. 'Here are you and I, Milly, banished to this horrible hole of a place, merely because our husbands have not had the strength of mind to pass dishes at dinner which they know are bad for them. Why Dr Rowntree insisted on my coming—a clever man that. He said, "You must be constantly at his elbow, Lady Nugent. You must worry him, plague him, get him, if possible, into a low state. That is why I am sending him to Aix. He would enjoy himself at Homburg, and one wants him to connect the result of his—well, his habitual over-eating, not with enjoyment, but the reverse. He will not enjoy Aix in August; it is hot and relaxing. Nor, I am afraid, will you."'

'I shan't elope with your husband, dear,' Millicent said. 'He is too disgusting. So is mine. But we might elope together. Do let us. I really am getting enfeebled in this place. Let us go away for a couple of days up to Mont Revard, you and I, quite alone. Let us get free from all these tiresome people. I won't take Clarice; you won't take Angelique; and we will neither of us take our husbands.'

Lady Nugent's methods, when her mind was made up, were marked by extreme rapidity, and having announced her intention at dinner that evening to her husband, she telegraphed for rooms, and the two left by the funicular railway up into the hills early next morning. Angelique saw them off at the station, and dexterously transformed her obsequious smile of adieu into something more humanly satisfied as the train departed. For, as there are two sides to every question, Angelique could probably (and with equal truth) have given another and vivid account of what passed when she attended the toilette of her mistress.

It is hard to say who enjoyed their departure most—they or their husbands, or their maids. Deep peace, at any rate, descended on Lord Nugent and Harold Fane as they sat at lunch that day, and they both gently overate themselves, and took liqueur with their coffee. The two French maids went with a party of compatriots on the Lake, where Angelique, apart from the natural vivacity of her manner, had a great success in a new hat of her mistress! Clarice had no need to borrow; her own clothes were smarter than Mrs Fane's.

Two days of peace and mountain-top were all that the ladies had originally contemplated, and all concerned laid themselves out to make the best of it. But the two days were doubled, and when one morning they came down it was not to return to the hotel, but merely to get some more clothes. Both their maids were out, it appeared, but as the morning was very hot, they were not ill-content to sit in the verandah waiting their return.

Suddenly shrill French laughter strangely familiar to Lady Nugent sounded close beside them round the corner of the verandah, and Angelique's voice said, '*Ah, vous êtes très gentile, monsieur.*'

Then there came into sight Harold Fane walking with Angelique.

Angelique stared at her mistress for one half-second, then she burst into a sudden explosion of white-toothed laughter, for close at hand, in a voice strangely familiar to Mrs Fane, came the words, '*Ah, vous êtes très gentile, monsieur.*'

And round the other corner of the verandah came Lord Nugent and Clarice.

The situation was beyond words; Angelique's laughter ceased as if a tap had suddenly been turned off, and all six looked blankly at each other. Then the masculine common sense of the party made a move, and the two men strolled gently away together. In another half second Angelique and Clarice had whisked away through the open hotel door, and Lady Nugent and Millicent alone remained. They looked at each other blankly again for a moment, and then by common impulse burst into shrieks of uncontrollable laughter. Again and again one or the other would make an heroic effort to be grave, but she would catch the eye of the other, and be again seized by the demon of hopeless mirth.

At last from exhaustion the end came.

'Oh, my dear, what a pity,' said Lady Nugent. 'We shall have to come back to Aix.'

'I suppose so,' said Millicent tremulously.

Mr Carew's Game of Croquet

THE air was laden with the scents of summer, and as
Mr Jocelyn Carew's taxi purred gently along the road in
Richmond Park he inhaled with great pleasure the delicate per-
fume of the flowering limes. They smelled warm and sweet: theirs
was a slightly sophisticated odour. There was the hint of the
country about them, but also the hint of Bond Street; you would
have said that they had been touched up at some scent
manufactory and thus rendered the more palatable to civilized
nostrils.

Mr Carew himself looked very civilized too; he was attired
for the country in light grey clothes and a straw hat, neat
white spats, and pale yellow gloves, and though rural, his rural-
ity was more suggestive of Richmond Park than of the untamed
moorland.

It had been said of him that his age varied in inverse proportion to the number of countesses present. This sounds a little
cryptic, but without doubt the epigrammatist meant that in the
society of the brilliant and high-born he became young and animated, and in their absence his years were multiplied.

Like all epigrams, it contained a germ of truth, though not the
whole truth, for the undivided attention of one countess was
sufficient to rejuvenate him so that he bubbled with youth and
high spirits. Distinguished folk of any sort, indeed, had the same
felicitous effect on him, and it was only in the society of the
obscure and mediocre that he became middle-aged and, occasionally, rude and disagreeable.

Today his plump, fresh-coloured face was positively boyish,
for though for the moment he was alone with his taxi-driver,
who could not be supposed to evoke his latent juvenility, he was
very shortly to be plunged in the most invigorating atmosphere.
He was to spend the weekend at the house of Lady Loring, who
was entertaining the sort of party which made him young for
a fortnight afterwards. Best of all, she had rung him up this

morning to ask him to come down early in the afternoon, for her
party, with the exception of the Duchess of Whitby, would not
get back from Henley till shortly before dinner-time. She, however, had refused to go with them, and it would be delightful of
him to solace her solitude. No doubt he knew her.

So Mr Carew was delighted to make himself delightful. He
did not know her, but that would soon be remedied.

The taxi dipped down the steep hill to Ham Gate, and presently turned into the gate of his earthly paradise. Learning that
Her Grace was somewhere out in the garden, he immediately
went forth on his agreeable errand, tossing his head backwards
and forwards two or three times in order to get a lock of his still
abundant brown hair to lie in a natural wisp over his forehead.

The garden was extensive and highly civilized. A big lawn ran
from the house down to the low fence that separated it from the
meadow beyond, and he was pleased to observe that it bore
indications of no more athletic pursuits than croquet. Lawn tennis
was anathema to him, for he loathed activity, and women, even
if they did not play themselves, watched the gladiators with an
interest they should have devoted to conversation. Croquet,
however, he could manage, and be very amusing over it.

At the edge of the lawn there were a couple of large roofed
shelters, comfortably furnished with tables and sofas and easy
chairs; this was an admirable device, for you could enjoy the
garden atmosphere without having eternally to stroll about, or
when utterly wearied of walking, rest in basket-chairs or deck-
chairs which squeaked, and if you were not careful, pinched you.
Here you could be rural in comfort, and he began to frame some
amusing sentences on the subject, which he would presently im-
provise when he found his august companion.

Mr Carew paused in one of these excellent shelters as he strolled
down the lawn in his quest. It showed signs of recent and exciting occupation, for on the table were half-a-dozen letters, opened
and thrust back into their envelopes, addressed to the duchess,
and the signs, in scattered stationery, that she had been answering them. He walked on, observing with great pleasure the exit
from the house of two footmen carrying the equipage of tea. He
would return presently after his stroll, at any point of which he
might meet his companion; if he missed her he would surely find
her here when he came back.

A winding walk between flowering shrubs skirted the lawn and the meadow beyond, and Mr Carew wandered along this, tasting at every bend in it the pleasures of anticipation, for at any moment he might meet her, and he kept perpetually on the tip of his tongue his graceful opening phrases. No sort of mutual introduction would be needed, for she was certainly expecting him, and there was no need to remind himself whom he expected. . . .

But the riband of path kept unravelling itself, and only disclosed fresh diapers of light and shade, and he made the complete circuit of the meadow without discovery. Then as he gained the lawn again on the far side from that on which he started, he saw that the shelter he had left a quarter of an hour ago was no longer untenanted, but there was a woman sitting there writing letters.

He hurried forward, with his opening sentences positively fizzing on the tip of his tongue. On his near approach she got up.

'How do you do, Mr Carew?' she said. 'I heard you had come, and I was just finishing a letter or two. But now my duty is clearly to give you tea, which is far more to my mind than writing letters.'

This was certainly quite to Mr Carew's mind also. In addition to being a duchess, she had everything a duchess ought to have—height, distinction, charm of manner, and above all, this delightful friendliness.

'That is too good of you,' he said. 'A cup of tea would indeed be a welcome refreshment. Somehow the country seems to predispose one to take nourishment at short intervals. I think it is the sight of cows perpetually eating that causes the suggestion of hunger. Wherever you look you see cows and sheep and horses perennially and perpetually taking what I believe is called a snack. Birds, too; observe that thrush on the lawn—or is it a sparrow?—tugging at a recalcitrant and succulent worm!'

She laughed.

'That's a most ingenious notion,' she said. 'I always used to think it was country air that made one hungry, but your idea is far more in accordance with modern theories. But would you call this quite the country?'

'Sufficiently so to produce hunger,' said Mr Carew. 'Indeed, to my mind suburbs represent the country at its best. You are surrounded by trees and cows, and all the regular rural furniture, and yet you know that our beloved London is within easy reach. How one misses the trees in London, but how, on the other hand, one misses the houses in the country! From where I sit I can see the roofs of Kingston, not too near to take away the impression of the country, but near enough to reassure me that I have not entirely lost touch with civilization however suburban. After all, we are gregarious animals.'

She laughed again.

'I'm afraid that I am a freak then,' she said. 'I adore being out sometimes on the moors or on some desolate sea-coast, knowing that there is not a single human being within miles of me! I don't say I want that often or for long, but I like being ungregarious now and then.'

'Dear lady, I hope this is not one of those moments,' said Mr Carew. 'But tell me if it is, and I will instantly transport myself, at the cost of the most vigorous pedestrianism, beyond the very furthest horizons.'

'Ah, don't do that,' she said, 'for in addition to losing the pleasure of your company, I should feel obliged to go on with these letters. And I should like to play croquet, too, if you have finished tea.'

Mr Carew jumped up.

'I consider it a sacred duty to keep you from your letters,' he said. 'Letters are like pitch, you cannot touch them without getting some sort of epistolary defilement. And am I not here for the set purpose of doing my best, my futile but fond best, to help you to pass the hours till our good Lady Loring returns with a cohort of delightful friends who will claim your attention, and, figuratively, snatch you from me. Let us at once play croquet. My ball, unskilfully propelled, seldom goes in the desired direction, and I invariably put my opponent's through hoops. I am, in fact, justly popular as an antagonist.'

They had just begun when there appeared from the house a rather shabby-looking little lady. Mr Carew quickly settled that she did not matter; she was no doubt some other guest of small importance. The idea of her wishing to join their game was a horrifying one, and so he turned his back on her, and was absorbed in watching his opponent. She, equally absorbed in her game, had not noticed the advent of this small female.

Presently, however, the small female arrived at the croquet lawn. Carew turned his back more relentlessly than ever (for she was evidently of the pushing variety), and was much annoyed to hear himself addressed.

'How are you, Mr Carew?' she said.

Mr Carew turned round, and apparently not noticing her out-stretched hand, bowed and took off his hat in that very distant and polite manner which paralysed common people. His rude-ness, in fact, took the odious form of exaggerated courtesy.

'I am extremely well, thank you,' he said.

He turned his back on her again. At the moment his oppo-nent's turn came to an end and he hurried across the lawn.

'After your brilliant performance,' he said, 'it is the poor worm's turn. Even worms, in the croquet sense of the word, have turns, though they are short and remarkably inglorious. Which, to use an odious colloquialism, is me?'

His opponent now for the first time saw the little lady.

'Do you want me, Fanny?' she asked.

Fanny gave a little croaking laugh.

'No, not in the least,' she said, and strolled away again.

Mr Carew inwardly congratulated himself. He knew as well as anybody how to expel intruders, and he had scored an undoubted success. It was not every day that you played croquet with a duchess, and his iced and acid politeness had quite choked off that dreadful woman.

He continued for the next half-hour to exert himself to the full in agreeable and witty conversation, and felt that he had never shone so effulgently. All possible disasters befell him in his game; he mobilized with his opponent instead of with himself, he sent her into required and coveted positions, and through them all he conducted himself with the liveliest good humour, with applause for her skill and amusing groans for his own misfortunes. He had never felt younger.

'I never played with such a sporting opponent,' she said. 'You and I must certainly play together on the same side, for I could do wonders with such an encouraging partner. But would it seem very rude of me if I suggested we should stop now? There are a few letters I really must write before the post goes.'

Mr Carew gave a little cry of despair.

'Ah, why are we not on your moors, or desolate beaches,

where there is no such thing as a post?' he said. 'But I see your benevolent plan; you wish to save me from the ignominy of complete rout. Be it so, dear lady, but you must remember and carry out your engaging, your sumptuous promise to adopt me as an honoured partner.'

She leaned her mallet against a hoop.

'Of course I will,' she said. 'But I also promised the duchess that I would finish those letters for her, and some are really rather important.'

For a moment, though his hearing was remarkably acute, Mr Carew thought he must have misunderstood her.

'You promised the duchess?' he said.

'Yes. She didn't want to interrupt our game, but I know she wants them finished.'

Mr Carew felt quite cold; it seemed like the chill of age. But he felt he had better know the worst at once.

'Was that the duchess who made a brief appearance here towards the beginning of our game?' he asked.

'Yes. How stupid of me not to have introduced you. I supposed you knew her.'

Mr Carew moistened his lips, which had become quite dry with rage and mortification. He had been extremely rude to the duchess, and he had been wasting his time with a female who, however agreeable, was clearly nothing more than the duchess's secretary. For the moment he quite forgot that this upstart secretary had called the duchess 'Fanny,' for he was entirely consumed with chagrin of the most bitter sort. It was she who was the intruder, and must be treated accordingly. It was all her fault; she ought to have told him at once that she wasn't a duchess, but only a secretary.

He became perfectly stiff and insolently polite.

'If I might then engage your attention for a second,' he said, 'I would ask you, with your permission, who you are?'

She stared at him in sheer incredulity, her face flushing a little at his impertinence.

'I help Fanny with her letters,' she said. 'I happen to be her sister, Miss Thornton.'

The Fall of Augusta

AUGUSTA PLAICE—such was her incredible name—
had experienced the ups and downs incidental to the
honourable career of a social climber, but the ups had distinctly
predominated, and she was already being numbered among the
very topmost boughs of the great and beautiful tree of fashion
and society. And then she made a mistake of the most dreadful
description on the very night when she was attaining to the very
zenith of her ambition, and came tumbling down from ever so
high. . . .

Tonight, then, to crown her climbings she was giving a large
dance, stupefyingly select, for there was somebody coming before whom she would make her lowest curtsey. It was a com-
petitive dance, too, for all this season she had been running
a neck-to-neck race with her detested compatriot, Alethea
Frisque—such was her incredible name—and Alethea had certainly not been among the fortunate folk who had received an
invitation. But only this morning a kind friend had thought it
wise to tell her that rumours were about that Mrs Frisque had
wagered fifty pounds that she would be present. In consequence,
Augusta had made up her mind that if so much as the end of
the snub nose of Alethea penetrated into her precincts she would
make her a short speech in a loud voice which Alethea would
remember to the last day of her ill-starred life, and very likely
afterwards.

Probably Alethea would come very late, when she herself had
deserted her post as hostess at the head of the stairs, and creep
like a mouse into the ballroom, get a witness for her presence,
win her bet, and go away again; but Augusta, though short-
sighted, felt sure that she would be enabled to see Alethea's snub
nose and pearls at the longest possible range. So she had been
very busy all morning, practising her curtsey and learning by
heart the two or three trenchant remarks which she intended to
address to Alethea.

Mrs Plaice, though careful about the selection of the fifteen hundred guests whom she had invited this evening, had been also rather reckless. She knew who the most intimate friends of her principal guest were, and had written little notes of invitation to them all, whether she had the privilege of their acquaintance or not. Among these was Lady Cynthia Matcham, whom she had never met. But she was well aware that Lady Cynthia was among the most coveted prizes of the hostess, and when she received Lady Cynthia's note of acceptance she felt that the birthday of her life had indeed come.

'She's harder to get than anybody,' she said to her husband, who, though strictly in the background, took a violent interest in these triumphs. He quickly turned up her name in a peerage, and looked disappointed.

'But she's only the daughter of an earl,' he said. 'And she only married Mr Matcham. Or perhaps she's a howling beauty.'

'I can't say, I'm sure, whether she is or not,' said Augusta, 'for I've never seen her to my knowledge. All I know is, that she matters more'n anyone almost. It's puzzling, I know, when there are so many of higher rank, but there it is.'

But what, oh what, was Mrs Plaice's guardian angel doing that day? He should, indeed, have given her some faint intimation of the danger she was in. He should have warned her that, so far from being a 'howling beauty', Cynthia Matcham had a snub nose and a lively manner, and that the Matcham pearls were as notable as those pertaining to Mrs Frisque. But he did none of these things, and Augusta rushed on to her doom. In blank ignorance of everything that he should have told her, she went on practising her curtsey and making up fresh stingers for Alethea. . . .

And all the time, by a crowning irony, there was no truth at all in the gossip that Alethea had wagered fifty pounds that she would be present at the great party. She had, as a matter of fact, a party of her own that night to which she had not asked Augusta Plaice, which was why Augusta did not know about it, and if she had mentioned fifty pounds at all—she was not in the habit of mentioning so paltry a sum—it must have been that, in general contempt and disdain, she said she would not have asked Augusta to *her* party for fifty pounds. . . .

And Augusta's guardian angel utterly failed to acquaint her

with any of this information, which would have been so useful to her.

Mrs Plaice had a nice little house in Park Lane, with an acre or two of marble hall and a tower of marble staircase and the largest ballroom in London. She received her guests at the top of the stairs, but soon the crush of them as they stormed the marble staircase became so irresistible that both she and Mr Plaice, though heroically struggling to maintain their position, were borne back in eddies and whirlpools into the entrance of the ballroom.

The majority of her friends did not know her by sight, and even fewer knew Mr Plaice, and in consequence they got quite mixed up in the crowd, and being small of stature, were hustled and shoved into corners, and were sundered both from each other and from the major-domo, who, being able to maintain an impregnable position on the top step of the staircase owing to his size and weight, bawled out as many names as he had time for.

Luscious and glorious names the majority of them were, but Mrs Plaice for some minutes was utterly unable to shake hands with any of their owners. Still they were there, which was all that really mattered, and the papers tomorrow would duly chronicle their presence. Then across the growing hum of voices as the swarm got even more dense, and across the rhythmic riot of the band, she found when, slightly dishevelled, she had forced her way back to her rightful position, that even those stentorian tones were inaudible.

The ballroom by now was thickly populated, but as yet there had appeared, as far as she was aware, neither her principal guest nor she to whom Augusta proposed to address the few trenchant remarks which she had by heart. But just as she regained her place again, she saw the crowd on the stairs below parting and making way and curtseying as her guest came up the stairs. Just then the dance in the ballroom behind came to an end, and the sonorous name was clearly audible.

Mrs Plaice made her curtsey, received a few gratifying re-marks, and His Royal Highness lingered a few minutes on the landing close to her, speaking to his friends. And then close after him came a little lady with a snub nose and ropes of pearls. She had passed the major-domo, apparently, without giving her name.

Mrs Plaice peered short-sightedly at her for a moment, and

saw red, for she also saw, so she entirely believed, Alethea Frisque, who, considering the scandalous nature of her errand, looked remarkably calm and collected. And Mrs Plaice, still seeing red, realized that the encounter could not have arrived more suitably, for the Prince's advent had caused a certain hush to fall, and her remarks would be clearly audible to a gorgeous audience. Everyone should know how she dealt with these pestilent upstarts from God knew where, who pushed their way into houses where they had not been asked, and made bets about it.

She took one step forward, put her hands behind her back, and spoke in her shrill and penetrating voice.

'You have come, I fear, to the wrong house,' she said. 'I did not give myself the honour of asking you. I will ask you instead to leave my house as quickly as is convenient to you. I will wish you good-night!'

The person she addressed stared at her for a moment in blank surprise.

'Yes, I have clearly come to the wrong house,' she said.

Just then her principal guest turned and saw her.

'Ah, how delightful,' he said. 'Will you give me the next dance?'

'I'm afraid I can't, sir,' said she. 'I have been informed by my hostess that I have come to the wrong house, and have been asked to go away.'

She turned and went.

Mrs Plaice had no time for misgivings, even if she had felt disposed for them, for guests were still streaming up the stairs. Also, her triumph over the odious Alethea was complete; she need fear no further rivalry there. Alethea was disposed of in the most public and satisfactory manner. All London would be talking of her well-deserved discomfiture next day, and Augusta had the further brilliant idea of inserting in the evening papers a short paragraph to the effect that Mrs Frisque had come uninvited to Mrs Plaice's party.

One thing only caused her slight regret; it might have been better, when her principal guest asked Alethea for a dance, to have permitted her to stop. But it was all very pleasant without these additional coals of fire.

Presently the stream of incomers slackened and ceased, and, flushed with triumph, Mrs Plaice began to circulate among her guests, and obtained several very nice introductions. But gradually it became borne in upon her that something was going on; she was aware that people were talking to each other on some subject which dropped as she approached.

And then she grew completely puzzled, for late arrivals told her that they had come on from Mrs Frisque's dance, and early departures remarked that they were going there. Then, still without realizing what she had done, she remembered that she had not yet seen Lady Cynthia Matcham, whom she was very anxious to know.

When Augusta Plaice desired a social advantage, there was no false pride about her that stood in the way of her obtaining it. She sought out Mrs Holmsworth, whom she knew was a friend, in order to get the introduction. Still swollen with triumph, she introduced first the subject of Mrs Frisque.

'Well, it is pleasant to see so many friends,' she said. 'And did you ever hear of such impertinence as that of Alethea Frisque? I heard that she had bet fifty pounds that she would be here tonight, though I had not asked her, and I felt it no less than my duty to tell her that she had better go away again. She must have left her own party—I'm told she's got a little party tonight—just to show herself here and win her bet. I put it pretty straight to her; perhaps you heard what I said. And now, Mrs Holmsworth, I want you to be so kind as to introduce me to Lady Cynthia Matcham, who said she would be here tonight.'

An extraordinary variety of expressions seemed to cross Mrs Holmsworth's face during this speech. At first she looked what Mrs Plaice would have called 'a bit stand-offish', then she assumed the eagerness of entranced and absorbing interest; finally she burst into a shout of laughter.

'But you introduced yourself,' she said at length. 'You told Cynthia that she had come to the wrong house, and had better go away at once. Of course, she's the image of Mrs Frisque ... Oh, my dear, how perfectly screaming ...!'

The Male Impersonator

MISS ELIZABETH MAPP was sitting, on this warm September morning, in the little public garden at Tilling, busy as a bee with her water-colour sketch. She had taken immense pains with the drawing of the dykes that intersected the marsh, of the tidal river which ran across it from the coast, and of the shipyard in the foreground: indeed, she had procured a photograph of this particular view and, by the judicious use of tracing-paper, had succeeded in seeing the difficult panorama precisely as the camera saw it: now the rewarding moment was come to use her paintbox. She was intending to be very bold over this, following the method which Mr Sargent practised with such satisfactory results, namely of painting not what she knew was there but what her eye beheld, and there was no doubt whatever that the broad waters of the high tide, though actually grey and muddy, appeared to be as blue as the sky which they reflected. So, with a fierce glow of courage she filled her broad brush with the same strong solution of cobalt as she had used for the sky, and unhesitatingly applied it.

'There!' she said to herself. 'That's what he would have done. And now I must wait till it dries.'

The anxiety of waiting to see the effect of so reckless a proceeding by no means paralysed the natural activity of Miss Mapp's mind, and there was plenty to occupy it. She had returned only yesterday afternoon from a month's holiday in Switzerland, and there was much to plan and look forward to. Already she had made a minute inspection of her house and garden, satisfying herself that the rooms had been kept well-aired, that no dusters or dishcloths were missing, that there was a good crop of winter lettuces, and that all her gardener's implements were there except one trowel, which she might possibly have overlooked: she did not therefore at present entertain any dark suspicions on the subject.

She had also done her marketing in the High Street, where she had met several friends, of whom Godiva Plaistow was coming to tea to give her all the news, and thus, while the cobalt dried, she could project her mind into the future. The little circle of friends, who made life so pleasant and busy (and sometimes so agitating) an affair in Tilling would all have returned now for the winter, and the days would scurry by in a round of housekeeping, bridge, weekly visits to the workhouse, and intense curiosity as to anything of domestic interest which took place in the strenuous world of this little country town.

The thought of bridge caused a slight frown to gather on her forehead. Bridge was the chief intellectual pursuit of her circle, and, shortly before she went away, that circle had been convulsed by the most acute divergences of opinion with regard to majority-calling. Miss Mapp had originally been strongly against it.

'I'm sure I don't know by what right the Portland Club tells us how to play bridge,' she witheringly remarked. 'Tilling might just as well tell the Portland Club to eat salt with gooseberry tart, and for my part I shall continue to play the game I prefer.'

But then one evening Miss Mapp held no less than nine clubs in her hand and this profusion caused her to see certain advantages in majority-calling to which she had hitherto been blind, and she warmly espoused it. Unfortunately, of the eight players who spent so many exciting evenings together, there were thus left five who rejected majority (which was a very inconvenient number since one must always be sitting out) and three who preferred it. This was even more inconvenient, for they could not play bridge at all.

'We really must make a compromise,' thought Miss Mapp, meaning that everybody must come round to her way of thinking, 'or our dear little cosy bridge evenings won't be possible.'

The warm sun had now dried her solution of cobalt, and, holding her sketch at arm's length, she was astonished to observe how blue she had made the river, and wondered if she had seen it quite as brilliant as that. But the cowardly notion of toning it down a little was put out of her head by the sound of the church clock striking one, and it was time to go home to lunch.

The garden where she had been sketching was on the southward slope of the hill below the Church square, and having packed her artistic implements she climbed the steep little rise. As she skirted along one side of this square, which led into

Curfew Street, she saw a large pantechnicon van lumbering along its cobbled way. It instantly occurred to her that the house at the far end of the street, which had stood empty so long, had been taken at last, and since this was one of the best residences in Tilling, it was naturally a matter of urgent importance to ascertain if this surmise was true.

Sure enough the van stopped at the door, and Miss Mapp noticed that the bills in the windows of 'Suntrap' which announced that it was for sale, had been taken down. That was extremely interesting, and she wondered why Diva Plaistow, who, in the brief interview they had held in the High Street this morning, had been in spate with a torrent of miscellaneous gossip, had not mentioned a fact of such primary importance.

Could it be that dear Diva was unaware of it? It was pleasant to think that after a few hours in Tilling she knew more local news than poor Diva who had been here all August.

She retraced her steps and hurried home. Just as she opened the door she heard the telephone bell ringing, and was met by the exciting intelligence that this was a trunk call. Trunk calls were always thrilling; no one trunked over trivialities. She applied ear and mouth to the proper places.

'Tilling 76?' asked a distant insect-like voice.

Now Miss Mapp's real number was Tilling 67, but she had a marvellous memory, and it instantly flashed through her mind that the number of Suntrap was 76. The next process was merely automatic, and she said, 'Yes'. If a trunk call was coming for Suntrap and a pantechnicon van had arrived at Suntrap, there was no question of choice: the necessity of hearing what was destined for Suntrap knew no law.

'Her ladyship will come down by motor this afternoon,' said the insect, 'and she——'

'Who will come down?' asked Miss Mapp, with her mouth watering.

'Lady Deal, I tell you. Has the first van arrived?'

'Yes,' said Miss Mapp.

'Very well. Fix up a room for her ladyship. She'll get her food at some hotel, but she'll stop for a night or two settling in. How are you getting on, Susie?'

Miss Mapp did not feel equal to saying how Susie was getting on, and she slid the receiver quietly into its place.

She sat for a moment considering the immensity of her trove, feeling perfectly certain that Diva knew nothing about it all, or the fact that Lady Deal had taken Suntrap must have been her very first item of news. Then she reflected that a trunk call had been expended on Susie, and that she could do no less than pass the message on. A less scrupulous woman might have let Susie languish in ignorance, but her fine nature dictated the more honourable course. So she rang up Tilling 76, and in a hollow voice passed on the news. Susie asked if it was Jane speaking, and Miss Mapp again felt she did not know enough about Jane to continue the conversation.

'It's only at Tilling that such interesting things happen,' she thought as she munched her winter lettuce. . . .

She had enjoyed her holiday at the Riffel Alp, and had had long talks to a Bishop about the revised prayer book, and to a Russian exile about Bolshevism, and to a member of the Alpine Club about Mount Everest, but these remote cosmic subjects really mattered far less than the tenant of Suntrap, for the new prayer book was only optional, and Russia and Mount Everest were very far away and had no bearing on daily life, as she had not the smallest intention of exploring either of them. But she had a consuming desire to know who Susie was, and since it would be a pleasant little stroll after lunch to go down Curfew Street, and admire the wide view at the end of it, she soon set out again.

The pantechnicon van was in process of unlading, and as she lingered a big bustling woman came to the door of Suntrap, and told the men where to put the piano. It was a slight disappointment to see that it was only an upright: Miss Mapp would have preferred a concert-grand for so territorially sounding a mistress. When the piano had bumped its way into the rather narrow entrance, she put on her most winning smile, and stepped up to Susie with a calling-card in her hand, of which she had turned down the right-hand corner to show by this mystic convention that she had delivered it in person.

'Has her ladyship arrived yet?' she asked. 'No? Then would you kindly give her my card when she gets here? *Thank* you!'

Miss Mapp had a passion for indirect procedure: it was so much more amusing, when in pursuit of any object, however trivial and innocent, to advance with stealth, under cover, rather than march up to it in the open and grab it, and impersonating Susie and Jane, though only for a moment at the end of a wire, supplied that particular sauce which rendered her life at Tilling so justly palatable. But she concealed her stalkings under the brushwood, so to speak, of a frank and open demeanour, and though she was sure she had a noble quarry within shot, did not propose to disclose herself just yet. Probably Lady Deal would return her card next day, and in the interval she would be able to look her up in the Peerage, of which she knew she had somewhere an antique and venerable copy, and she would thus be in a position to deluge Diva with a flood of information: she might even have ascertained Lady Deal's views on majority-calling at bridge.

She made search for this volume, but without success, in the bookshelves of her big garden-room, which had been the scene of so much of Tilling's social life, and of which the bow-window, looking both towards the church and down the cobbled way which ran down to the High Street, was so admirable a post for observing the activities of the town. But she knew this book was somewhere in the house, and she could find it at leisure when she had finished picking Diva's brains of all the little trifles and shreds of news which had happened in Tilling during her holiday.

Though it was still only four o'clock, Miss Mapp gazing attentively out of her window suddenly observed Diva's round squat little figure trundling down the street from the church in the direction of her house, with those short twinkling steps of hers which so much resembled those of a thrush scudding over the lawn in search of worms. She hopped briskly into Miss Mapp's door, and presently scuttled into the garden-room, and began to speak before the door was more than ajar.

'I know I'm very early, Elizabeth,' she said, 'but I felt I must tell you what has happened without losing a moment. I was going up Curfew Street just now, and what do you think! Guess!'

Elizabeth gave a half-yawn and dexterously transformed it into an indulgent little laugh.

'I suppose you mean that the new tenant is settling into Suntrap,' she said.

Diva's face fell: all the joy of the herald of great news died out of it.

'What? You know?' she said.

'Oh, dear me, yes,' replied Elizabeth. 'But thank you, Diva, for coming to tell me. That was a kind intention.'

This was rather irritating: it savoured of condescension.

'Perhaps you know who the tenant is,' said Diva with an unmistakable ring of sarcasm in her voice.

Miss Mapp gave up the idea of any further secrecy, for she could never find a better opportunity for making Diva's sarcasm look silly.

'Oh yes, it's Lady Deal,' she said. 'She is coming down—let me see, Thursday isn't it?—she is coming down today.'

'But how did you know?' asked Diva.

Miss Mapp put a meditative finger to her forehead. She did not mean to lie, but she certainly did not mean to tell the truth.

'Now, who was it who told me?' she said. 'Was it someone at the Riffel Alp? No, I don't think so. Someone in London, perhaps: yes, I feel sure that was it. But that doesn't matter: it's Lady Deal anyhow who has taken the house. In fact, I was just glancing round to see if I could find a Peerage: it might be useful just to ascertain who she was. But here's tea. Now it's your turn, dear: you shall tell me all the news of Tilling, and then we'll see about Lady Deal.'

After this great piece of intelligence, all that poor Diva had to impart of course fell very flat: the forthcoming harvest festival, the mistake (if it was a mistake) that Mrs Poppit had made in travelling first-class with a third-class ticket, the double revoke made by Miss Terling at bridge, were all very small beer compared to this noble vintage, and presently the two ladies were engaged in a systematic search for the Peerage. It was found eventually in a cupboard in the spare bedroom, and Miss Mapp eagerly turned up 'Deal'.

'Viscount,' she said. 'Born, succeeded and so on. Ah, married——'

She gave a cry of dismay and disgust.

'Oh, how shocking!' she said. 'Lady Deal was Helena Herman. I remember seeing her at a music hall.'

'No!' said Diva.

'Yes,' said Miss Mapp firmly. 'And she was a male impersonator. That's the end of her; naturally we can have nothing to do with her, and I think everybody ought to know at once. To

think that a male impersonator should come to Tilling and take
one of the best houses in the place! Why, it might as well have
remained empty.'

'Awful!' said Diva. 'But what an escape I've had, Elizabeth. I
very nearly left my card at Suntrap, and then I should have had
this dreadful woman calling on me. What a mercy I didn't.'

Miss Mapp found bitter food for thought in this, but that had
to be consumed in private, for it would be too humiliating to tell
Diva that she had been caught in the trap which Diva had avoided.
Diva must not know that, and when she had gone Miss Mapp
would see about getting out.

At present Diva showed no sign of going.

'How odd that your informant in London didn't tell you what
sort of a woman Lady Deal was,' she said, 'and how lucky we've
found her out in time. I am going to the choir practice this
evening, and I shall be able to tell several people. All the same,
Elizabeth, it would be thrilling to know a male impersonator,
and she may be a very decent woman.'

'Then you can go and leave your card, dear,' said Miss Mapp,
'and I should think you would know her at once.'

'Well, I suppose it wouldn't do,' said Diva regretfully. As
Elizabeth had often observed with pain, she had a touch of
Bohemianism about her.

Though Diva prattled endlessly on, it was never necessary to
attend closely to what she was saying, and long before she left
Miss Mapp had quite made up her mind as to what to do about
that card. She only waited to see Diva twinkle safely down the
street and then set off in the opposite direction for Suntrap. She
explained to Susie with many apologies that she had left a card
here by mistake, intending to bestow it next door, and thus
triumphantly recovered it. That she had directed that the card
should be given to Lady Deal was one of those trumpery little
inconsistencies which never troubled her.

The news of the titled male-impersonator spread like influenza
through Tilling, and though many ladies secretly thirsted to know
her, public opinion felt that such moral proletarianism was impossible. Classes, it was true, in these democratic days were being
sadly levelled, but there was a great gulf between male imper-
sonators and select society which even viscountesses could not

bridge. So the ladies of Tilling looked eagerly but furtively at any likely stranger they met in their shoppings, but their eyes assumed a glazed expression when they got close.

Curfew Street, however, became a very favourite route for strolls before lunch when shopping was over, for the terrace at the end of it not only commanded a lovely view of the marsh but also of Suntrap. Miss Mapp, indeed, abandoned her Sargentesque sketch of the river, and began a new one here. But for a couple of days there were no great developments in the matter of the male impersonator.

Then one morning the wheels of fate began to whizz. Miss Mapp saw emerging from the door of Suntrap a Bath chair, and presently, heavily leaning on two sticks, there came out an elderly lady who got into it, and was propelled up Curfew Street by Miss Mapp's part-time gardener. Curiosity was a quality she abhorred, and with a strong effort but a trembling hand she went on with her sketch without following the Bath chair, or even getting a decent view of its occupant. But in ten minutes she found it was quite hopeless to pursue her artistic efforts when so overwhelming a human interest beckoned, and, bundling her painting materials into her satchel, she hurried down towards the High Street, where the Bath chair had presumably gone. But before she reached it, she met Diva scudding up towards her house. As soon as they got within speaking distance they broke into telegraphic phrases, being both rather out of breath.

'Bath chair came out of Suntrap,' began Miss Mapp.

'Thought so,' panted Diva. 'Saw it through the open door yesterday,'

'Went down towards the High Street,' said Miss Mapp.

'I passed it twice,' said Diva proudly.

'What's she like?' asked Miss Mapp. 'Only got glimpse.'

'Quite old,' said Diva. 'Should think between fifty and sixty. How long ago did you see her at the music hall?'

'Ten years. But she seemed quite young then.... Come into the garden-room, Diva. We shall see in both directions from there, and we can talk quietly.'

The two ladies hurried into the bow-window of the garden-room, and having now recovered their breath went on less spasmodically.

'That's very puzzling you know,' said Miss Mapp. 'I'm sure it wasn't more than ten years ago, and, as I say, she seemed quite young. But of course make-up can do a great deal, and also I should think impersonation was a very ageing life. Ten years of it might easily have made her an old woman.'

'But hardly as old as this,' said Diva. 'And she's quite lame: two sticks, and even then great difficulty in walking. Was she lame when you saw her on the stage?'

'I can't remember that,' said Miss Mapp. 'Indeed, she couldn't have been lame, for she was Romeo, and swarmed up to a high balcony. What was her face like?'

'Kind and nice,' said Diva, 'but much wrinkled and a good deal of moustache.'

Miss Mapp laughed in a rather unkind manner.

'That would make the male impersonation easier,' she said. 'Go on, Diva, what else?'

'She stopped at the grocer's, and Cannick came hurrying out in the most sycophantic manner. And she ordered something— I couldn't hear what—to be sent up to Suntrap. Also she said some name, which I couldn't hear, but I'm sure it wasn't Lady Deal. That would have caught my ear at once.'

Miss Mapp suddenly pointed down the street.

'Look! there's Cannick's boy coming up now,' she said. 'They have been quick. I suppose that's because she's a viscountess. I'm sure I wait hours sometimes for what I order. Such a snob! I've got an idea!'

She flew out into the street.

'Good morning, Thomas,' she said. 'I was wanting to order— let me see now, what was it? What a heavy basket you've got. Put it down on my steps, while I recollect.'

The basket may have been heavy, but its contents were not, for it contained but two small parcels. The direction on them was clearly visible, and having ascertained that, Miss Mapp ordered a pound of apples and hurried back to the garden-room.

'To Miss Mackintosh, Suntrap,' she said. 'What do you make of that, Diva?'

'Nothing,' said Diva.

'Then I'll tell you. Lady Deal wants to live down her past, and she has changed her name. I call that very deceitful, and I think worse of her than ever. Lucky that I could see through it.'

'That's far-fetched,' said Diva, 'and it doesn't explain the rest.

She's much older than she could possibly be if she was on the stage ten years ago, and she says she isn't Lady Deal at all. She may be right, you know.'

Miss Mapp was justly exasperated, the more so because some faint doubt of the sort had come into her own mind, and it would be most humiliating if all her early and superior information proved false. But her vigorous nature rejected such an idea and she withered Diva.

'Considering I know that Lady Deal has taken Suntrap,' she said, 'and that she was a male impersonator, and that she did come down here some few days ago, and that this woman and her Bath chair came out of Suntrap, I don't think there can be much question about it. So that, Diva, is that.'

Diva got up in a huff.

'As you always know you're right, dear,' she said, 'I won't stop to discuss it.'

'So wise, darling,' said Elizabeth.

Now Miss Mapp's social dictatorship among the ladies of Tilling had long been paramount, but every now and then signs of rebellious upheavals showed themselves. By virtue of her commanding personality these had never assumed really serious proportions, for Diva, who was generally the leader in these uprisings, had not the same moral massiveness. But now when Elizabeth was so exceedingly superior, the fumes of Bolshevism mounted swiftly to Diva's head. Moreover, the sight of this puzzling male impersonator, old, wrinkled, and moustached, had kindled to a greater heat her desire to know her and learn what it felt like to be Romeo on the music-hall stage and, after years of that delirious existence, to subside into a Bath chair and Suntrap and Tilling. What a wonderful life! . . .

And behind all this there was a vague notion that Elizabeth had got her information in some clandestine manner and had muddled it. For all her clear-headedness and force Elizabeth did sometimes make a muddle and it would be sweeter than honey and the honeycomb to catch her out. So in a state of brooding resentment Diva went home to lunch and concentrated on how to get even with Elizabeth.

Now, it had struck her that Mrs Bartlett, the wife of the vicar of Tilling, had not been so staggered when she was informed at the choir practice of the identity and of the lurid past of the new parishioner as might have been expected: indeed, Mrs Bartlett had whispered, 'Oh dear me, how exciting—I mean, how shocking,' and Diva suspected that she did not mean 'shocking'. So that afternoon she dropped in at the Vicarage with a pair of socks which she had knitted for the Christmas tree at the workhouse, though that event was still more than three months away. After a cursory allusion to her charitable errand, she introduced the true topic.

'Poor woman!' she said. 'She was being wheeled about the High Street this morning and looked so lonely. However many males she has impersonated, that's all over for her. She'll never be Romeo again.'

'No indeed, poor thing!' said Mrs Bartlett; 'and, dear me, how she must miss the excitement of it. I wonder if she'll write her memoirs: most people do if they've had a past. Of course, if they haven't, there's nothing to write about. Shouldn't I like to read Lady Deal's memoirs! But how much more exciting to hear her talk about it all, if we only could!'

'I feel just the same,' said Diva, 'and, besides, the whole thing is mysterious. What if you and I went to call? Indeed, I think it's almost your duty to do so, as the clergyman's wife. Her settling in Tilling looks very like repentance, in which case you ought to set the example, Evie, of being friendly.'

'But what would Elizabeth Mapp say?' asked Mrs Bartlett. 'She thought nobody ought to know her.'

'Pooh,' said Diva. 'If you'll come and call, Evie, I'll come with you. And is it really quite certain that she is Lady Deal?'

'Oh, I hope so,' said Evie.

'Yes, so do I, I'm sure, but all the authority we have for it at present is that Elizabeth said that Lady Deal had taken Suntrap. And who told Elizabeth that? There's too much Elizabeth in it. Let's go and call there, Evie: now, at once.'

'Oh, but dare we?' said the timorous Evie. 'Elizabeth will see us. She's sketching at the corner there.'

'No, that's her morning sketch,' said Diva. 'Besides, who cares if she does?'

The socks for the Christmas tree were now quite forgotten and, with this parcel still unopened, the two ladies set forth, with Mrs Bartlett giving fearful sidelong glances this way and that.

But there were no signs of Elizabeth, and they arrived undetected at Suntrap, and enquired if Lady Deal was in.

'No, ma'am,' said Susie, 'Her ladyship was only here for two nights settling Miss Mackintosh in, but she may be down again tomorrow. Miss Mackintosh is in.'

Susie led the way to the drawing-room, and there, apparently, was Miss Mackintosh.

'How good of you to come and call on me,' she said. 'And will you excuse my getting up? I am so dreadfully lame. Tea, Susie, please!'

Of course it was a disappointment to know that the lady in the Bath chair was not the repentant male impersonator, but the chill of that was tempered by the knowledge that Elizabeth had been completely at sea, and how far from land, no one yet could conjecture. Their hostess seemed an extremely pleasant woman, and under the friendly stimulus of tea even brighter prospects disclosed themselves.

'I love Tilling already,' said Miss Mackintosh, 'and Lady Deal adores it. It's her house, not mine, you know—but I think I had better explain it all, and then I've got some questions to ask. You see, I'm Florence's old governess, and Susie is her old nurse, and Florence wanted to make us comfortable, and at the same time to have some little house to pop down to herself when she was utterly tired out with her work.'

Diva's head began to whirl. It sounded as if Florence was Lady Deal, but then, according to the Peerage, Lady Deal was Helena Herman. Perhaps she was Helena Florence Herman.

'It may get clearer soon,' she thought to herself, 'and, anyhow, we're coming to Lady Deal's work.'

'Her work must be very tiring indeed,' said Evie.

'Yes, she's very naughty about it,' said Miss Mackintosh. 'Girl Guides, mothers' meetings, Primrose League, and now she's standing for Parliament. And it was so like her; she came down here last week, before I arrived, in order to pull furniture about and make the house comfortable for me when I got here. And she's coming back tomorrow to spend a week here I hope. Won't you both come in and see her? She longs to know Tilling. Do you play bridge by any chance? Florence adores bridge.'

'Yes, we play a great deal in Tilling,' said Diva. 'We're devoted to it too.'

'That's capital. Now, I'm going to insist that you should both dine with us tomorrow, and we'll have a rubber and a talk. I hope you both hate majority-calling as much as we do.'

'Loathe it,' said Diva.

'Splendid. You'll come, then. And now I long to know something. Who was the mysterious lady who called here in the afternoon when Florence came down to move furniture, and returned an hour or two afterwards and asked for the card she had left with instructions that it should be given to Lady Deal? Florence is thrilled about her. Some short name, Tap or Rap. Susie couldn't remember it.'

Evie suddenly gave vent to a shrill cascade of squeaky laughter.

'Oh dear me,' she said. 'That would be Miss Mapp. Miss Mapp is a great figure in Tilling. And she called! Fancy!'

'But why did she come back and take her card away?' asked Miss Mackintosh. 'I told Florence that Miss Mapp had heard something dreadful about her. And how did she know that Lady Deal was coming here at all? The house was taken in my name.'

'That's just what we all long to find out,' said Diva eagerly. 'She said that somebody in London told her.'

'But who?' asked Miss Mackintosh. 'Florence only settled to come at lunch-time that day, and she told her butler to ring up Susie and say she would be arriving.'

Diva's eyes grew round and bright with inductive reasoning.

'I believe we're on the right tack,' she said. 'Could she have received Lady Deal's butler's message, do you think? What's your number?'

'Tilling 76,' said Miss Mackintosh.

Evie gave three ecstatic little squeaks.

'Oh, that's it, that's it!' she said. 'Elizabeth Mapp is Tilling 67. So careless of them, but all quite plain. And she did hear it from somebody in London. Quite true, and so dreadfully false and misleading, and *so* like her. Isn't it, Diva? Well, it does serve her right to be found out.'

Miss Mackintosh was evidently a true Tillingite.

'How marvellous!' she said. 'Tell me much more about Miss Mapp. But let's go back. Why did she take that card away?'

Diva looked at Evie, and Evie looked at Diva.

'You tell her,' said Evie.

'Well, it was like this,' said Diva. 'Let us suppose that she heard the butler say that Lady Deal was coming——'

'And passed it on,' interrupted Miss Mackintosh. 'Because Susie got the message and said it was wonderfully clear for a trunk call. That explains it. Please go on.'

'And so Elizabeth Mapp called,' said Diva, 'and left her card. I didn't know that until you told me just now. And now I come in. I met her that very afternoon, and she told me that Lady Deal, so she had heard in London, had taken this house. So we looked up Lady Deal in a very old Peerage of hers——'

Miss Mackintosh waved her arms wildly.

'Oh, please stop, and let me guess,' she cried. 'I shall go crazy with joy if I'm right. It was an old Peerage, and so she found that Lady Deal was Helena Herman——'

'Whom she had seen ten years ago at a music hall as a male impersonator,' cried Diva.

'And didn't want to know her,' interrupted Miss Mackintosh.

'Yes, that's it, but that is not all. I hope you won't mind, but it's too rich. She saw you this morning coming out of your house in your Bath chair, and was quite sure that you were *that* Lady Deal.'

The three ladies rocked with laughter. Sometimes one recovered, and sometimes two, but they were re-infected by the third, and so they went on, solo and chorus, and duet and chorus, till exhaustion set in.

'But there's still a mystery,' said Diva at length, wiping her eyes. 'Why did the Peerage say that Lady Deal was Helena Herman?'

'Oh, that's the last Lady Deal,' said Miss Mackintosh. 'Helena Herman's Lord Deal died without children and Florence's Lord Deal, my Lady Deal, succeeded. Cousins.'

'If that isn't a lesson for Elizabeth Mapp,' said Diva. 'Better go to the expense of a new Peerage than make such a muddle. But what a long call we've made. We must go.'

'Florence shall hear every word of it tomorrow night,' said Miss Mackintosh. 'I promise not to tell her till then. We'll all tell her.'

'Oh, that is kind of you,' said Diva.

'It's only fair. And what about Miss Mapp being told?'

'She'll find it out by degrees,' said the ruthless Diva. 'It will hurt more in bits.'

'Oh, but she mustn't be hurt,' said Miss Mackintosh. 'She's too precious, I adore her.'

'So do we,' said Diva. 'But we like her to be found out occasionally. You will, too, when you know her.'

CRANK
STORIES

M.O.M.

HENRY ATTWOOD at the age of twenty was left an orphan, and cursed with a competence.

Some natures are so strong that this blighting influence of a competence has no effect on them, and, like good citizens, they continue to work like galley-slaves in order to turn their competence into affluence, and pay taxes on the higher scale obligingly provided by the Chancellor of the Exchequer in order to penalize industry. But Henry Attwood was not one of these strong natures.

He found the world so amazingly pleasant and interesting that, being without expensive tastes of any kind, he contrived to spend delightful and strenuous days on four hundred and fifty pounds a year until the fatal and almost universal experience of falling in love drove him to acquire the vast fortune that he is quite incapable of spending. It is true that his charming wife does all that can be expected of a mere woman in this direction, but the wealth that flows in a continual Pactolus into his bank balance seems to defy her most earnest endeavours.

So, at the age of twenty, Henry Attwood, in the year 1890, was left with an income of four hundred and fifty pounds a year, and instantly abandoned the routine of medical studies which he was following at a London hospital, with the idea of being a doctor. It was not that they did not interest him—for they interested him enormously—but, unfortunately, other things interested him enormously, too, and he wanted just now to win the amateur championship at golf more than he wanted anything else.

He talked this over with his friend Hugh Ingleton—with whom he shared lodgings in Westminster Bridge Road—in his usual extravagant and vivid manner.

'I don't give up my profession, Hughie,' he said; 'and really, if you come to think of it, winning the championship will bring me in a far larger practice than seeing more arms and legs cut off. It amazes me that you don't see why! You are bound by materialistic views. You don't know how a little excitement and interest pulls a patient round. You and I, for instance, if we were called in to prescribe for a case of influenza, would certainly do exactly the same thing from a medical point of view. But if the man was a golfer at all—and most men think they are—he would be far more stimulated by an amateur champion than by you. We all know perfectly well that no medicine ever cured anybody. What cures is the stimulus you give. Then I shall learn a lot about art. I shall learn to play the piano. I shall learn about gardening. All for the same reason. Hypnotism, too—suggestion. I shall go to Paris and study there. It is suggestion really that cures, and here in England, at present, you are thought a quack if you dream of such a thing.'

'All this will take time,' remarked Hugh.

'Yes, dear child. *Ars longa, vita brevis.* Very likely I shan't ever be a doctor at all. You were going to say that, so I save you the trouble. I may become a professional golfer, I may become a gardener, or a mesmerist, or a musician, with long elfin locks. Really, at the age of twenty, no fellow ought to know what he is going to become, unless indigence drives him to become something. It's too early to choose. One should not choose until one has seen more what choices there are. Everyone ought to be supported by the State till he is forty. Then he is probably past work, you will say, and ought to be painlessly put out of the way.... Again, I've often thought of becoming a clergyman, not a country parsonage kind of buffer, with a glass of port wine after lunch, but a real parson down in the slums. But whenever I think of becoming anything, I feel that I've got a vocation for it.'

Hugh Ingleton, with grim, serious face, rose and tossed him a pair of boxing-gloves.

'Then I'll prove you haven't got much of a vocation for a boxer,' he said.

'Right O! Give me two minutes to change. If there's one thing I can do, it's to box.'

'I'll knock the nonsense out of you,' said Hugh.

An hour afterwards, when the two friends were dining at a small Italian restaurant over the way, it appeared that this result had not been attained, for Attwood expanded with fresh extravagances over Chianti.

'Wine!' he said. 'Could one be an Omar Khayyám on four-fifty a year, do you think? I really don't ask any more than to play golf all day, have twenty minutes with the gloves—Jove, I could do without the gloves, for I believe you've broken a rib for me!—and then drink enormous quantities of rough, strong wine. One would get gouty, of course, but by that time I should be a Christian Scientist, and so get rid of that. And then—oh, Hughie!—then some poor white-faced devil, like that man there, comes in—he's half-blind, too, and I diagnose lead-poisoning—and one feels that it is only the brutes that perish who don't give their whole lives to trying to help a few of such sufferers out of the myriads. I wonder if suggestion would have any effect in definite organic disease? I don't see why not. Definite organic disease can assuredly be set up by nerves and worry, so why should it not be cured through the nerves also? I want to test that. But, first of all, I shall win the amateur championship.'

'Marriage?' asked the laconic Ingleton.

'With regard to me? No, I'm too busy for the present to think about it. It is necessary to have a good deal of leisure to think about marrying, while, as far as one can judge, there's not much leisure afterwards. Now, will you please finish that Chianti, or shall I? No, I think neither of us will. We'll send it over to that poor, white-faced fellow with our compliments.'

So for the next seven years Henry Attwood lived, with all his heart, mind, and soul, the delectable life so proper to the years between twenty and thirty, when the powers both of enjoyment and of learning are so keen, doing with all his might the things that seemed to him most worth while.

With him these pursuits were always innocuous—he did not, for instance, take up the career of an Omar Khayyám—and generally laudable. A year and a half of incessant golf-playing secured for him the amateur championship, while a year of strenuous piano-playing proved to him that he would never make a pianist. Then followed a couple of years in Paris, where he studied medicine at the Sorbonne, and mesmerism in the Charcot School, and then it suddenly struck him, with a force that was inevitable and overwhelming, that he was living a life as selfish and self-centred as that of the merest sensualist.

He had acquired quantities of delightful knowledge, but he

had done it all to please himself, and was conferring by his superb physical fitness and mental equipment no shadow of benefit on any outside himself, while the 'white-faced man', so to speak, had earned from him nothing more than vague pity and the dregs of a bottle of Chianti. Nor had he even come near the less culpable selfishness of falling in love; he had lived as completely for himself as the drunkard or the drug-drinker.

So within a month he was attached in a lay, not a clerical, capacity to an East End mission, and had become a 'real person down in the slums'. His reality, indeed, was something amazing, if by reality we mean the 'touch' he had with life.

Nothing came amiss to him, and he poured into his work all that he had previously pent up in himself. He superintended soup-kitchens, he taught in schools, he organized and performed in penny readings and other entertainments, and presented himself every evening as a target at which the youth of Hackney aimed blows with boxing-gloves. But all these energetic affairs were to him no more than pastime; his real work, as his head acknowledged, lay with the sick and the dying.

Assuming, as was indeed the case, that their spiritual requirements had been attended to by his clerical brethren, he coaxed or scolded the sick into a revival of their nervous energies which might combat their real or imaginary diseases, while if they could combat no more, he brightened the way into the dark valley with a lamp compounded, so to speak, of foolish nonsense and those little pleasant trivialities of this world of ours, which retain their interest even when the darkness is immediately and inevitably going to close round us. He dispersed shadows, and was the dispenser of pleasure and encouragement, and by his very presence seemed to relieve pain. He moved like some fresh wind through wards and miserable dwellings.

All the time his conviction that at least three-quarters, if not four, of the illness and *malaise* of the world is due to the imagination, and can be cured through the imagination, grew to a gospel certainty within him.

On this he descanted to Hugh Ingleton, who had come down to see him one Saturday evening.

'I'm always at leisure on Saturday evening, Hughie,' he had said, 'because I let all the fellows in the boys' club do exactly what they choose that night.'

'I should have thought that was the very night you would look after them more,' said Hugh.

'Well, that's not my plan. If they are going to lead decent lives, and most of them are, they must lead them in spite of temptations. Now, when the boys' club is open, they really find it far more attractive than the streets—they don't want to go into the pubs and get into beastly messes. So once a week I turn them all loose, and they've got to protect themselves against filth and boozing. It answers all right. Of course, some of them get into scrapes or drink too much; but usually, on reflection, they find they didn't enjoy it so tremendously. Men have got far more imagination than you think; they think of themselves as being strong and hard-working and clear-eyed, and that has a great effect on their lives. Imagination! Heavens, if one could only use imagination up to its true value! There's no other force in the world to compare to it.'

'Charcot?' asked Hugh.

'Oh, it's beyond what Charcot dreamed of. There's no limit to the power of the imagination over the body and the mind. But we all want "an outward and visible sign", as the Catechism says. If you tell a dyspeptic man that there is nothing wrong with him sufficiently powerfully, he will perhaps improve, but only a little. But give him a pill to take after dinner, and tell him that it is bound to put him all right, he will improve a great deal.'

'It depends what the pill is made of,' said Hugh.

'Not very much; though, of course, you can do a little by drugs. But the main work of the pill will be done by the man's belief in its efficacy. I'm thinking out a medicine now which I expect will cure almost everything. It will cure, in any case, all the ailments that lead to organic disease.'

'I shall expose it in *Secret Remedies*,' said Hugh.

'No, you won't, because I'm going to tell you all about it now, this minute, in confidence, and you will certainly agree that, taken as I prescribe it, it is admirable. Besides, it won't be for sale, nor will it be advertised. I shall have it on tap at our sick-clubs, and shall direct the use of it myself. I'm going to call it "My Own Mixture". They'll remember that, and it will spread like mad. M.O.M., you know. You can't forget it. Bottle of Mom.'

'I think I should prefer Mumm,' said Hugh. 'But let's hear all about it.'

Henry Attwood deposited his long, big limbs in a chair that only just held him. His ruddy boyish face, with its blue eyes and crisp curling hair, showed like a sort of sun through the clouds of tobacco smoke which he puffed from a briar-wood pipe. Outside, a sudden flood of wind-vexed rain beat on the window, and he jerked his thumb over his shoulder.

'I hate a wet Saturday night,' he said, 'because it drives my lambs into the pubs. But they've got to learn to stand on their own feet, bless them! Well, about My Own Mixture. It's going to be made chiefly of camomile and salt. Have you ever tasted camomile and salt? You would remember it, if you had, for it is impossible to conceive a more loathsome and nauseating flavour.'

'Then why prescribe it?' asked Ingleton.

'Chiefly because it tastes so utterly abominable. It tastes strong and awful, and consequently people will think—my sort of people, I mean—that it must be doing them good. They like medicine to be beastly; it is part of the outward and visible sign. I thought of adding a little quinine, but it's too expensive. But that's not the whole point. Here's a dried camomile flower for you. I ask you to chew it for a minute. You will then be able to understand what follows.'

'Anything in the cause of science,' said Hugh.

Attwood waited a couple of minutes.

'That's enough,' he said. 'Now have a cigarette.'

'Part of the plan?' asked Hugh.

'Yes.'

Hugh lit his cigarette, took one whiff of it, and instantly threw it into the fireplace.

'Good Heavens, what foul tobacco!' he said.

Attwood chuckled.

'Not at all. It's what you've been smoking all the evening. But you won't want to smoke again for another hour. Now have some whisky and soda to console you.'

'Still science?' asked Hugh.

'Still science.'

Hugh mixed himself a glassful, took a sip, and strongly shuddered.

'But it's poison!' he said.

'Not at all. It's a good whisky. But *are* you beginning to see something of the inwardness of M.O.M.? After a dose of it, as I shall prescribe it, you wouldn't be able to smoke or drink alcohol for three hours at least. Now, as I said, there's not only camomile but salt in M.O.M. That'll make them thirsty, and they'll be driven to drink water. Well, a lot of my fellows are constantly rheumatic, and if there is one thing more likely than another to help your rheumatism, it is drinking quantities of fluid. You know that. So incidentally—only incidentally, mind—M.O.M. is in future to be given to the rheumatic and gouty and acid, and, instead of smoking and drinking whisky and beer, they will drink water. I shan't tell them to do that—they would utterly despise water if recommended them—but they'll be thirsty.'

Hugh sniffed at his whisky again, and again postponed it.

'Go on,' he said.

'Well, three-quarters of my flock—not the young 'uns, of course, but the working-men and the slaving women, suffer most of all from fatigue, which they patch up with stimulants. Now, what's my prescription for them? Three tablespoonfuls of M.O.M. mixture in a pint of hot water, to be drunk with a teaspoon directly after supper. That will take them the best part of half an hour. I shall tell them to take it sitting down, not standing up, and with their eyes closed, I think. They won't want to go round to the pub, after that, and, being tired, they will, I hope, go to bed. Have you ever drunk hot camomile tea? It makes you sleep like a top. And in the middle of the night they will awake drowsily and drink some water. And they'll feel far brisker next morning than if they had spent half the night in the pub. They want to be brisk and not tired; they drink spirits because they are tired. But most of them love medicine, and they will give M.O.M. a trial, if it's only because I tell them to.'

Attwood, not having partaken of camomile, lit another pipe.

'Even all this is only incidental,' he said. 'It certainly will do them good, but the real good it will do them will be their belief it's doing them good. That is far more important. That you don't believe, I expect, because you are blinded by your English ignorance. But if you had been through the Charcot School, you would recognize the illimitable power of suggestion. For dyspeptics, too! There's a lot of dyspepsia here, not among the very poorest, but chiefly among those who, when they feel rather unwell, set themselves down to get through a piece of beefsteak, which they think will "strengthen" them. For such I shall prescribe them M.O.M. half an hour before dinner. Have another try at the whisky, Hugh.'

Such was the inception of M.O.M., and marvellous was the growth of its use and success.

With the cachet of Attwood's name and recommendation, its success was unrivalled. Somehow drunkards, fatigued, dyspeptic, with the image of that cheerful and vital young giant in their mind, sat themselves meekly and hopefully down with bowls of the nauseous mixture and a teaspoon, and sipped and shuddered, and shuddered and sipped.

Greater yet was the army of those who had nothing the matter with them, but who, in the damp and sunless autumn, needed their vital force not increased, but aroused. Of this class were wives and daughters of tradesmen in comfortable but stuffy circumstances, and from them the marvellous healing and invigorating powers of the abominable mixture spread far and wide beyond the confines of Hackney, and a serious situation began to develop.

For M.O.M. was not a patent medicine to be obtained 'at every chemist's'—it was the brew of one man, prepared by himself on a secret recipe, to make which public, as he saw quite well, would be to rob his invention of its efficacy. He gave it to members of his flock, but with the growing and imperious demand for it, it was certainly ascertained that his flock sold it to other enquirers for it on advantageous terms, and applied for more.

It was impossible that Mrs East, for instance, had consumed a whole bottleful of the essence between Tuesday and Friday—she would have been no more than a brine-pickle if that was the case. It was impossible not to connect Bob Flash's new coat with the three bottles he had emptied in little less than a week, even accepting the incredible statement that his children preferred it to their bread and milk for supper!

Already a large local chemist had offered to prepare the stuff in cauldrons, if only Henry Attwood would give him the recipe, supply it at a reasonable figure, and share the profits with its inventor. His conscience would not allow him to make a profit out of so fraudulent a decoction, even though the decoction—or, rather, the spirit in which the decoction was imbibed—produced such successful results.

And all the time the demand grew unbridled, and Attwood lived in a briny atmosphere of camomile.

Then came the final and determining factor. On his holiday he saw Her for Whom he and the world were made, daughter of a small country squire, with eyes of night set in a flower-like face, and the inexorable need for human personal love shot up in him sudden and strong, like the flowering of an aloe. Marriage on four hundred and fifty pounds a year, with two rooms in a celibate mission in the East End, did not appear to a shrewd and impoverished father a practical scheme.

That is why we can all get M.O.M. at two-and-ninepence a bottle, and the larger size, containing twice the quantity, at four-and-sixpence.

The Adventure of Hegel Junior

THE practised traveller will often have observed, even if he has not visited, a seaport station in the bottom left-hand corner of Scotland called Stranraer. From there a north-west passage plied by paddle-steamers conducts you to five tall chimneys and some ragged children in the top right-hand corner of Ireland, which are called Larne. These paddle-steamers slap the water at the most prodigious rate, and are furnished with comfortable cabins and excellent breakfasts, but they have no control (as far as I could judge) over the movements of the sea. They are called a 'line'—so much is stated in 'Bradshaw'—but the rails are badly laid.

The three travellers about whom I shall have occasion to speak had a modest luggage, which consisted chiefly of golf-clubs. There were snub-nosed drivers of a whippy sort, truculent-looking brassies, wry-necked irons, and putters apparently of fine gold, and these and they journeyed still westwards till they came to a place pronounced Fawn (though spelled catchily, and I do not remember how), which is on the further side of the other end of nowhere, though on the near side of Lough Swilly. From there a curious lop-sided, cross-eyed craft bore them to their journey's end.

This craft went by steam, and had a decided bias, like a bowl; and its captain, after the exchange of a few soft words, allows one to take the wheel. For me it was an experience, and an experience it was also, I doubt not, for those of the passengers who were fit to observe our course, for the Atlantic had been angry the day before.

The captain only laughed. He was a man of iron nerve.

Of these three passengers, I, as is obvious, was one, Buck was another, and a person whom we called Hegel was the third. His real name was not Hegel: but his real name is beside the point, and we called him Hegel because he was a philosopher.

He had just gone through the Moral Science Tripos at

Cambridge, in which he had taken a first. But his philosophy lay far deeper than this, for a Tripos may be only a sort of fungus-growth on a man (at least, so Buck and I thought, and we, also, were not unacquainted with Triposes), and Hegel was a philosopher to his heart's core. For instance, on our north-west passage, when danger-flags of green were flying on his face, and the throe was imminent, he assured us that so-called sea-sickness was pure imagination, and that he personally, by an effort of will, had never felt better. And an incredibly short time afterwards, his ruling passion still so dominated him that he reappeared, and continued to be tedious.

Also at golf he never allows, in his own case, that any innate malignity of the ball can be called 'bad luck'. Indeed, more than once, when a magnanimous opponent has said 'Bad luck' to him, in consolation at the punishment of a brilliant attempt of any kind, he has been known to reply quite calmly—'If I had hit the ball correctly it would have gone where I wished it to.' Now that sort of thing shows philosophy of the deepest dye.

Arrived at that delectable end of the earth, for two days we played golf, and the third being Sunday, and the unwritten law of the place indicating its observance, we walked northwards along Lough Swilly. The day was one of a hundred thousand; the sun shone with the most magnificent lavishness of light; clouds, broad-bosomed and dazzling white, chased over the blue field above, and their shadows over the shining Lough below, and the wind was as soft as the brogue of the grey-eyed Irish folk who gave us 'Good-morning!'

Our walk lay on the edge of cliffs, which rose ever higher from the tumbled water that boomed at their feet; and starting from sea-level, where the ear was filled with the tumult of a boisterous sea, we had in half an hour, though still on the very margin of the Lough, got to such a height that the noise of the waves was only a murmured mutter, such as you may hear in a shell, and the scream of the pebbles, dragged out in the back-wash, but a faint sibilance. Here the cliff plunged with a noble suddenness into the water, the path still leading along its extreme edge, and was marked for those who have to travel here by dusk or night with big stones at short intervals on the seaward side, whitewashed over.

Here and there on the gigantic wall were little juts and

terraces, a foot or two wide, on which blown grass-seed and crevice-loving flowers had unaccountably anchored and sprung up in tufts of spiky leaf and blossom, but never have I seen a rock which leaped so bold and sheer three hundred feet or more on to the narrow shingle that at low tide fringed the sea. But when the tide is high, sufficient depth of water runs up to the base of the cliff, and the unspent surges hurl themselves at it in living walls of translucent sapphire.

At the supremest height and the extremest edge of this huge bastion we threw ourselves down on the short sweet turf, and talked lazily and by fits, and smoked with steady industry, as is meet on Sunday morning. Then Hegel, as often happens, became serious and 'jawed'. His monologue, some of which I give, was constantly interrupted, it must be understood, by loud laughter, as in the police reports.

'Will you never cease to be boys?' he said. 'Will you eventually turn into those horrible bald people who sit in clubs with their backs to the window, when they are in town, and who in the country just potter about the farm with the bailiff, or, worse than that, live in health-resorts to cure the gout which port-wine has brought on? They have never grown up; they are not men. Fancy playing golf, too, when you are forty! You will, Buck, you know; and so will the other idiot. Do you really suppose that that is all one has to do in this life? About the next life I haven't make up my mind: I think there probably is one; at least, I cannot imagine that I, this Ego, stop when I die.'

(You must remember that Hegel was only twenty-two, and Buck settled the little point by telling him that he had no imagination. That sort of thing is good for Hegel, but after a moment's pause he continued.)

'But in the interval I believe in the Progress of Mankind,' he said; 'and that, and nothing else, really concerns me. Yes, I see your future perfectly. You will have a few more years' ('"A few more years shall roll,"' said Buck) 'in which you will enjoy, so you think, amorous adventures, and talk as you talked last night about "gurls"' (this was libellous), 'and then perhaps you'll marry and settle down, so you call it, just as if you weren't sufficiently sunk already, and read the paper, and shoot, and drink port: and, in Heaven's name, what is the end of it all? You will go before your Maker—if you have one, and I fully believe you have—able

to shoot a crossing pheasant with moderate—only moderate—
certainty, and to lay an iron shot dead once out of twenty times.
That is what you will have learned in your sixty or seventy years
of life! And you will beget children, who will inherit the indescribable stupidity of yourselves. Your children will certainly
inherit that (though I think Max Nordau and people push hered-
ity too far), because it is the one thing you were born with and
have cultivated. It was born with you, but I am afraid it will not
die with you.'

Here Buck choked, and we had to pat him on the back; and,
notwithstanding the benefit it would be to mankind if he had
there and then died childless, according to Hegel, the latter exhibited a visible concern, inconsistent with what he had said, but
amiable. But when Buck had recovered he went on just as
before—

'It is awful to think what useless lives we lead,' he said. 'Nine
out of ten of fellows in our class of life—which is a beastly
expression, because we are all equal—go into the City all day,
add up sixteenths and thirty-seconds till their fathers die. Then
if they are eldest sons they go into Parliament, and oppose all
attempts at remedying existing abuses, or become JPs, and get
pilloried in *Truth*. And if they are not eldest sons they continue
adding up until they become partners in a firm, and get other
young men to do it for them. Why, an engine-driver on a
luggage-train is of more practical use than fifty of them!'

Hegel, in fact, was at his worst that morning, and it would be
tedious to give more of his preposterous conversation. It was
also useless to argue with him, for he is an ingenious beast, and
makes what one says mean the opposite of what one meant to
say, which he calls the Socratic method.

Eventually we put wisps of grass down his neck behind, and
strolled home, feeling hungry after the sermon, lunched heavily, and tasted supreme content. Then letters arrived, and one
of Hegel's excited him—Socratically perhaps, but we thought
at least Platonically—and he borrowed all our keys in order
to open a closed bookcase in the library, which contained
ordnance-maps. Later on he sent a telegram, reply paid.

In the evening came revelations. Considering how Hegel had
sermonized that morning, we were justified in retaliating by un-
seemly conjectures, often repeated, as to the destination of the

telegram. This made him so obviously uncomfortable that having ascertained that no one near or dear was dying or dead, we continued till he confessed.

There was a She in the case, and She was staying with some people he knew, not six miles off. The telegram he had sent proposed that he should dine and sleep there next day, and the answer, which he had already received, said 'Delighted!' And the prudent Hegel had arranged to send his bag by the lop-sided steamer and walk along the cliff himself. He had meant to steal off next afternoon without telling us, for he is secretively inclined.

In spite of this opening of the gate of Paradise, Hegel played golf next morning with the most fiendish precision. There had been heavy rain in the night, and though his luggage went on before lunch by the lop-sided steamer, and he had no change, he still lay down on sopping greens to study his putt. This is a process which takes time, but Hegel always made up for it by subsequently holing out, which made it more annoying.

The afternoon clouded over, and before we had started to play again a heavy rain came from the north-west. All morning the sea had been rising, and by four o'clock a thunderous surge drove on to the beach, and Hegel's manifest anxiety about the arrival of the lop-sided steamer was comical, for as it started at noon, it really did seem within the range of probability that it should do its six miles before evening. 'But, thank God, you're not steering!' said Hegel to me.

His own departure also he put off, hoping that the weather would clear, and sunset brought an hour of clean-washed blue sky, and promised a fair evening. So about six Buck and I set off with Hegel northwards to put him on his way.

But the amendment in the weather was short, and by the time we had reached the jut of headlong rock where we had sat under Hegel's discourse all the morning before, a threatening rack of cloud driving up blind and black from the west, and obscuring in a very short time the sunset half of the sky, warned us homewards. Hegel would assuredly get very wet, but at the end he would bask in the smile of Her. So should not we, and we turned to go back to our bachelor home. Even as we turned, Buck called over his shoulder—

'Don't get thinking of Her, and walk over the edge, old man.'

But Hegel's reply was drowned in a scream of wind.

We began by walking, but soon we ran. In an incredibly short time the light was sucked from the sky, and night, falling like the stroke of a black wing, brought with it in streaming downpour the arrears of a month's drought. But the flood meant no slackening of the gale: wind and rain together hissed and howled like demented things, while beneath us on the left, growing ever louder as we approached sea-level, rose the tumult of the Atlantic, pent by the narrowing land. But black as it was, the white stones kept us to the path, and half-an-hour saw us, drenched to the skin, passing the illuminated squares of hotel-windows, and into shelter.

Hegel (here I write that of which I was not eye-witness) parted from us on that outstanding bluff, and went northwards.

On him, too, night and tumult descended with sudden and extreme uproar, but the whitened stones kept him to the path. For a couple of miles this path leads along the sheer edge, but he went cannily, and with a blithe heart. Then in a moment, about a mile after we had left him, various things happened.

His foot stepped into vacancy: he saw that what he thought was a white stone was a wave breaking over a reef three hundred feet below; his elbow was knocked up across his face; a mad gust of wind nipped his cap from his head, and he clutched out wildly and backwards and sideways with his hands. They caught, first one and then the other, on something, slipped, and caught again on an edge of rock; his body swung sheer, and he was left hanging in darkness to the extreme verge of the cliff, and his feet dangled in the air. Straight below, so it seemed, but very distant, roared the rollers.

It has been said that Hegel was essentially philosophical, and as the business of the philosopher is to observe constantly and always, even when asleep (and then he puts down his dream when he wakes, and sends it to the Society for Psychical Research), Hegel observed now.

'First of all,' said Hegel afterwards, 'it flashed across me with extraordinary clearness that I was quite irredeemably dead, so it was no use bothering oneself. Then—and this was more bitter— it struck me that I was rather young; and, thirdly—and this was most bitter of all—that in an hour's time I should have been dining with Her. My place would be laid for me, and perhaps they would wait dinner a little.

'Thought is exceedingly rapid, and not till I had considered these three things did I know that I had cut my knee, which must have been done the moment I fell. Immediately afterwards—yet it was hardly afterwards, for I thought so quickly—I felt that my cap had blown away, and I wondered with great curiosity whether it had fallen into the sea or had dropped on to the shingle. In the latter case I knew that you would find it if the tide had not come up again, as well as—well, as well as me—that is to say, if you found either.

'Not till then did it occur to me that since I had fallen over the cliff and had had the good fortune to catch hold of the edge, I had better scramble up again at once; and as my fingers seemed to have a good hold, I gave up being irredeemably dead, and began pulling myself up. But the edge on which I had caught bulged outwards, and I could not by mere hauling get up. There was a small sharp tooth of rock I could feel pointing downwards, which caught in my coat just below the elbow and held me. However, a quick jerk might get over that, though—I remembered this at the time—it would tear my coat, which was nearly new. So I made a sudden jerk upwards from the elbows, and I felt the rock to which I was hanging move slightly. And then I knew that I was clinging, not to the cliff, but to some big loosened stone stuck in the earth, which would not stand jerking. Then I felt along, first with one hand and then the other, right and left. On both sides there was only loose earth. After that I hung quiet for a moment or two.

'It was a cold night, but quite suddenly the sweat began to pour from my face. I felt large drops gather on my forehead, and one trickled down my nose, and another into my eye. Then more came, and the drop on my nose got larger, and fell. After that, there was so much that I do not remember what happened to it. My body, so to take it, was very much frightened, but it was not so bad.

'Then, for a moment or two, I suppose, but it seemed longer, I thought about life and death and God. The whole of my life did *not* appear to me, as one is told happens, but the wind or the sea or something sang, "Hark, my soul, it is the Lord"—just one line, and no more. Then I thought about my people for just a second, and then about you and Buck, and whether you would play golf next morning. And I wondered whether you would get very wet going home, and if there would be lobster for dinner.

Then I said quite aloud, "What a cursed nuisance this all is!" and then I began thinking again whether my cap had fallen into the sea or on to the shingle.

'After that I told myself again that I was certainly going to die in a few minutes, and I thought about my rooms at Cambridge, and a pipe that was in my pocket which ought to have the ash cut away, and about Blanche—that's her name, you know—and whether I had been away from home so long that my fox-terrier wouldn't be sorry. And then I thought about my cap again.

'Then my left arm got tired and began to ache, and I wondered what on earth was the use of hanging on any longer. Suddenly it struck me that I had not shouted for help, and I began to shout—Heavens! how I shouted, and how futile it appeared to me even then! I could hear my voice carried away over the Lough by the wind like tobacco-smoke when you lean out of the window of an express. I shouted twenty times more after I had begun to count, and then I thought about my cap again.

'As you know, it was raining tremendously, and about then I heard even above the wind a little whisper just by me, like a person sighing in his sleep, and my elbow just grated against an edge of rock. So I guessed at once that the rain had loosened the stone to which I hung, and that it was giving way. I very much wanted it to be quick and go, because I was so bothered about what had happened to my cap.

'It must have been almost immediately that it went, but in that time I thought about all these things again, and especially about my cap. Then it whispered more loudly, and began to slide. It is all rot talking about a drowning man clinging to a straw, because as soon as I felt it was really off, I let go, and swore just once. Lucky I did let go. It just grazed my shoulders, for I ducked my head, and I fell, I suppose, eight inches on to the ledge where you found me. Minutes afterwards, it seemed, I heard the stone go smash on the shingle, so I concluded that my cap had fallen there too, for as soon as it was over the edge it would be out of the wind.

'I stood on the ledge for some time, holding on like grim death—though there was no need—with my face to the cliff, like a child put in the corner. I was not consciously frightened before, but, by Jove, I paid for it then! After that the rain stopped, and soon the moon came out; but I stood clinging to the rock,

and seeing my shadow cast there for a long time before I dared
look round. Then I saw I was safe. The ledge I had dropped
upon was firm, and two feet wide, I should think. Also, as you
saw, there was a little upstanding rock, behind which I could put
my head and not see the drop below, for the depth of it made
me feel sick. And that is all.'

The interim is shortly told. In the morning came another telegram for Hegel, which Buck and I opened, to send on if necessary. It repeated the invitation of Sunday, said his bag had arrived,
and supposed that the storm had delayed him. And so with white
lips we set out: one party below on the beach, with a boat against
the incoming of the tide, the others at the top of the cliffs. At a
certain point we—I went with the party on the top—were hailed
by a loud and unphilosophical voice.

'At last!' it said. 'What an age you have been! Lie down one
of you, and stretch a hand over. Oh, you've brought a rope.'

We let down a rope's end, and in a moment Hegel was standing with us. Then he burst out into loud laughter, and immediately afterwards cursed, in marrowy language, the sea, the rocks,
us, the white stones, and his cap.

But we gave him brandy, and he got better, and now, a week
later, he is playing golf again with the same old fiendish precision. Also he is reading Schopenhauer, because the affair at the
house northwards has not gone very successfully—in fact, She is
engaged to somebody quite different.

Hegel says that Schopenhauer is a splendid fellow, and the
secret of life, and Heaven knows what. I have not read any
myself, nor has Buck, but we disagree with Hegel on principle.
Besides, since his disappointment, he says such awful things about
women. I expect he got them out of Schopenhauer.

The Simple Life

THE Duchess of Shrewsbury was sitting in a small, wooden sort of shelter on the lawn of what she called her cottage near Goring (which, however, has battlements and a tower), without any shoes and stockings on, because she was leading the simple life. A croquet-mallet stood by her, which she had used for two hours already that day, shrieking, because 'it tickled so', as her fairy footsteps (for she was an immensely large woman) trod the grass.

But the game was over, and just now she was explaining the principles of the simple life to one of the Vernon twins. Both in body and mind they were exactly alike, and she was never quite sure to which she was talking. They were her nephews, however, so she could and did say practically anything to either of them.

'My dear, I feel ever so much better already,' she was saying now, 'and I've only tried the simple life really strictly, you know, since last Monday. It makes all the difference to one's happiness, I find; and if you'll only stick to it——'

Here she was interrupted for a moment by the arrival of a footman with two telegrams, which she tore open. There was also a telephone on the table of the shelter, and simultaneously it began to ring. She had had a particularly powerful bell put on it, so that she could hear it from any part of the garden.

'Just see who it is, dear,' said she to the Twin, 'while I read these. Oh, how angelic of him! Antonelli will come down directly he has finished at the Opera, so he'll catch the half-past twelve train.

'Oh, and did I tell you that those two dears from the Comédie are coming, and they will do *the* farce together after dinner? Yes; the motor will have to go in to meet the last train,' she said to the footman, 'and there must be a little supper ready for M. Antonelli. Just some soup, and a cutlet, and some fruit. Now, what's the other?'

The Twin had got into communication with someone

unknown, and was saying 'Who are you?' at short intervals like a minute-gun. He also, like his aunt, was sitting without shoes and stockings, which was pleasant on so hot a morning; and an iced drink, a box of cigarettes, and a plate of fruit by his side indicated that one might be simple without being uncomfortable.

The telegram was from the duke, asking his wife if there was a bed for him.

'How unfortunate!' she said. 'I think Antonelli fills us completely up.'

'I can go and sleep at the inn, aunt,' said the young man.

'No; the rooms are so badly ventilated. I am sure you would catch all sorts of things, and not get enough oxygen.'

'Or I'll sleep here in the shelter,' said he. 'That's part of the simple life, isn't it?'

'Oh, do; but I hope you won't catch cold. I don't like telling Shrewsbury there isn't room. I see so little of him. Thank you, dear. So his Grace will come down this afternoon,' she added to the footman, 'but he doesn't say when, so both trains must be met. And tell Mr Vernon's man—which are you, dear?—yes, Mr Jack Vernon's man, that he will sleep here. And who is that ringing, Jack?'

Jack, however, was saying 'Yes, yes,' and did not answer at once.

'It's your broker,' he said. 'South Africans are buoyant, and he wants to know——'

The Duchess snatched the receiver from him.

'Yes, my dear man,' she said, 'it's me. Yes, yes. No? How delightful! So you've sold them? How much? Two hundred and forty pounds? Fancy! Yes. Quite so. You'll let me know about that then later? Thanks.'

The Twin lit a cigarette.

'Well, the simple life——' he suggested.

'Ah, yes, we simplify, you know. We do without all the things you would think one couldn't possibly do without, and are ever so much better for it. For instance, six months ago I couldn't possibly have done without hats. I shall save thousands. Boots, too; you couldn't guess what my boot-bill is. And meat, which is not only most expensive, but is really after all a sort of solidified gout.'

Again the telephone rang violently, and the Duchess held a brilliant conversation through it. While this was going on a small tray with plasmon, blancmange and lemonade was brought out for her by a footman, to which, when the telephone business was over, she addressed herself with extraordinary appetite.

'You see, I got up at seven,' she said ('Oh, Jack, this plasmon is too delicious, and so supporting—five mutton chops here at least), and played croquet for two hours. Then I did my exercises. You have to kick yourself, and slap yourself, and make all manner of movements; and after that deep breathing——

'My dear, it's heavenly. And you see I've only had one cup of tea yet, without anything to eat, and this is the first thing I've eaten today. And I don't feel in the least exhausted.'

Jack was naturally critical, and certain questions occurred to him.

'But surely, dear aunt,' he said, 'would it not have been simpler for everybody if you had had some of that—that cold shape, when the others were having breakfast? It seems to me that not a moment passes without some sort of meal being brought out for somebody. There's the telephone again.'

A pause in their conversation naturally followed; but when the Duchess was again disengaged he continued.

'That telephone rather complicates things, doesn't it?' he said. 'You never get a moment to yourself.'

'Ah, but the telephone simplifies things so for the other end,' said she. 'Think how many telegrams it saves, and notes too, which I shouldn't get in time.'

'Unless people took the trouble to write the day before,' remarked Jack.

'Yes; but how complicated all that is! You don't grasp the whole question of simplification yet, dear; you must take a larger view.

'Take a mutton chop, now. No, not literally. How can you be so silly? But the butcher has to kill the poor chop, take an innocent animal's life, which is dreadful.

'Oh, there's a wasp. Hit it with a tennis-racket. There! It won't wasp any more.

'Yes, the poor sheep has to be killed, and the butcher's man has to drive over, and the chef has to cook it for twenty minutes. All that instead of one teaspoonful of plasmon.'

Jack's attention wandered.

'There are Miss Armstrong and my brother making violent signs from the other side of the river,' he said.

The Duchess rang the electric bell which communicated with the house.

'How stupid of me! I quite forgot,' she said, 'they insisted on going to look at the church, which was very rash, as I am told that churches are perfect hotbeds of microbes; and I promised to send the punt over for them when they returned.'

A frightfully harassed-looking footman accordingly punted across, and in a few minutes Miss Armstrong, another guest, and the other Twin joined them in the shelter. The other Twin cleared his throat.

'Dear aunt,' he said, 'you like simplicity. We're going to be married.'

The Duchess gave a violent start, and swallowed a large lump of plasmon.

'Oh, it's so bad for one to be startled,' she said. 'You dears, have you just settled it?'

Congratulations, however, were cut short by the relentless telephone-bell, and the Duchess had to attend. Also at this moment a loud splash sounded from the direction of the river, and the harassed footman, who had overreached himself with the punt-pole, was observed floundering to the shore. Altogether, in fact, Jack felt that the simple life was not necessarily uneventful.

During the afternoon constant relays of people arrived, some coming down for the afternoon merely, others to spend the first weekend of August with the Duchess.

Dinner was eaten on the terrace by the river, and the garden was charmingly lit with hundreds of fairy lights. This meal was somewhat complicated, for some half-dozen of the Duchess's guests were vegetarians and teetotallers, and the rest neither, so that two complete dinners were simultaneously served to the end of the meats.

After dinner the 'two dears' from the Comédie did their screaming little French farce. In the middle, however, the Duchess had to hurry to the telephone, which rang so loudly as to make it impossible to hear what the two dears were saying, and tried to conduct a conversation with her stockbroker in whispers. But, hearing from him the word 'slump', she cut him off altogether.

Antonelli, finally, the tenor from the Opera, arrived rather importantly at about ten minutes to one, and ran straight into Miss Armstrong, who had refused him heart and hand, root and stock, two days before. He didn't wait for his supper, but vanished again into the night.

Bridge was then played into the rather larger hours; and, since Jack was sleeping in the shelter, he could not go to bed until the last of the guests had gone into the house. This was not long after three in the morning.

An hour later the garden was resonant with the chirping of birds, who, in their horrid, complicated way, scoured about looking for worms. Whereas, he thought sleepily, if they would only live the simple life, and eat grass at rational hours instead of gobbling flesh-food in the middle of the night, the disciples of a simpler plan of life might get a wink of sleep.

Mrs Andrews's Control

MRS ANDREWS was certainly an Athenian by nature, and it was her delight not only to hear some new thing, but to put it in practice. Enjoying excellent health, she was able to take almost any liberties with her constitution, and for a long time was absorbed in the maelstrom of diets, each of which seemed to suit her to perfection.

For a couple of months she adopted the Pembroke treatment, and droves of sheep were sacrificed to supply her with sufficient minced mutton, while the utmost resources of the kitchen boiler were needed to give her the oceans of hot water which she found it necessary to drink all day except at meals. Having obtained the utmost benefits derivable from this system, she nourished her ample and vigorous frame, by way of a change, on pyramids of grated nuts, carefully weighed out, and it cannot be doubted that she would enthusiastically have fed herself on chopped up hard-boiled egg, like a canary, if she could have found any system of diet that inculcated such a proceeding.

Her husband, for all his mild and apparently yielding disposition, must at bottom have been a man of iron soul, for he absolutely refused to embark on any of these experiments, though he never dissuaded his wife from so doing, and stuck firmly, like a limpet, to his three solid and satisfactory meals, not disdaining minced lamb, nor even a modicum of milled nuts, when he felt that they would be agreeable, but adding them to his ordinary diet, without relying on them. The two, childless and middle-aged, lived in extreme happiness and comfort together, and no doubt Mrs Andrews's enthusiasms, and the perennial amusement her husband derived from them, served to keep the sunlight of life shining on them. They were never bored and always busy, which, perhaps, even more than diet, secured them serenity of health.

But the time came when Mrs Andrews, in an unacknowledged despair of feeling better and more vigorous physically than she always did, turned her Athenian mind towards mental and psy-chical fads. She began by telling the fortunes of her friends in Oakley by means of cards, and, though she could always say how she knew, following the rules of her primer, that her hus-band had had scarlet fever when he was twenty-three, yet the fact that she knew it perfectly well without the help of the cards made the discovery rather less amazing.

She tried Christian Science, though only for a short time, since no amount of demonstration over false claims could rid her one day of the conviction that she had a raging toothache, whereas the dentist convinced her in a moment, by the short though agonizing application of the pincers, that he could remove the toothache, which had resisted all the precepts of her temporary creed. An excursion into the realms of astrology succeeded this, and conjointly a study of palmistry, and at this point her hus-band, for the first time, began to take an interest in his wife's preoccupations.

It certainly did seem very odd that his horoscope should test-ify to the identical events which the lines in his hand so plainly showed his wife, and certain apparent discrepancies were no doubt capable of explanation. When he knew that the right hand indi-cated what Nature meant him to be, and the left what he had made of himself, it could not but be gratifying to find he had lived so closely up to his possibilities, and it was pleasant, again, to find his wife so enthusiastic about his plump, pink palm.

'A most remarkable hand, my dear,' she said. 'I never saw evidence of such pluck and determination. And look at your Mount of Jupiter! Splendid!'

Mr Andrews did not know exactly what the Mount of Jupiter was, but he knew what pluck and determination were.

'Upon my word, my dear,' he said, 'there may be something in it. I will borrow your primer, if I may. And now about the future.'

Mrs Andrews was already peering eagerly into the future. This was as splendid as the Mount of Jupiter.

'Such a line of life!' she said. 'Let me see, you are fifty-eight, are you not? Well, on it goes—sixty, seventy, eighty, without a break in it. Why, I declare it reaches ninety, Henry!'

This was very gratifying, and it showed but only ordinary politeness on Henry's part to enquire into his wife's prospects.

'Ah, I haven't such a line as you, dear,' she said. 'But, after all, if I live in perfect health till I am eighty-two, which is what my hand tells me, I'm sure there's no reason to complain.'

But when Mrs Andrews had told the fortunes of her husband and all her friends, and secured them, on the whole, such charming futures, it was no wonder that she went further into matters more psychical and occult. A course of gazing into the most expensive crystal proved disappointing, since she could never see anything except the reflection of the objects in the room, while her husband, now actively taking part in these investigations, merely fell asleep when he attempted to see anything there.

They both hoped that this might not be ordinary sleep, but the condition of deep trance which they found was one of the accompanying phenomena, and productive of great results; but these trances were so deep that no recollection of what occurred therein ever remained in his mind, with the exception of one occasion, on which he dreamed about a boiled rabbit. As he had partaken of this disgusting provender at lunch that day, both Mrs Andrews and he regarded this dream as retrospective in character, and as not possessed of prophetic significance.

It was about this time that they both became members of the Psychical Research Society, and their attention could not but be struck by the wonderful phenomena brought into being by the practice of automatic writing. If you had a psychical gift in this direction—and it was now the dream of both Henry Andrews and his wife to find that they had—all apparently that had to be done was to hold a pencil over a writing-pad conveniently placed, abstract your mind from the hand that held the pencil, and sit there to see what happened.

The theory was that some controlling spirit might take possession of the pencil and dictate messages from the other world, which the pencil would record. Back numbers of the psychical journals warned them that patient practice might be necessary before any results were arrived at, the reason being that the control must get used to the novel instrument of communication, and warning was given that they must not be discouraged if for a long time nothing was recorded on the paper except meaningless lines. But it appeared that most people, if they would only be patient enough, would be rewarded by symptoms of the presence of a control before very long, and when once a beginning was made, progress was apt to be very rapid. It was recommended also that practice should be regular, and, if possible, should take place at the same time every day.

The idea fired Mrs Andrews at once.

'Upon my word, dear Henry,' she said, 'I think it is very well worth trying, for the crystal is yielding no results at all. Psychical gifts are possessed by everybody in some degree, so this very interesting article says, and if ours do not lie in the direction of crystal-gazing, it makes it all the more probable that we shall achieve something in automatic writing. And as for a regular time for practising it, what could be more pleasant than to sit out in the garden after tea, when you have come in from your golf, and enjoy these warm evenings, with the feeling that we are occupying ourselves, instead of sitting idle, as we are apt to do?'

Henry distinctly approved of the suggestion. He was often a little fatigued after his golf, though he was going to live till ninety, and the prospect of sitting quietly in a chair in the garden, instead of feeling that he ought to be weeding, was quite a pleasant one.

'Then shall we each sit with paper and pencil, dear?' he asked.

Mrs Andrews referred to the essay that gave elementary instruction.

'Certainly,' she said. 'We will try that first. They say that two hands holding the pencil often produce extraordinary results, but we will begin, as they suggest, singly. I declare that my hand feels quite fidgety already, as if the control was just waiting for the means of communication to be prepared.'

Everything in Mrs Andrews's house was in apple-pie order, and it took her no time at all to find two writing-pads and a couple of sharpened pencils. With these she rejoined her husband on the paved walk, where they had had tea, outside the drawing-room, and, with pencil in hand, fixed her eye firmly on the top of the mulberry tree at the edge of the lawn, and waited. He, with left hand free for his cigarette, did the same, but his mind kept going back to the boiled rabbit he had dreamed of after crystal-gazing, which still seemed to him a very unusual occurrence, for, to the best of his recollection, he had never dreamed of boiled rabbit before.

Within a few days' time very promising developments had

taken place. Almost immediately Mrs Andrews had begun to trace angled lines on the paper, which, if they did not suggest anything else particular, were remarkably like the temperature chart of a very feverish patient. Her hand, seemingly without volition on her part, made energetic dashes and dabs all over the paper, and she felt a very odd tingling sensation in her fingers, which could scarcely be put down to anything else than the presence of the control.

Her husband, scarcely less fortunate, also began to trace queer patterns of irregular curves on his sheet, which looked very much as if they were words. But though they were like words, they were not any known words, whichever way up you attempted to read them, though, as Mrs Andrews said, they might easily be Russian or Chinese, which would account for their being wholly meaningless to the English eye. Sheets of possible Russian were thus poured out by Mr Andrews, and whole hospital records of fever charts on the part of his wife, but neither at present came within measurable distance of intelligibility. The control seemed incapable of making itself understood.

Then on a memorable day Mr Andrews's pencil evinced an irresistible desire to write figures, and after dictating 'one, two, one, two', a great many times, wrote quite distinctly 4958, and gave a great dash as if it had said its last word.

'And what 4958 indicates, my dear,' said he, passing it over to Mrs Andrews, 'I think we must leave to the control to determine.'

She looked at it a moment in silence; then, a great thought splendidly striking her, she rose in some excitement.

'Henry, it is as plain as plain,' she said. 'I am forty-nine; you are fifty-eight. Our ages are thus wonderfully conjoined. It certainly means that we must act together. Come and hold my pencil with me.'

'Well, that is very curious,' said Henry, and did as he was told.

At this point their experiments entered the second phase, and the pencil thus jointly held at once developed an intelligible activity. Instead of mere fever charts and numerals, it began to write whole sentences which were true to the point of being positive truisms. Before they went to dinner that night, they were told, in a large, sprawling hand, that 'Wisdom is more than wealth', and that 'Fearlessness is best', and that 'Hate blinds the eyes of

Love'. The very next day more unimpeachable sentiments were poured forth, and at the end was written, 'From Pocky'.

Pocky, then, was clearly the control; he became to Mr and Mrs Andrews an established personality with a fund of moral generalities. Very often some practical application could be made of his dicta, as, for instance, when Mr Andrews was hesitating as to whether to invest quite a considerable sum of money in a rather speculative venture. But, recollecting that Pocky had said that 'Wisdom is better than wealth', he very prudently refrained, and had the satisfaction of seeing the speculative concern come a most tremendous smash very soon after. But it required a good deal of ingenuity to fit Pocky's utterances into the affairs of daily life, and Mr Andrews was getting a little tired of these generalities, when the curtain went up on the third phase.

This was coincident with the outbreak of the German war, when nothing else was present in the minds of husband and wife, and Pocky suddenly became patriotic and truculent.

For a whole evening he wrote, 'Kill them. Treacherous Germans. Avenge the scrap of paper,' and very soon after, just when England generally was beginning to be excited over the rumour that hosts of Russians were passing through the country to the French battle-front, he made the final revelation of himself.

'The hosts of Russia are with you,' he wrote, 'Cossacks from the steppes, troops of the Great White Czar. Hundreds and thousands, Russia to England, England to France. The Allies triumph. From Pocksky.' The pencil gave a great dash and flew from the fingers that held it.

It was all most clearly written, and, in a voice that trembled with excitement, Mrs Andrews read it out.

'There, my dear,' she said, 'I don't think we need have any further doubt about the Russians. And look how it is signed— not Pocky any longer, but Pocksky. That is a Russian name, if ever there was one!'

'Pocksky—so it is,' said Mr Andrews, putting on his spectacles. 'Well, that is most wonderful. And to think that in those early days, when my pencil used to write things we couldn't read, you suggested it might be Russian!'

'I feel no doubt that it was,' said Mrs Andrews firmly. 'I wish now that we had kept them, and my writing, too, which you used to call the fever charts. I dare say some poor fellow in hospital had temperatures like that.'

Mr Andrews did not feel so sure of this.

'That sounds a little far-fetched, dear,' he said, 'though I quite agree with you about the possibility of its being Pocksky who wrote through me. I wonder who he was? Some great general, probably.'

You can easily imagine the excitement that pervaded Oakley in the weeks that followed, when every day brought some fresh butler or railway-porter into the public press, who had told somebody who had told the author of the letter in question that he had seen bearded soldiers stepping out of trains with blinds drawn down, and shaking the snow off their boots. It mattered nothing that the whole romance was officially denied; indeed, it only made Mrs Andrews very indignant at the suppression of war news.

'The War Office may say what it likes,' she exclaimed, 'and, indeed, it seems to make it its business to deny what we all know to be true. I think I must learn a few words of Russian, in case I meet any soldier with a beard—"God Save the Czar!" or something of the kind. I shall send for a Russian grammar. Now, let us see what Pocksky has to tell us tonight.'

That no further confirmation of Pocksky's announcement on this subject ever came to light was scarcely noticed by the automatic writers, for Pocksky was bursting with other news. He rather terrified his interpreters, when there was nervousness about possible Zeppelin raids, by saying: 'Fires from the wicked ones in the clouds. Fourteen, twelve, fourteen, cellar best,' since this could hardly mean anything but that a raid was to be expected on the fourteenth of December; and Mr and Mrs Andrews— and, indeed, a large number of their friends—spent the evening in their cellars, coming out again when it was definitely after midnight.

But the relief at finding that no harm had been done speedily obliterated the feeling that Pocksky had misled them, and when, on Christmas Eve, he said, 'Spirit of Peace descends', though certain people thought he meant that the War would soon be over, the truce on the Western Front for Christmas Day was more generally believed to bear out this remarkable prophecy.

All through the spring Pocksky continued voluble. He would not definitely commit himself over the course that Italy was to take, but, as Mrs Andrews triumphantly pointed out, Italy would not definitely commit herself either, which just showed how right Pocksky was. He rather went back to the Pocky style over this, and said: 'Prudence is better than precipitation; Italy prepares before making decision. Wisdom guides her counsels, and wisdom is ever best. From Pocksky.' Intermittently the forcing of the Dardanelles occupied him.

Now, here a rather odd point arose. Mr Andrews at this time had to spend a week in town, and Pocksky managed the pencil which his wife held alone. In all these messages Pocksky spelled the name of the straits 'Dardanels', which, for all I know, may be the Russian form. But two days ago Mrs Andrews kindly sent me one of his messages, which I was glad to see was most optimistic in tone. She enclosed a note from herself, saying—

'You will like to see what Pocksky says about the Dardanels. Isn't he wonderful?'

So Mrs Andrews, writing independently of Pocksky, spells Dardanelles the same way as Pocksky does when he controls the pencil. I cannot help wondering if the control is—shall we say?—quite complete. I wonder also how the straits will get themselves spelt when Mr Andrews returns. It is all rather puzzling.

George's Secret

WHAT George's secret was we shall never know, because George has lost it as irretrievably as you lose the Nice Rapide at the Gare de Lyon, if you are unwise enough to take the Ceinture Railway round Paris. But Tom and I saw George in the full possession of his secret for two long June days, that secret which set him on a pinnacle higher than the kings of the earth, and as Tom can never even hear it alluded to, much less allude to it himself, without becoming blasphemous, it is left for me to recount its manifestations.

It was on this wise:

Tom is fonder of fishing than anyone else I have ever seen, and I am much more devoted to fishing than Tom. Therefore, it happened that one long vacation we rushed away from Cambridge as soon as term was over to a stream which I shall call Euphrates, because it is a river of Paradise.

Pison, the first river of Paradise, is in Ross-shire, and the salmon of Pison are as strong as bullocks, and as pink as the rosy-fingered morn. Gihon is in Norway, and the salmon there are as strong as the four-year-old bulls and as nobly born as the Lady Clara Vere de Vere, and the salmon-trout are as the sand of the sea for number. Hiddekel is in Hampshire, and the trout of Hiddekel are as shy as the red deer on the mountains over Gihon; yet if you go like Agag, delicately, they will yield themselves over to the dry fly, that siren in whose hands even Ulysses would have been as wax.

But Euphrates is in Devonshire, and the man who has not fished Euphrates in June knows not the joy of the rivers of Paradise. Brawling down between the knees and elbows of Exmoor it goes, and it knows not drought nor dearth. Here it burrows between walls of good red rock, chafing for the sea, and here it lies with a stretch of meadow land on each side, and overhung with alders and slim poplar trees, loitering along from shallow to weir, and weir to pool, and it is below the weir in the flat meadow land, and all down the pools to where they begin to break into foam and ripple again, that the big trout lie.

Far be it from me to speak against the dry fly — for have I not fished in Hiddekel? — yet, in many moods, wet fly fishing pleases me more. With the dry fly, you spy your trout as if he were a stag, and then proceed to inveigle him. What you gain in diplomacy you lose in mystery.

But in the Euphrates you may cast your fly upon the waters blindly and at random. There are many trout in all the pools, and big ones in each, and who knows but that each cast may not be just over the snout of some giant intent on feeding? But though the trout of Euphrates will take the wet fly well and eagerly, they are no fools. The fly must be cast to their liking, it must touch the water with less noise than the echo of a dream, its touch must be as light as Titania's kiss, or they will have none of it, and the gut must be as fine as gut can be, for there is nothing finer than gut. Such at least were the demands of the Euphrates trout, before George's secret revolutionized their habits, and such are their demands now that George has lost his secret.

But for two days the laws of the Medes and Persians were repealed. George repealed them, and the annoying thing about it is that he has not the least idea what laws he substituted for them.

George had never fished before, he told us, and when we saw him begin we saw no reason to doubt his word. The first evening we were there we rushed out for an hour or two; but George said he would only come and watch us. He attached himself to me, and hardly took the trouble to conceal his contempt when I caught nothing for ten minutes. He also began pitching pebbles into the water until he was stopped. However, in the course of the hour I caught six, and George said he thought it looked pretty easy.

Next morning, after breakfast, we all went down to the stream. I was a few minutes behind the others, and when I got down George had put on his waders and was just stepping into the water. I asked him what flies he had on, and he said he didn't know their names. My horror was intensified when I saw attached to a rope of gut a bluebottle, a thing like a hornet, and a sort of tortoiseshell butterfly. At the same time I excused him for not knowing their names, for they were unnameable. He said he had bought them in Manchester. I told him he might as well fish with a couple of kittens and a retriever puppy; but he laughed scornfully. Next moment the tortoiseshell butterfly whisked by my nose, and it, the bluebottle, and the hornet fell sonorously on to the water. I shrugged my shoulders and took off my boots, in order to get into my waders. Then I heard George calling to me.

'I've caught something,' he said. 'What am I to do?'

'It's a snag,' I called out; 'if your flies won't come loose, you must wade out and disentangle it.'

I heard him splashing about in the stream, and thanked my stars I was going to fish above him, and, having got my waders on, I went into the water to cross over to the other side. George was just poking about with a landing-net a few yards below me, and I waited.

Something splashed on the top of the water, and George swooped at it as if he were catching butterflies. I stumbled down to him, seized the landing-net from him, and landed his fish. It was one of the finest fish I had ever seen taken in the Euphrates, and its upper lip was firmly impaled on the tortoiseshell butterfly.

'How did this get here?' I asked George sternly.

'I don't know,' said George. 'It seems to have taken my fly.'

'But it's impossible,' I said. 'No self-respecting fish would take that thing.'

'I know nothing of its character, my dear fellow,' said George, 'but I fancy it will taste the same.'

The idea of a fisherman thinking of the taste of his fish was bad enough, but my curiosity strove with my desire to begin fishing myself, and prevailed.

'I shall stop with you a bit,' I said. 'You'd have lost that fish landing him.'

'Do you think so?' said George.

George cast again, and the hornet caught in an overhanging branch of alder. He wrenched it free — the gut would have held the sea-serpent — and the three nameless insects fell into the water in a lump, with a large piece of green leaf garnishing the tail of the hornet. I suggested to George that he should take it off, and George answered that it didn't matter.

Three times more he hurled his flies at the unoffending water, like Zeus hurling a thunderbolt, and then another fish rose to him, but missed the flies. George chucked his menagerie at it and hooked it. It had taken the hornet.

I stood and watched George for an hour on that creamy June morning, when the water was in beautiful condition and the fish were on the feed, although I would not have waited one minute of it to look at the finest fly-fisher living. He rattled his flies on the water; he churned the still pool into foam; he knocked at it as if it was the closed door, and he the five foolish virgins; he struck it as with a rhinoceros-hide whip; he beat it; he flogged it; he banged it; he slapped it; he did everything but fish it. The unnameable insects flew this way and that through the astonished air; they stooped on to the water like cruel hawks, or lions springing at unsuspecting fawns; but what made it worse was that George caught fish. He caught many heavy fish.

For two days George continued to catch many heavy fish, and I was seriously thinking of writing to the *Field* about him, illustrating my article with photographs of the water as the flies struck the surface, and with full-sized tracings of the flies themselves.

The first day he caught thirty-five fish, and the second day forty-one. Then the end came. No man can catch good baskets of fish without wishing to catch better, and George's evil genius prompted him to practise fishing with a somewhat lighter hand. After dinner that night we were smoking on the lawn, and George brought out his fishing-rod and asked us to show him how we cast without making such a splash. If he mastered the rudiments of fishing, it seemed to him, not unreasonably, that if to his unquestionable genius for catching fish there was added art, he would at once rise to a position which had never yet been attained. So, until it grew quite dark, George made the quiet air hideous with the bluebottle, the hornet, and the tortoiseshell butterfly.

Next morning he fished steadily from breakfast-time to lunch, and caught nothing. The fish were on the rise for a full hour and a half that morning, and Tom and I both caught a fair lot. At lunch George was morose, and inveighed against Art, saying that Nature was the only guide, and that he would go back to his state of innocence and ignorance. So all that balmy afternoon he fished as no man but he had ever fished before: his flies fell heavily in a lump, and cruelly and vindictively beat upon the stream, yet no fish rose. The secret was gone.

For two more days he persevered, and even now, though he fishes well, sometimes the sweet madness of the secret comes on him again, and he hurls large flies at the tender trout, but without result. The secret is irretrievably lost.

I do not attempt to explain George's secret. Whether the fish were all mad, or whether they were so much surprised that in mere absence of mind they rose at George's thunderous attack I do not know. I can only state that for those two days they rose at him like one man, when, to judge by all we know about the habits of fish, they ought to have hidden themselves under stones until the tempest was overpast. In any case their conduct for those two days only confirms my opinion of the Euphrates trout: that you can get quite exceptional fishing among them.

Buntingford Jugs

MRS AYLWIN was having tea very comfortably all by herself on a dark, inclement afternoon early in October. The fire was prospering, the windows had their curtains drawn to shut out the depressing prospect of the dripping wind-swept garden of Brompton Square, and she, between sips of tea, was indulging in the only sort of literature which had any attraction for her, namely, catalogues of forthcoming sales at the London auction rooms.

Pictures did not interest her—in fact, she hated pictures, having once bought a magnificent Romney which proved to have been painted over an atrocious daub of William IV in naval uniform—and she turned over, without looking at a single item, two pages of Mortlake tapestries shortly coming under the hammer. She threw this sumptuous catalogue into her waste-paper basket, but the next, which was issued by a very modest firm of auctioneers in East Street, Hampstead, seemed to merit considerable attention.

Mrs Aylwin was certainly comely; she could also have been called buxom. Her age might have been forty-five, but it was fifty, and she found fifty a very pleasant age to be. She had been a widow for ten years, and these ten years had been the busiest and far the happiest of her life.

Her husband had been a small spider-like man with a passion for second-rate bric-à-brac and a pathetic belief in his own taste. He had a furniture and curiosity shop just off the Brompton Road, and his judgement as a purchaser was invariably deplorable. He was convinced up to the last day of his life that heavy mahogany Victorian sideboards and wardrobes would shortly be in great demand, and at his death his widow had parted with a forest of these gloomy receptacles at staggering loss. He had held the same mistaken conviction with regard to steel engravings and many other unmarketable objects.

Mrs Aylwin, in consequence, at his death, had been left badly

off; but the constant environment of her husband's purchases
had given her a great shrewdness as to what *not* to buy, and she
had learned to see at a glance, even if she knew nothing about
the fabric in question, whether it had distinction and character.
Character was the great thing: a piece might be hideous, but if
it had character her purse was open.

The shop 'Aylwin & Sons'—though she had never had either
son or daughter—still did a good trade, but it was not there that
she made her best deals. The shop, in fact, was rather a blind for
what went on in this comfortable little house of hers in Brompton
Square. It was here that she made her 'collections'.

Sometimes she collected Aubusson carpets or Persian rugs,
sometimes Queen Anne furniture, sometimes Crown Derby
china, sometimes even globular paperweights with curious deco-
rations of glass flowers or objects that resembled confectionery
seen under water embedded in them. For Mrs Aylwin—and in
this lay her genius—had discovered a fact as yet not sufficiently
recognized by the trade, namely, that there are many rich people
(and she cared now to deal only with thoroughly rich people)
who would not think of buying one piece of Queen Anne furniture or one piece of Crown Derby, but who would eagerly
pay twenty times the price of one for ten collected specimens of
it. Just now the collection appeared to be ornaments made of
shells. There were a clock and a pair of candlesticks under glass
shades made of shells, a couple of baskets of shell-flowers on the
table, and a cabinet by the window was full of boxes encrusted
with shells.

Though Josephine Alwyn was at present alone, she rather expected a visitor, namely, her old friend Anthony Coleham, for
whom she entertained a strong regard. She also rather expected
that before he left her he would introduce a certain subject,
namely, that of matrimony. Of late he had been alluding to the
woes of loneliness, and had asked her if she was not conscious
of the same. But though she lived alone and saw few people, she
was not the least conscious of loneliness, for she was invariably
busy with that pleasant work of buying and selling in which she
was so successful. Also for other reasons it would never do, for
he, though not a dealer, was a very ardent collector, with ample
means to indulge his hobby, and if they were married he could
hardly help exercising a certain influence on her dealings, and

she much preferred independence. But, after all, he might be coming in, as he often did, only for a chat.

The other alternative, however, had vividly occurred to her, and, though she meant to refuse him, she had, with a feminine instinct which would not be denied, done her hair in a very becoming fashion and put on a dress which he much admired.

She had barely finished going through her catalogues when he appeared.

'You look charming today,' he said, 'but then you always do!'

This made it seem probable that she had been right about the object of his visit. But she wanted to have a chat first. If he proposed to her straight off and she refused him, it would be difficult to chat quite at ease afterwards; there would be an awkwardness.

'Nonsense, my dear. I'm an old woman,' she said, 'and old women are invariably hideous. What a day! It was good of you to come out in such a deluge.'

The same train of thought had perhaps occurred to his mind, for he did not combat her pessimistic view about old women, but sat comfortably down. He was a large man, pleasantly furnished with flesh, and filled a chair beautifully.

'And how have things been going?' he asked. 'Business prosperous?'

'Of course; it always is with me,' she said. 'Collections! That's the secret of successful dealing, and, like all true philosophies, very simple. If I, for my own satisfaction, buy a Chinese Chippendale chair, what do you suppose I want next? Why, of course, another Chinese Chippendale chair. And when I've got two, I want a set, and after I have got a set I want another set. That's human nature.'

Anthony Coleham had been looking round the room. 'And I suppose that's why this room, which used to be so nice when it was empty, with just your beautiful rugs on the floor, is now an abominable array of shell ornaments,' he said. 'How a woman like you, who really has taste, can surround herself with such artificial and Victorian monstrosities, I cannot think. Look at those awful candlesticks encrusted with the meanest objects of the sea-shore!'

Josephine Aylwin felt that she was quite right in her determination what to say in a certain eventuality. It would never do to have a husband like that: he would discourage her, he would cause her to doubt her own judgement. Also there was something to be said for shell ornaments.

'Yes, my dear, I knew you would think them hideous,' she said. 'But they have character—bad character, perhaps, but that is so much better than no character. They mean something; they are a fine reflection of the mind of the persons who must have taken years in making them. I don't say I admire them much, but they are a unique collection.'

'I regard them with suspicion,' he said. 'I have known you make a collection for purely business purposes, and then, by degrees, get so fond of it that you could hardly bear to part with it. Chelsea figures, for instance! How you cried when you got so large an offer for them that you couldn't refuse it!'

'Yes, that was an awful morning,' she said. 'But you needn't be frightened about these shell ornaments, though they are ingenious little things.'

'I hope you'll sell them at once,' he said. 'They make me feel rather unwell; I feel as if I was in a lodging-house.'

She laughed. 'Well, you won't be uncomfortable for long,' she said, 'for I've had an offer for them, and I shall take it. There won't be a single shell ornament left when next you come to see me.'

'And what will the next collection be?' he asked.

'You ought to know very well that I shan't tell you,' she said. 'I never let anyone know what my collection is till I have got together a good quantity of it. If a dealer in London knew what I was collecting, it would be all over the place in no time, and the prices would go up. As soon as I've got together all I think I want, I let it be known, and up go the prices, and my little lot becomes far more valuable. But I like to get a good start first.'

'I hope you're doing so,' he said.

'I am indeed. I've got quite a lot of my new collection already.'

'But haven't they found out what you're after?' he asked.

'Not a bit of it,' said she. 'I'm being very cunning over this, for there's not very much of it about. I pick up a piece now and then in a shop, but I never myself attend an auction where there is any of it. I send my maid instead.'

'With *carte blanche* to buy?' he asked.

'No. But the price never comes near the limit I give her. A couple of pounds is as much as I've paid for any piece yet. Of course I go and look at the—the things before the auction begins, to make sure that they are all right, but if I'm seen examining fifty lots with a perfectly blank face, who's to tell which is the one I have got my eye on?'

'I wish you would tell me,' said he; 'I might find pieces for you.'

She shook her head. 'No,' she said, 'it would do me no good. Dealers would begin to see that there was a demand for it. And I like doing a thing quite on my own, too.'

He had already begun to fidget in his chair; there was something on his mind, and this speech of hers bore on it. He was silent a moment.

'Josephine, I wish you didn't like conducting life on your own,' he said at length. 'I wish you would let me have a hand in it. I believe you're fond of me, and I should love to be allowed to take care of you. I should account it the greatest privilege and joy. Josephine, will you marry me?'

She was suddenly touched. She had expected this, but she had not known what a delightful companion he was till she had to refuse his permanent companionship.

'Oh, Tony, my dear,' she said, 'I'm sorry, but I won't marry you. I like you immensely—quite as much as you like me—but it wouldn't do. We're not in love with each other, of course, in the least. We'll leave that out, for it would be nonsense to pretend it. We'll continue to be very good friends, just as we are. If any other man in the world offered to marry me, I should laugh in his face. But I'm sorry, really sorry, that I can't marry you. I don't laugh—I am sorry.'

'But why?' he asked. 'You say you like me immensely.'

'And that is true. But I am so happy *as* I am. I'm busy, I'm successful.'

'I should help you to be more successful,' said he.

'No, my dear, you wouldn't. You would be a handicap to me. I should try to bring your ideas in line with mine, or you would try to bring mine in line with yours. We should have jars and bickerings every day of our lives if we were one firm. You've told me already that my room is like a lodging-house and makes you feel ill. I should hate to have you feel ill all the time I was amassing shell ornaments, and I should hate to give up my collection, whatever it was, in order that you might feel better.'

Anthony Coleham was seated opposite the door while she made these depressing remarks. Even as she spoke it opened and there appeared a maid carrying, carefully in both hands, a china jug. It and she were vividly illuminated, and he saw the jug pretty distinctly. It was of white, fluted ware, and in front, under the spout, it had as decoration a wreath of flowers in blue.

'The Buntingford jug, ma'am,' she said.

Mrs Aylwin got very nimbly to her feet, and, as Mr Coleham distinctly noticed, her eyes lit up with pleasure. But she kept the pleasure out of her voice.

'Put it down anywhere,' she said, and turned to Anthony. 'It's just a little nothing. Rather pretty, though. A jug for water when I'm arranging flowers.'

She had taken the jug from the maid, and herself put it down in a rather remote corner of the room.

'That's what I feel, dear Tony,' she said. 'We should quarrel, we should bicker, and I should so hate that. As for your feeling lonely, you know quite well that I am always so delighted to see you. You can't come here too often or stop too long. But as regards the other, no. Do you forgive me?'

He got up. 'Not till you consent to marry me,' he said. 'You're unforgiven at present.'

'That's rather horrid of you. And are you really going?'

An idea had begun to bubble in Mr Coleham's brain. He had noticed that her eyes kept wandering to the remote corner where stood the Buntingford jug. He therefore carefully avoided looking in that direction or making any allusion to it. It was part of his idea not to appear to take the slightest interest in it.

As he sat at his solitary dinner that night, the idea matured. He believed that he had guessed what her new collection was, and the name of it was Buntingford ware. He guessed, too, that Buntingford ware was already dear to her, the collection she was making had got a place in her heart, and it would wring her heart when the day came for selling it, as had been the case with her Chelsea figures. But it would be even more heartbreaking, he thought, if she could not get on with her collection. Of course he might be wrong about it all, but those lover-like glances she cast towards the obscure corner....

He went next morning to the Victoria and Albert Museum, and after some search discovered in a show-case of miscellaneous English china two jugs exactly similar to the one he had seen last night, with the label 'Buntingford Ware'. The curator of the section was a friend of his, and he learned from him that little was known about this obscure factory.

'It was one of those small industries,' he was told, 'that have never attracted any attention. It is coarse stuff, of no interest. Pieces come up occasionally at auction, and are knocked down for thirty shillings or so. Who would want a collection of those things? A couple of specimens are enough for the Museum. There's no beauty about them, as you can see for yourself.'

Mr Coleham's heart leaped inside his fine fur coat. 'No, ugly stuff,' he said. 'But it was new to me, and I take an interest in anything new. Bitter cold morning, isn't it? Come and see my Heppelwhite card-table some evening, and have a bit of dinner. It's a peach, that table.'

Mr Coleham's catalogues of sales were as numerous as Mrs Aylwin's, and he hurried home to study them. He found that out of a dozen approaching sales there were two which contained an item of Buntingford ware, and in each case these were jugs. He consulted his large-paper edition of Fountain's *English Porcelain*, and turned up the page relating to Buntingford ware. There were only a few lines devoted to it. It gave the mark of the fabric, a capital B in a circle, and informed the reader that only jugs, of coarse and uninteresting workmanship, were known as a product of that factory. It suggested that these were possibly inferior Salopian ware, not up to the standard of the Caughley Works, and contemptuously dismissed the subject.

This delighted him; it was so like Josephine's cleverness to have taken up a class of porcelain about which nobody knew or cared, and he felt convinced of the correctness of his guess. Proof, if proof was needed, came a few days later when he attended the sale in East Street, Hampstead, and saw Mrs Aylwin's maid there. He had taken his valet with him, and instructed him, while he himself kept prudently out of sight, to bid and go on bidding for Lot 217.

An insignificant duel took place, but he knocked the opponent out at four pounds, which his valet paid on the spot. He returned home with a Buntingford jug. A fortnight later he got his second Buntingford jug, but he had to pay five pounds for it.

Anthony Coleham was getting very stout, but, preferring that to taking exercise, had long acquiesced in Nature's obese decrees. But now he had an object, and day after day he used to go from shop to shop, not asking for Buntingford jugs, but scrutinizing with the collector's eye the contents of the most unimportant and frowsy stores. Every now and then he came across one of these ugly jugs and bought it for a song, while at the larger dealers in porcelain, where he was already well known, he confidentially told the proprietors that he was looking out for specimens of this ware, and would be much obliged if they would send him any such that came into their shops. After a month of incessant walking in slummy places, he had purchased half a dozen of these jugs, and dealers had sent him half a dozen more. The price was rising a little, but, being very rich, he did not mind that. All he minded was the coarse appearance of his purchases; but he put them on the table in his billiard-room, which he never used, and turned the key on them.

On Christmas Day Josephine, as usual, came to dine with him. In spite of the festival she appeared dejected, but nothing was said on either side about her latest collection. Prudence (for she put two and two together with remarkable quickness and accuracy) dictated reticence on one side, depression on the other. But she congratulated him heartily on his slimmer appearance and briskness of movement, and he confessed that he had taken quite a lot of walking exercise of late.

He continued to see her with his usual frequency, but her dejection not only continued, but deepened. It was particularly marked on one bright afternoon in the early spring, when there had been a sale in a well-known auction room, and three Buntingford jugs had come up. The price she was willing to pay had evidently risen considerably, though no one but his valet and her maid bid for these treasures, and he had to give an average of twelve pounds for each. But he had, of course, obtained them, and his billiard table was getting crowded.

She sighed heavily as she gave him his cup of tea, and he asked her if anything was the matter.

'Yes, I've been having a check,' she said. 'I don't know if I told you, one day in the autumn, that I had made a good beginning with a new collection.'

He made a face as if trying to recollect. 'I rather fancy you did,' he said. 'I can't remember what it was; perhaps you didn't tell me.'

'Naturally I didn't,' she said with a certain asperity, 'and I'm not going to tell you now. But I can't get on with my collection. If a piece turns up in the auction room, I never can secure it. I've raised my limit, but it's no use. There's somebody else making a collection.'

'It sounds rather like it,' said he.

'Whom do you think it can be?' she asked.

He was perfectly on his guard. 'My dear Josephine,' he said, 'as you have not allowed me to know what you are collecting, how can I possibly tell who else is collecting it? Now, I don't ask to know; I don't want to know. It may be waste-paper baskets or walking-sticks.'

'But I'm not going to be beaten,' she said with energy. 'I like opposition: I fight it; I overcome it.'

'Bravo!' said he. 'It does me good to see your spirit. And you've not been able to get on with your collection? Too bad! And is your annoyance only professional, so to speak, or had you, as in the case of your Chelsea china, got to love this new collection?'

'Ah, I adore it!' she said. 'I go and gloat over the few pieces I've got. I love it more than anything that I've ever collected.'

'Poor Josephine!' said Mr Coleham with much feeling.

Her energy waned; she sank back languidly in her chair.

'It's a wretched feeling never being able to get what one so much wants,' she said.

'Horrid, isn't it?' said Mr Coleham. 'Especially when you know that it is in somebody's power to give it you.'

'What's that?' she said. 'Oh, you mean the horrible person, whoever it is, who always outbids me.'

'No, I was thinking of myself,' he said, 'and of you who could give me what I want.'

'Oh, that!' said she. 'Yes, I'm sorry. I said I was sorry before. But really I can think of nothing else except what I want so terribly. It has become an obsession with me. If I could only get together a fine number of these pieces, I should be so happy.'

He rose. 'Do you know, Josephine,' he said, 'that it's rather dull for me hearing you talk about something the very nature of which you refuse to divulge to me?'

'Well, I can think of nothing else,' she said. 'I can't talk about anything else. Only today three pieces were sold in London, and I couldn't secure one of them.'

'Bad luck,' said he.

It was still light when he left her, and he strolled along the Brompton Road, looking into the shop windows. He was sorry for Josephine, who clearly was very unhappy, but her spirit was still unbroken, and he wanted to reduce her to despair before he disclosed his plot. She must be in a condition to realize that it was no use fighting him either in the field of matrimony or in that of Buntingford jugs. She must learn that he was stronger than she.

He had turned into a side-street where there were many curiosity shops, and his progress was slow. Then he gave a gasp of amazed wonder, and his eyes started from his head. There in an inconspicuous shop facing him was a tea-set—tea-pot, sucrier, milk jug, bread-and-butter plate, and six cups and saucers—all of Buntingford ware. And the foolish experts knew of no such thing; they had never heard of anything but Buntingford jugs.

It was impossible, of course, to be certain without examination, and he entered the shop and in a trembling voice asked to be allowed to see the tea-set in the window.

'Very sorry, sir,' said the proprietor, 'but I'm keeping that for one of my customers. It oughtn't to be in the window at all.'

Mr Coleham had one of those inspirations which are the hallmark of genius. He was convinced also in his own mind that the apparently outrageous lie he was about to tell was literally true.

'You mean Mrs Aylwin, of course,' he said. 'That's all right; I am buying it for her.'

There was that quiet conviction in his voice which always produces its effect. The man hesitated, but only for a moment.

'Well, in that case,' he said, 'I suppose I am right to let you have it.'

'Certainly, certainly,' said Mr Coleham. 'And what price are you asking for it?'

The price was moderate enough compared with those he had been paying lately, and presently it was packed and paid for, and he took it home in a taxi, hugely exulting. He felt sure that Josephine could not possibly resist a Buntingford tea-set.

She was coming to lunch with him in a few days, and he arranged his collection to the utmost advantage. All round the billiard table, nicely spaced, was a row of Buntingford jugs, and in the middle the tea-set. He inspected it just before she came, and locked the door.

Mrs Aylwin was in excellent spirits again, all her dejection had passed, and she was her cheerful self.

'I've been making myself miserable, Tony,' she said as they lunched, 'and I'm tired of it. I've been beaten. I don't like being beaten, but when you are beaten, the best thing to do is to acknowledge it, and begin on something else.'

'Oh, your latest collection,' said he.

'How unfeeling you are! I've never cared for anything so much in my life. The only consolation is that the price has gone up immensely, and I have no doubt I shall sell the pieces I've got at a great profit.'

'Perhaps, then, you might tell me what it is,' he said.

'Why, I forgot you didn't know,' said she. 'Naturally there's no secret about it now. I sent my pieces down to the shop this morning. Buntingford jugs. I suppose you've never heard of Buntingford ware?'

'Tell me about it,' said he.

'Well, it is an English fabric of which nobody thought anything six months ago. I got hold of one piece, and tried to find out something about it, but nobody knew. Nothing, in fact, is known about the ware, but it entirely consists of jugs; they only made jugs at Buntingford. You saw one once, though you never knew it, and heard the name of it, but you weren't attending.'

'When was that?' he asked.

'My maid brought one in when you were sitting with me. I whisked it away, because my collection was young then, and I thought you might guess what it was. But my collection hasn't grown any older, so I am making a clean sweep of it. Come round to the shop afterwards and look at it. I sent it down this morning.'

He rose. 'I've been making a collection, too,' he said. 'Come into the billiard room and see it. It has been getting on beautifully.'

He unlocked the door and she entered. For a moment she stood stricken to stone, and then turned to him.

'So it was you?' she said. 'You beast! I'll never speak to you again!'

'I'm sorry for that,' he said. 'I hoped to give it you all as a wedding present.'

She stamped her foot. 'Never, never!' she cried.

'Very well. Then as soon as you have gone I shall smash it, piece by piece, with a hammer.'

She had taken a step nearer the table, and now her hand closed round one of the beloved objects.

'You can't, you can't,' she said. 'It would be murder!'

'Indeed I shall. You may as well have a look at them, for no one but the dustman will ever see them again. And there's a Buntingford tea-set there. Unique, of course.'

'A tea-set?' she said in a trembling voice.

'Yes, there it is. I got it only the other day.'

Her eye fell on it, and she drew it towards her and examined it.

'Oh, Tony,' she said, 'oh, Tony! And you'll give me this, too?'

'As a wedding present. Otherwise——'

She threw her arms round his neck. 'Oh, my dear, how lovely of you! How perfectly wonderful of you! When shall we be married?'

Suddenly, with a scream, she let go of him.

'The telephone,' she cried, 'the telephone! Ring up the shop, Tony! I must tell them to take all the jugs out of the window. Heavens, I hope none of them has been sold yet!'

SPOOK
STORIES

By the Sluice

MY friend Louis Carrington, with whom I was to spend a liberal weekend, met me in his car at Whitford Station on Friday afternoon. There had been a long spell of damp and windless weather, and the fog which had been so thick in London was scarcely less dense down here; the whole of Surrey seemed to be blanketed in this white opacity. Even when we got free of the town we could do no more than crawl along the road with prolonged hoots at every turn and corner. Occasionally, when the air was somewhat clearer, a glimpse could be seen of a sombre copper-plate low in the west, which one supposed was the sun, for the reason that it could scarcely be anything else.

Louis was unusually silent; his attention, of course, was largely taken up by this blind progression, but I soon became aware, through that perception which long intimacy gives, that there was something on his mind. In answer to a direct question he admitted this was so, and said he would tell me about what he called 'this very painful affair' when we got home. It did not, he relieved me by saying, directly affect him or his immediate circle, but it was a very sad thing, very sad indeed, and he fell to silence and knitted brow again.

We arrived at the end of our four-mile drive without accident, and found his wife in the jolly, spacious hall which they used as general sitting-room. It was pleasant to come out of that inhospitable dimness into the warmth and light, but over Margaret also there was this same shadow of anxiety or suspense, and even as she greeted me she said to him:

'Any news yet about him, Louis?'

'No, poor chap, not a word,' said he; 'I've communicated with the police, and search parties are going out.'

'And you've advertised?' she asked.

'Yes: county and London papers, telling him to come back without any fear. I signed it myself, and I think he trusts me.

Now I'm going to tell Frank the whole story to see if there is anything else he can suggest.'

The story certainly was a painful one, though to me, personally, it concerned a man whom I had never seen in my life, and of whose existence till this moment I had never heard. . . . Louis is the manager of the local branch of a big banking house in Whitford, and his sub-manager, Thomas Oulton, had worked his way up through thirty years of industrious and honourable service to his present position. He was respected and liked in the town, he had a good salary with an ample pension ahead, and, as far as was known, he had no money worries of any kind.

'And then without warning,' said Louis, 'only yesterday came the crash. A client of ours came to see me about some securities we held for him. Among them were a hundred shares of a certain cement company, which had lately offered new shares to its holders at a price considerably below the market quotation. They had the right to purchase at par one new share for every four they held; our client therefore could buy twenty-five of these for twenty-five pounds. We had advised him to do so, and at his orders had applied for them, and in his pass-book there duly appeared this sum in payment of them. His list of investments, which we held for him, had lately been made up, and we noticed that though he was debited with the payment of them, they did not appear in it.

'I felt sure that there was some explanation of this; probably the new certificates had not been issued yet, and sent for Oulton. My clerk came back, saying that Oulton had left the bank, saying he was going out for lunch, a few minutes before; he had left, in fact, when he saw this client of ours come in and ask to see me.

'Half an hour passed, and an hour. Oulton did not come back at all. I sent round to the restaurant where he usually had his lunch, but he had not been there. Soon after I rang up his house in the village here to know if he had been home. He had been in, and told his wife that he had to go up to our head office in London over some business, and might not get back, if the fog was bad, till next morning. Accordingly he took away with him a suitcase with the few things he would want. Now I knew there was nothing connected with the bank that could have taken him to London, but I rang up the head office. He had not appeared there. Then, still almost incredulous that there could be anything wrong in the case of so steady a man, I went into the affair myself. I found that the certificates had been issued some days before, and soon there was no longer any doubt that Oulton had debited our client's account with this paltry sum and taken the money.'

'And then I suppose you found other defalcations?' I asked.

'Not one. All other accounts with which he had anything to do were perfectly in order. I am quite positive that Oulton had never done such a thing before. He knew that our client was a very rich man, and that the chances were a hundred to one that he would never notice so small an omission. But he just happened to do so. Oulton must have known, too, that if he had come to me and told me what he had done I could have managed something. I should not have proceeded against a man who had served us so long and faithfully for a sudden madness— for it was no less—of this kind. But I suppose that the sight of the client he had defrauded coming in and asking to see me broke his nerve, for he must have guiltily guessed what his errand was. Even now, if he can only be found, or if, seeing my advertisement, he comes back, I shall somehow get him out of trouble. I daresay it is my duty to have him prosecuted, but I consider it no less my duty to save a man with a long and blameless record like his from ruin. And when duties conflict you have to choose between them.'

We assented to this and sat silent a few moments. But there seemed nothing more that could be done; Louis's advertisement was the best chance of getting hold of the unfortunate man, and the only course at present was to wait in the hope that some news of him, or, best of all, he himself, should turn up. Soon other, more cheerful, topics unfolded themselves, and we talked of agreeable schemes for the spending of the next few days, should the fog permit us to do anything at all.

Golf was one, for there was a good links near by on the stretch of sandy, heathered country outside Louis's wooded domain; another, particularly dear to him in this season of April, was observing the arrivals of migrating birds. The open heath, the woods below his house, and his fine sheet of water that lay deep within them, ringed with copses and banks of sedge, should all be alive with movements of the northerly travelling hosts.

To the best of my belief Oulton was not mentioned again that evening, but I have to record what now seems to me the first in the series of those odd occurrences which I do not profess to explain. At the time it struck me as a mere fanciful impression on my part, but in the light of what soon happened it seems more reasonable to suppose it was a manifestation—faint, and scarcely coming 'through'—of the power (whatever that was) which soon gave clearer evidence of itself.

Louis, after tea, went to his room to finish up some business, and Margaret to the nursery to play with her two small children, and thus I was left alone in the hall, thinking, as far as I am aware, of birds and golf rather than Oulton. As I mused, rather drowsily, by the fire, I thought I heard a very faint tinkle from the telephone at the far end of the hall. It certainly was not the usual peremptory summons, and I lazily waited for it to be repeated.

It came again, still faint and far-away, and I went to the instrument. There were little clicks and buzzings to be heard, and then I thought I heard a voice in a whisper saying something inaudible.

'Who is it?' I asked. 'I can't hear you.'

I had hardly spoken when a voice from the exchange said, 'Number, please?' I explained that there was some message coming through, and was told that no connection had been made through the exchange. But, though I felt sure there had been someone there, I might have been mistaken. The bell that summoned me had not sounded as it generally did. The impression, however, remained that someone wanted to communicate with this house.

The evening passed in a perfectly normal manner. We dined and played cut-throat, but all the time, still fancifully I suppose, the idea remained in my head, sometimes growing very insistent, that there was someone trying to make his presence felt. We went to bed shortly after midnight, and I instantly fell asleep.

I awoke out of a perfectly dreamless sleep with the impression that I had heard the bell of the church clock strike; indeed, some vibration of it still lingered in the air. It was perfectly natural that I should have done so, for the church stood only a few hundred yards away, at the bottom of the steep slope by the garden.

I was drowsy, but certainly still awake, when I heard it again; it struck one, but now I was sure it was not the chime of the clock, but one of the church bells. After an interval it came again, and yet again; the bell was tolling as if for a death. It was odd that it should be rung in the middle of the night, and I wondered what the reason for that could be.

And then, quite suddenly, there came into my mind the thought that Oulton was dead. Where, so to speak, it came from, I had no idea, but it instantly crystallized into a conviction.

My room was almost completely dark; from the windows came no ray of light at all, but there was still a red coal or two smouldering out in the fireplace. And then I was aware that over the end of my bed there was forming in the air a patch of something dimly luminous, an oval of greyish light. It seemed to hang unsupported, and as I watched it, not exactly frightened, but in some numb suspense of the mind, it defined itself a little more and took the shape of a human face. The outline grew complete and firm; I could see the form of ears jutting out rather prominently from the side of the head, but of features there was no trace at all.

Then suddenly the suspense of my mind broke, and in an access of panic terror I felt for the switch of the electric light, still keeping an eye glued to that developing face, and throttled by the horror of perhaps seeing eyes and mouth form themselves in the blankness of it. Then the room leaped into brightness, and there was nothing there but the safe-curtained emptiness of it, with the dying embers clinking in the grate.

As I recovered from the grip of the terror, my curiosity, I suppose, awoke, and it cured my cowardice. I turned out my light again and watched, but there was no sign of it now, and the tolling of the bell had ceased. Already it seemed to my normal consciousness quite unreal, and I wondered if I had dreamed it all. But if so, the night-hag had ridden me with a spur, for my forehead dripped with the dews of that moment's terror.

I slept late, and found Louis and his wife already at breakfast. Just as I entered I heard him say to her:

'But the child must have dreamt it. The bell could not have been tolling in the middle of the night. . . . Ah, good morning, Frank; fog as bad as ever, I'm afraid. Putting on the hearthrug, and books about birds instead of the real thing.'

'But what's that about a bell tolling?' I asked. 'Did one of your children hear it? Because I did, too.'

'Both dreaming,' said Louis. 'How is it possible?'

'The only explanation I can think of is that somebody was ringing it,' I said.

He had finished breakfast and got up.

'Well, I'll make a bet with you,' he said, 'that no one was. I've got to go down to the village, and I'll enquire. Any other adventures last night?'

I decided at once not to tell him about the other adventure, for, horribly real as it had been at the time, it seemed, over eggs and bacon, to be too fantastic to recount. But still somewhere in the back of my mind there was the idea that some wave from the infinite sea which laps round the coast of material things had at that moment hissed up to me on the shore and withdrawn again.

'The adventure of a great many hours' uninterrupted sleep,' I said.

The day outside was certainly desolation; the fog pressed its grey face close to the windows, and it was scarcely possible to see across the terraced walk that ran along the house. But the prospect of a snug morning indoors was not disagreeable, and when Louis set off to the village, I encamped myself very comfortably by the fire in the hall. He was back in half-an-hour and joined me there.

'The church was locked all night,' he said, 'and opened again by the vicar at eight for morning prayers. My errand, of course, you can guess. I went to see Mrs Oulton, in case she had heard anything from her husband. But there was nothing. Surely, don't you think he must see my advertisement this morning? If we hear nothing today I shall begin to be afraid——Well, it's no use thinking about that yet.'

He had seated himself on the window-seat, and was looking out into the denseness. Suddenly he sprang up, pointing.

'Look!' he said. 'Why, that's he! The man who walked by the window just then. Didn't you see him?'

I had seen nothing, but now I followed Louis as he rushed across the hall, and ran out with him from the front door into the fog. We sped round the corner of the house on to the terrace, and along it to the end, where a flight of stone steps descended to the garden, without seeing a sign of any human being.

'But where is he, where is he?' cried Louis. 'He can't have gone more than a dozen yards since I saw him. Perhaps he has gone to the back door. I'll go round there, and you go down the steps into the garden. He must be quite close somewhere.'

I ran down the steps, and searched this way and that, and found no one but a gardener coming up with vegetables to the house. He had passed nobody on his way, and presently I came up on to the terrace again from the far end of it, and heard Louis calling me.

'I've been all round the house,' he said, 'and to the garage, but there's not a trace of him.'

'But are you sure it was he?' I asked.

'Not a doubt of it. Besides, whoever it was, what has happened to him? I must ring up the police at Whitford and tell them. And yet I wonder if that's wise. The poor chap may have seen my advertisement and be wanting to steal back quietly to see me. When we ran out together he wouldn't be able to see who we were in the fog, and may have thought that there were two men running to capture him. He may be hiding till he can get at me alone. And yet where can he have hidden?'

So Louis decided, for fear of scaring the man, to postpone his information to the police that he had seen him. Oulton, he believed, had concealed himself somewhere (and, indeed, this fog made the idea feasible) till he could slip into the house undetected, and Louis settled to remain quietly at home all day, strolling perhaps in the garden so as to give him his opportunity.

This sounded sensible, and yet even while we were discussing it, the futility of such a plan struck me. I knew in my own mind that the figure Louis had seen was not that of a living man, any more than that white sketch of a human face which had hung in the darkness of my room last night was an effect of material light and shadow, or the imagining of a dream. Something was astir in the discarnate kingdom, some soul seeking to manifest itself.

During the afternoon the fog began to clear, and about four o'clock I went out with my binoculars for an ornithological tramp. Louis would not join me, for he was determined to stay close to the house so that Oulton might find him, and I set off across the heath with the intention of making a wide circuit there, and then walking through the woods and home by the lake. But though my occupation was congenial, and since one had to keep the eye very alert it should have claimed my close attention, I found myself barely heeding where I went or what I saw. Some invisible influence was at work; I was being detached from the myriad points of contact between myself and the material world, and there was waking within me the perception of things occult that, perhaps luckily for us, is usually dormant, and only enters the field of consciousness for rare and brief periods.

Just as the comprehension of some difficult idea slowly dawns on the mind, so now (I can express it in no other way) I felt that some inward eye was being unsealed. At present there was nothing for it to look on, its horizon was empty, but it was ready for the moment which I felt sure was coming, when there should appear to it, perhaps very horribly, in the manner of that blank face in the darkness last night, some phantom from the unseen world. A hundred times I tried to recall myself to the normal sights and sounds about me, but they were becoming more and more meaningless, and had no reality compared with the reality for which, shuddering in spirit, I waited.

I had made a long beat across the open, and was working round towards the belt of woods through which I purposed to go, when once more the fog began to gather. I had no mind to be caught by it on this huge unfeatured upland, for one might wander far and long if all landmarks were blotted out, and I hastened to get into the woods, for there, as I knew, a path would lead me down to the lake, and passing the head of it, take me back to the house.

I found the gate at the entrance to this path just before the fog grew suddenly much more dense, and I congratulated myself on having got off the open before it gathered like this, and entered the wood.

It was very dark under the trees, and the wind which earlier in the afternoon had cleared the air outside had not penetrated here, and the mist hung thick and white between the veiled forms of the tree-trunks. Darker yet it grew as the light from the sky outside was expunged by the fog, but I could just see the path ahead of me, and I went quickly, for there was closing in upon me not the fog alone, but some nameless horror of the spirit.

What exactly I feared I could not have said; but something, as yet unseen, was stirring, and in this forlorn dimness of the wood

I longed for any companionship from the familiar world. Once I stopped to listen for any sound that would give evidence that there was life, even if only of birds or woodland beasts, somewhere near me, but not a note nor the patter of feet in the undergrowth came to me. The path was mossy and even my own footfalls were dumb.

Suddenly I heard the rustle of dead leaves from my feet, and I saw that I had somehow got off the path. I scouted this way and that for it, and retraced my steps, but in the deep, thick dusk I was quite unable to find it again, and the only thing to be done was to keep on going downhill, for somewhere at the bottom I knew that I must strike the lake or the stream that flowed from it, and could orientate myself again. The ground was uneven, and more than once I stumbled over some root, caught my foot in a spray of bramble, and all the time I was fighting with this rising tide of fear.

At last the darkness began to lift a little, and ahead there was no longer the same density of trees, but an open space to which I quickly drew nearer, and there in front of me lay the lake. I had greatly miscalculated my direction, for I found that instead of being at the upper end of it I had come to the lower end, where was the sluice from which the water poured down a steep bank and formed the stream that passed by the village.

A belt of thick undergrowth lay between me and the path that led along the banks of the sluice, and I was threading my way slowly through this when once again I stumbled against some unseen obstacle and fell. I picked myself up unhurt, and then looked to see what had caused me this fall. I saw that it was a small suitcase.

In a flash I remembered that Oulton had gone home from the bank and packed a few things for his pretended visit to London. I lit a match, and found his initials, 'T. O.', stamped on the side of it. I took it up, and with it in my hand struggled out on to the open path, past the sluice. I must clearly carry it home to Louis, for it might prove a valuable clue in the search for the missing man. He had certainly been in this wood, bewildered perhaps by the thick fog, and having missed his way as I had done. But I wondered how he came to be here at all, for if he had been going up to London he would have gone from his house to the station. Or——

I had come to the sluice; on my left the mist-veiled lake lay leaden and deep, and a row of young willows edged the bank. I saw forming itself in the air just above them a pale oval of light. It oscillated slightly, as if stirred by some breath of wind, and as I watched it the outline grew firm and definite. Terror screamed to me to run from the place, but the same terror held me fast.

On each side of the face, blank as yet, there grew the form of rather prominent ears, and then above them came the semblance of grey hair hanging down over the forehead in dank straight lines, as if dripping wet. The shadowed eye-sockets appeared below thick-arched eyebrows, a nose long for the face ruled itself downwards between them, and below that a mouth, slack and open, with tongue lolling over the livid underlip. And now the eye-sockets were empty no longer; eyes with the lids half shut down on to them peered at me, though fixed and glassy, with an infinite and despairing sadness.

Then, like a screen picture coming into better focus, smaller details fixed themselves. I saw the puckered skin at the outer corner of the eyes, the darkness of the shaved jaw and upper lip, the modelling of the high cheekbones, an upright crease between the eyes. All the time the face oscillated gently sideways.

How long I watched it with cold horror clutching at my heart I do not know. A few seconds, I expect, was the duration of this unbodied vision, but such moments are immeasurable in terms of time. Then it was there no more; in front of me was the mist-swathed lake and the row of young willows just stirring in the air, and in my hand the suitcase of Thomas Oulton.

But with the vanishing of the vision, of the hallucination, whatever you may call it, the terror vanished too, and there I was, hearing the suck and splash of the sluice, master of myself, and knowing that the manifestation I had abjectly dreaded was part and parcel of all that is. The kindly woodland lay about me, the earth was drinking in, like a baby at the breast, the moisture of its nourishment, and beyond and behind, imminent and remote, was the power which had let me look through the transient veil of material limitation. What I had seen, what for the moment had filled my soul with the ultimate terror, was no more shocking than the wild whirling of the planets in space, or the sudden melody of the thrush that bubbled from the covert by the waterside, for all were subject to the same law that 'moved the sun and the other stars'.

The sequel can be told very shortly, though the reconstruction of the whole history can never be known for certain. I described the face that I had seen to Louis, and it answered so closely to the appearance of the missing man that the lake just above the sluice was dragged, and the body found there. In the breast-pocket of the coat was an envelope addressed to him; the ink had run owing to the long immersion in the water, but his name was still legible. In it were twenty-five Treasury notes of a pound each. Oulton's intention therefore seems clear, but there are several hypotheses which roughly fit to facts.

Perhaps he left his home, having told his wife that he was summoned up to London on business, with the intention of going there and of trying to evade pursuit. Against that there is the fact that he did not go to the station, but went, with his suitcase, into the woods through which a path led to Louis's house. But the two are reconcilable, for we may suppose that though he meant to disappear, he wanted first to restore the money of which he had defrauded the bank. Again, though his leaving his suitcase in that thicket where I found it, and the recovery of his body from the deep water not fifty yards away, might indicate that he deliberately committed suicide, it is yet possible that he hid his suitcase there with the intention of coming back for it after he had left the envelope at the house, and that in the dense and blinding fog he accidentally fell into the water. The path by the sluice is very narrow, and such a mishap perfectly possible. He was encumbered with a long greatcoat, and a false step on the slippery stone edging there might easily have been fatal.

Of the other phenomena recorded I have no explanation to give, but only suggest that the veil between the seen and what we call the unseen is of thinnest gossamer, and that ever and again we have glimpses of what lies outside our mortal vision.

Atmospherics

THERE is nothing more delightful to the thoroughly unscientific mind than to control some scientific machine which yields entertaining results, and which one does not in the least understand. That, so I concluded, was, at any rate, one of the reasons why I neglected all other duties, and most other pleasures in order to enjoy my new wireless.

'Ad Astra' was the name of it, and a very suitable one, for it put me into communication with places that seemed as remote as the planets, and evoked from them the very music of the spheres. It had eight valves (whatever 'valves' might be) and two switches and two dials, and an index which made it perfectly easy to choose, as in a dinner at a restaurant, whatever one liked.

Daventry and London, and Hilversum and Paris, and Berlin and Vienna were waiting with their dishes. A little adjustment of the switches and manipulation of the dials was all that was necessary, and then, after a few loud howls and whistlings, I could get into touch with singers and pianists half-way across Europe.

This was all romantic enough for a prosaic age, but secretly I cherished even wilder romances in connection with my 'Ad Astra'. It was, I am proud to say, the very last word in wireless, and every now and then it seemed, to my ignorant view, to emit noises that came from none of the localities on its sumptuous index. Below the blare of an orchestra from Berlin, I sometimes caught the sound of a human voice; below a lecture delivered in the studio in London, I caught the sound of singing. Scientific friends who also heard these mutterings appeared to me to be a little puzzled about them, but they bravely asserted that they were 'atmospherics'.

Yet they did not seem quite casual enough for mere accidents of the ether; voices certainly made coherent remarks, unexplained instruments of music played fragments of tunes, and somehow I had got into my head that this wonderful 'Ad Astra' could, intermittently and fortuitously, catch sounds that were outside the

range of its professed radius. After all, as Mr Einstein has proved
to those who are able to understand what he says, time and space
are both dimensions of the same huge whole, and I wondered
whether it was not possible that 'Ad Astra' was reproducing
sounds not only distant in space, but distant in time.

But I have no scientific attainments, and the professors,
though sometimes a puzzled look furrowed their serene brows
when they heard these extraneous noises, continued to say
'Atmospherics'.

Just now 'Ad Astra' was clad in its neat serge travelling-suit,
and placed on the seat next me in the train that was taking me
to the old Cinque Port town of Tillingham, where I was to
spend a weekend with my friend Harry Armytage in his house
called 'Mayor's Orchard'. He had just bought this house, I had
never been there before, and knew nothing whatever of it and its
surroundings, except that I was aware that the sea had retreated,
and that Tillingham, which was once a port, was now a couple
of miles inland.

As I approached my destination, it looked as if I should not
for the present get any clearer idea of it, for we slid into a thick
sea-fog, and after innumerable hootings and stoppages, I stepped
out into the most impenetrable mist I have ever encountered.
Harry had sent down a servant to meet and conduct me, who
told me that 'Mayor's Orchard' was but five minutes' walk from
the station, and I followed him through the dense white dusk
up the hill.

I carried 'Ad Astra' myself, and presently he threw open a
door, and I found myself in a delicious Queen Anne interior. In
a little parlour off the hall I found them at tea, Harry and his
wife Evie and her sister and brother-in-law, all old friends.

I consented, of course, without any pressing at all, to demon-
strate the marvels of my new toy, but never have I experienced
a greater fall to my pride. We got a little scrannel jazz music
from London, but no other station would come through at all.
The fog no doubt was thick in the Channel, and the Channel
was populous with fog-bound ships, and we could get nothing
whatever except the incessant dot-and-dash of Morse code, ship
calling to ship. Paris and Hilversum and Berlin and Vienna were
all as mute as mackerel; there was nothing but this silly, unintel-
ligible gabble.

'Frightfully interesting,' said Harry at length, 'but a shade monotonous. How about bridge?'

'I don't want to play,' said Evie. 'You four play.'

That was amiable, but false: Evie always wants to play bridge. Besides, every now and then, through this silly babble, I knew I had heard something, which was not Morse code, and I only wanted to be left with 'Ad Astra', and find out what it was. So after a few politenesses on the part of the others, I found myself alone with my machine.

I could cut out these tiresome noises altogether, but I found that when I did that, I also cut out the intervening something, which I so much wanted to catch, and that when the dot-and-dash of this inter-ship signalling was most audible, so also was this unexplained impression of what sounded sometimes like a voice, and sometimes like faint musical notes.

Wholly unscientific as I am, I realized that it was not far distant in space, at any rate, from these stupid cacklings. It had something to do, in space if not in time, with them.

And then as, hairbreadth by hairbreadth, I shifted the dials, I heard, not from the machine at all, but from close outside, the sound of wind: a strong breeze was rising, and the fog no doubt dispersing, for almost immediately these dot-and-dash noises completely ceased. And now that they were silent, I knew that I was right in thinking that there was something going on below them: it emerged, growing gradually louder.

There was the noise of a drum and of a fife, and of a cornet, and they were playing 'God save the King', in a windy and elementary manner, but surely with enthusiasm. Then there was the sound of a door opening, and the tune swelled out suddenly, as if the door of the house where I sat had been opened, and the players were just outside. The door shut again, the tune ceased altogether and I heard a man's voice speaking in English, but with a strong guttural German accent.

'Olso, it is most kind of you, Mr Mayor,' he said. 'To be sure, I shall be very comfortable. That goddam fog, terr-r-ible, and a fool of a captain. Yes: a little supper: very pleasant. I will first to my room go.'

The voice ceased, but surely there were steps in the hall just outside and on the stairs. I looked out, but there was no one there, and now, not a whisper came from my apparatus. This way and that, hairbreadth by hairbreadth, I moved the dials, but there was nothing of any sort audible.

Presently Harry came in from the room where they were playing bridge, and found me still endeavouring to recapture that strange intrusion. Where had it come from? And *when* (so I could not help asking myself) had it come from . . .?

'Still tinkering?' he said. 'The stars seem to be a bit in eclipse tonight. A rocket went up just now from the sea. There must be some ship run aground in the fog. I'm dummy at the moment, so I came to see if you would like to be shown your room. You're in the King's room, Evie said.'

I made a final attempt, and got up.

'Yes, do show it to me,' I said. 'But why the King's room?'

He led the way upstairs.

'Oh, an old story,' he said, 'but I believe quite authentic. George the Second was once visiting the Cinque Ports in his yacht, and there came on a thick fog just like there was tonight, and he ran aground in shoal-water opposite Tillingham. He was brought to land in a small boat, and came up to the town. The mayor met him with all the pomp that could be arranged at a moment's notice, and they brought him along here, with a fife and a drum playing "God save the King".'

'And then?' I asked.

'He slept here: the house belonged to the mayor. Mayor's Orchard you know. There are some extremely old apple trees in the garden——'

'Interesting,' said I. 'And I'm going to sleep in the room he had?'

'Yes. Here it is. Jolly panelling, isn't it? There's a picture of the King. Thoroughly German. But, after all, he was German. He spoke English, though, which his father couldn't do, but with a strong German accent.'

Harry went back to his game, and it is hardly necessary to state, I instantly fetched 'Ad Astra' up to my room.

Berlin was ready to my summons now, and Vienna and Paris had never been so splendidly audible. But not a whisper more could I catch coming across the years from the night when the King slept at Mayor's Orchard.

'Ad Astra' nobly vindicated its ability to give me all that it professed to give, but gladly would I have sacrificed all that for a few whispers more in that guttural voice, or a few more bars of that very imperfectly rendered National Anthem. Atmospherics, indeed!

Boxing Night

HUGH GRAINGER was spending Christmas with us, and, as usually happens when he is present, the talk turned on the topics that concern the invisible world, which, though it is sundered from our material plane, sometimes cuts across it, and makes its presence perceived by strange and inexplicable manifestations. He held that evidence of its existence, communications from the unseen to our mortal sense, were established beyond any doubt.

'Ghosts, clairvoyant visions, true presentiments, and dreams are all glimpses of the unseen,' he said. 'Such messages and messengers come from we know not where, and we know not how they come, but certainly they do come. Often the very act of communication appears difficult: those beyond the ken of our normal perceptions find it hard to get into touch with us, and often the messages get distorted or bungled in transit.'

'So as to be quite trivial or meaningless,' said someone.

'That is so,' said he. 'But, again, sometimes the message seems to be rendered more convincing by the very errors it contains. Error is so likely in such a tremendous transmission. I heard a story at first-hand the other day which illustrates that very aptly.'

There was an encouraging murmur of invitation, and Hugh drew from a drawer in the writing-table a sheaf of manuscript.

'I heard it in considerable detail,' he said, 'and I have only turned it into narrative form. It just happened like this.'

He sat down by the lamp, and read to us.

Woollard's Farm lay remote and solitary in the green lap of the Romney Marsh. Not a house stood within a mile of it as a bird would travel, and the curve of the farm road following the big drainage dyke made that distance half as long again for wheeled traffic. For a foot passenger, a couple of railed plank bridges crossed the dyke, and by cutting off the curve made a directer route, but now, in mid-winter, the flood water was high and the footbridges awash; deep pools lay in the intervening pastures, and any who would go into Rye must make the longer circuit before he struck the high road.

The farm took its name from the family which for two hundred years, so the tombstones in Brooklands churchyard testified, had owned its once ample acres. Today these acres were sorely dwindled, and dwindled, too, was the yeoman stock which had once more prosperously tilled it. The last proprietor of the diminishing line had begotten no son, and though one at least of his two daughters to whom he had left it had a masculine grip in her efficient management, they were both unmarried and middle-aged, and no doubt, at their death Woollard's Farm, though it might retain its patronymic style, would pass into the hands of strangers.

They knew of no other paternal relation except their Uncle Alfred, who was a town-bred man and would surely, if he survived them, sell this marshland property. There was more than an off-chance of this, for, twenty years younger than their father, he was but little their senior, and a gnarled, robust fellow. Often, indeed, had he urged his nieces to make the sale themselves, for houses such as theirs, with its spacious parlours, its solid oak floors and staircases, its pleasant brick-walled garden, were fetching high prices in the market. There had been several enquiries lately at his house-agent's office in Rye for just such a property, and he promised them a fine bid for it, and himself, no doubt, a fine percentage on the transaction. He was considerably in need of some such piece of business, for times were bad and money scarce with him.

But his hectoring persuasions had hitherto failed to convince his nieces; as long as they could get a livelihood out of the place, their affection for their home was impregnable to such suggestions. As for the loneliness of it, they were self-sufficient women, neither making friends nor needing them, undesirous of chatting neighbours, and content to get through the day's work and be ready for the next.

Lately affairs had gone very well with them: market-days at Rye and New Romney had enabled Ellen Woollard to amass a fat sheaf of notes from the sale of pigs and poultry, and a wallet with a hundred and fifty pounds in it was, on this evening of Christmas Day, safely stowed in the secret cupboard in the panelling of the parlour at the farm. Next week there were substantial purchases to be made at the Ashford market, and for that reason she had not paid her notes into the County Bank at Rye. Ready money, to be paid down then and there, made the best bargaining at a market, and to deposit and draw out again from the bank meant a half-day twice occupied with the excursion.

The two sisters lived with the utmost simplicity: they kept no servant, except a girl whom they had allowed to go for two days of Christmas holiday to her family in Rye; she, with Rebecca Woollard, the younger of the sisters, did the cooking and housework, while Ellen was busy all day with outdoor affairs. In general, they ate and sat in the big lattice-panel kitchen, but tonight, in honour of the festival, Rebecca had made ready the parlour, and here, after their supper, when doors were locked and windows curtained, they spent the evening among the Christmas tokens of holly and evergreens with which she had decked the room. On other evenings she would be busy with sewing and household mendings, while Ellen, tired with her outdoor activities, dozed by the fire, but tonight a cheerful, talkative idleness occupied them, the sober glow of past memories, and, in spite of the shadows of middle age, optimistic gleams for the future.

'Yes, that was a rare good sale last week at New Romney,' said Ellen. 'There'll be enough and to spare for the new linen you say you want.'

Rebecca held up her thin hands to the blaze; pretty hands they were, but weak and irresolute.

'Well, I like that!' she said. 'Fancy talking of the new linen I say I want! Why, there's more patches in the tablecloth than weaving, and as for the sheets, I only ask you, Ellen, to look at them before you get into bed. Not that it's any good to ask you that, for I'm sure you're half asleep always before you turn your bedclothes down.'

'And you've been sleeping better lately, Rebecca, haven't you?' said her sister.

'I've certainly lain awake less. But such dreams as I have now all night long! They fairly scare me sometimes, and I think I'd sooner lie tossing and turning and hearing the weary clock striking than go through such adventures.'

Ellen laughed.

'Dreams are all a pack of rubbish,' she said, 'fit to smile about and forget as you dress in the morning. I can dream, too, if it comes to that, for it was only last night as I thought Uncle Alfred came here with a couple of bailiffs and told us we must quit, for we couldn't pay our taxes; we were sold up and he'd bought the place. Why, if there's any sense in dreams, they go by the opposite. If I paid any heed to them, I should say that meant that the farm would prosper next year as it never did before. The thought of all that good money in the cupboard there was what made me dream so contrarily.'

Rebecca pursed her lips with a gloomy shake of her head.

'I see a deal of truth in your dream, sister,' she said. 'Certain and sure it is that if Uncle Alfred had a chance he'd turn us out of the farm, be the means foul or fair.'

'Maybe, but that wasn't my dream, Rebecca. I dreamed he did turn us out, and there's little likelihood of that with all going so well. But he's a disagreeable man, that's sure. Such an answer as he sent me when I asked him to take his Christmas dinner with us today, and bide over the holiday.'

'I wonder at your asking him year after year like that,' said Rebecca. 'He don't want to come, and the Lord knows we don't want him. Would you be the happier if Uncle Alfred was sitting with us now, finding fault with this, and scolding at that, and wanting us to be quit of the farm, and go to live in some mucky town where there's not a breath of fresh air from year's end to year's end, and never a fresh egg to eat, and the washing coming back all chawed up and yellow, and nothing but the gabble of neighbours all day? No, give me Uncle Alfred's room sooner than his company, and thank you kindly.'

The mention of Uncle Alfred always made Rebecca rage; Ellen was ready to have done with the obnoxious subject.

'Well, we won't bother with him, nor he with us,' she said. 'But he's father's brother, Rebecca, and it is but decent to bid him spend Christmas with us. To be sure there are pleasanter things to talk about. Your house linen, now; twenty pounds you shall have to lay out on it, and any bits of things you want, and that will leave me enough to get such pigs and hens as the farm hasn't been stocked with for the last five years. And who knows that before the year turns there won't come along some bright young fellow to court you——'

This was a long-standing joke, that, like sound wine, seemed to improve with years. It set Rebecca laughing, for, indeed, she was no more of a marrying sort than her sister, and presently afterwards they made the fire safe with regard to flying sparks, and went up to the raftered bedchamber, where they slept together.

Ellen, as usual, was the first to be down next morning, and, with the girl away, she lit the kitchen fire and put the kettle to boil, while she prepared the feed for her chickens. It was very dark still, for though the sun was risen, the sky was thick with leaden clouds, moving heavily in a bitter north-east wind, and promising snow. Her face was worried and troubled; she looked sharply from time to time into the dark corners of the room and out of the latticed panes, for despite the scornful incredulity she had expressed last night on the subject of dreams, a vision so hideously and acutely real had torn her from her sleep that even now she was up and dressed and actively engaged she could not shake herself free from the horrid clutch of it.

She had dreamed that she and her sister were sitting in the parlour after nightfall on Boxing Day when a tapping came at the front door, and going to open it she found on the threshold a soldier dressed in khaki, who begged a night's lodging, for outside a hurricane of snow was raging, and he had lost his way. In he came, pushing by her before she had bidden him to enter, and he walked straight down the passage and into the parlour. She followed him, and already he was breaking in with the butt of his rifle the panelled door of the cupboard which contained her money. It crashed inwards beneath his blows, and he put the fat wallet of notes into his pocket. 'Now we'll have no witnesses,' he cried, and next moment, with a swing of his rifle, which he held by the barrel, he had felled Rebecca with a terrific blow on the head, and there she lay bloody and battered on the floor. Then true nightmare began, for Ellen, trying to flee, found she could stir neither hand nor foot. She gave a thin, strangled cry as once more the murderous weapon was swung for the blow which she knew would crash down on her head, and with the shock of that mortal agony she awoke.

Busy herself as she might, Ellen could not shake off the convincing reality of the nightmare. It was not of dream-texture at all; it was on another plane, vivid and actual as the fire she had just lit or the bitter wind that whistled and rattled the panes. The thing had never happened, but it was of the solid stuff of reality. It was in vain that she reasoned with herself, and snapped an unconvinced finger: just here by the door she stood and saw the tall figure framed against the driving snow, and if none of this had happened, fulfilment would come to it. . . .

Then a foot on the stairs recalled her, and here was Rebecca coming down to prepare their breakfast on the morning of Boxing Day. It would never do to speak of this to her sister; it would scare her silly.

Rebecca went about her work in silence, laying the table and cutting the rashers. She had no spoken word for Ellen's greeting, but only a mumbling movement of her lips, and her hands were a-tremble. She bent over her work, so that Ellen got no clear sight of her face, and it was not till they were seated at the table, with a candle burning there, that she got a comprehensive look at it. And what she saw made her lay down her knife and fork.

'Goodsakes, what's the matter, Rebecca?' she asked.

Rebecca raised her eyes; there sat in them some nameless and abject terror.

'Nothing,' she said; 'it would only make you laugh at me if I told you.'

Ellen gave her a cheerful face.

'Well, I should like a laugh on this dark morning,' she said. 'One of your dreams, maybe?'

'Yes, that's right enough,' said Rebecca, 'but such a dream as I've never had before.'

In spite of the growing heat of the fire, it must have been still very cold in the kitchen, for suddenly, from head to foot, an icy shiver ran through Ellen.

'Tell me then,' she said. 'Get rid of it.'

Rebecca caught that shudder, and violently trembling, pushed her plate from her.

'I'll tell you,' she said, 'for, sure, I can't bear it alone. It wasn't a dream; it wasn't of that stuff that makes dreams. . . . I thought it was the evening of Boxing Day, the day that's dawned now——'

She told her dream. It was identical down to the minutest detail with Ellen's, except that it was she herself who had gone to the door, and that she had seen her sister battered down by a blow, and waited in the catalepsy of nightmare for the stroke that would follow.

Even to Ellen's practical and unfanciful mind, the coincidence— if coincidence it was—was overwhelming; the sanest and least fantastical could not but see in this double vision a warning that it would be foolhardy to disregard, and within an hour the two of them had locked up the house, and were in the pony-cart on the way to Rye. As it was Boxing Day, the bank would be shut, and their plan was to entrust their money to their uncle for safe keeping till tomorrow. They had agreed not to tell him the true cause of their expedition; it was reasonable enough that two women in a place so remote should not care to be keeping so large a sum in the house. Tomorrow one of them would call again and deposit it at the bank. They found him already at the whisky bottle, and acid and disagreeable as ever.

'Well, what brings you two here?' he said. 'Compliments of the season, or some such rubbish?'

They explained their errand.

'A pack of nonsense!' said he. 'I'll not have aught to do with your money. Supposing my house was broken into before to-morrow morning, and your notes taken, you'd have the law on me for their recovery. And I tell you that that's a deal more likely to happen in a town than that a thief should go traipsing half-a-dozen miles out into the marsh on the chance of finding a packet of banknotes at a lonely farmhouse!'

He got up, beat out the ashes of his pipe, and filled it again, frowning and muttering to himself.

'Burglars, indeed, at Woollard's Farm,' he said. 'I never heard such a crazy notion! If I had a bit of money in the house here— worse luck I haven't—it would be a deal more reasonable of me to ask you to take care of it. Who ever heard of a burglary at a house like yours? The man would be daft who tramped halfway across the marsh, and in a snowstorm, too—for there'll be snow before night, unless I'm much mistaken—on such a chance. Who's to know that you've got the worth of a penny piece in the house?—for I warrant you've told nobody.'

'Uncle Alfred, you might be kind and keep it for us,' said Ellen. 'It's only till tomorrow.'

'I might, might I?' he sneered. 'Well, I tell you I mightn't, and more than that, I won't. You've got safe places enough. Where do you keep it?'

'In the panel-cupboard in the parlour,' said Ellen.

'Aye, and a good place, too,' said he. 'I remember that cupboard; your father always kept his brass there. And do you figure a burglar smashing in all your panelling in the hopes of finding a cupboard there, and when he's hit on that, thinking to discover a wallet with banknotes in it? A couple of dreamy, timorous women—that's what you are. I wouldn't keep your money in my house, not if you paid me ten per cent of it for my trouble. Where should I be if it got stolen? Be off with you both, and don't bother me with your Christmas invitations!'

It was no manner of good to spend time and persuasions on the crusty fellow, and there was no one else whom they knew sufficiently well to approach on so unusual an errand. By midday the two were back again at the farm, glad to be indoors on this morning of shrewd snowy blasts, and the money, since assuredly there was no better hiding-place than this concealed cupboard in the panelling, was back once more in the cache.

Sullen and snarling as Uncle Alfred had been, there was certainly good sense in his view that this remote homestead was about the unlikeliest possible place for a burglar to choose for his operations, and Ellen, with more success than in the cold dawn, could reason herself out of her alarm. A dream was no more than a dream when all was said and done, and it was not for a sensible woman to heed such things. It was singular to be sure that the same vision had torn Rebecca from her sleep, but tomorrow by this time she would be laughing at the fears which had sent her twittering into Rye this morning.

Before the close of the short winter day the snow had begun to fall in earnest, and by the time the chickens and pigs were fed and made secure, and the thick curtains drawn, they could hear the thick insistent flurry of it as the wind drove it against the panes. But now that doors were locked and windows bolted, the squeal of the tempest shrill above the soft tapping of the snow-flakes only intensified the comfort of the swept hearth and the log fire that glowed in the open grate. Once again, as last night, they sat in the parlour, with the dark panelled walls gleaming sombrely in the firelight and the flames leaping as the wind bugled in the chimney. Eight o'clock, and nine, and ten sounded on the chimes of the grandfather clock, and as the last hour struck Ellen got up. The tranquil passage of the evening had quite restored the grip of her common sense, and she could even joke about her vanished apprehensions.

'Well, I reckon it's no use our sitting up for that soldier of yours, Rebecca,' she said. 'He's missed his connection, you might say, and I shall be off to bed, for tomorrow's a work-day again——'

Her sentence hung suspended and unfinished. There came a rap at the front door at the end of the passage, and the bell tingled. Rebecca rose to her feet with hands up to her ears, as if to shut out the sound.

'Who can it be at this time of night?' whispered Ellen.

Rebecca came close to her, white and palsied with fear.

'It's he,' she said. 'I know it's he. We must keep still, for there's no light showing, and perhaps he may go away. Dear God, let him go!'

A rattling at the latch had succeeded to the knocking, and then all was quiet. Presently it began again, and again the bell repeated its summons.

Then Ellen lit a hand-lamp; anything was better than this unbearable suspense; besides, if their visitor was some strayed wayfarer——

'I'm going to the door,' she said. 'It may be someone who has lost his way in the snow and the darkness, and on such a night he might well perish of cold before he found shelter. What should you and I feel, Rebecca, if tomorrow a woman, or a girl maybe, was found stiff and stark nigh the house, or drowned in the big dyke? That would be worse stuff than any dream.'

Trembling with fright but with an unshakable courage, and disregarding her sister's appeals, she went straight to the front door, drew back the heavy bolts, and opened it. On the threshold, framed against the fast-falling snow, stood a man in khaki. In the flickering light from her lamp she could not distinctly see his face, but over his shoulder was a rifle, of which he grasped the butt.

'I'm lost in the marsh, ma'am,' he said, 'trying for a short cut to Rye, but I knew there was a farm hereabouts, and thank God I've found it. I ask you for a lodging till dawn, for on a night like this there's death out there.'

'I can give you no lodging,' she said shortly. 'Follow the farm-road and you'll strike the highway.'

'But there's no seeing your hand before your face,' he said, 'and I'm half perished with cold already. Any outhouse will do for me, just shelter and a wisp of straw to wrap me in.'

The strangle of her nightmare was on her. Rebecca had crept along the passage, and in her ashen face Ellen saw her own heart mirrored.

'You can get no lodging here,' she said. 'Them as walk at night must get tramping.'

For answer he held out his rifle to her.

'Here, take that, ma'am,' he said. 'You're scared of me, I can see, but if I meant you harm would I give you my gun? I'll take off my boots, too, and my belt with its bayonet; a footsore man without boots or weapons can't harm you, and you may lock me into any cupboard or shed you please.'

His hands and face were bleached with the cold, and dream or no dream, she could not shut a man out in the cold of this impenetrable night.

'Come in,' she said. 'Take off your boots, and get you into the kitchen. Come what may, it's sheer death tonight in the marsh.'

At her bidding he walked into the kitchen while she had a whispered word with Rebecca.

'We can't do different, Rebecca,' she said, 'though strange it is about your dream and mine, and if it's God's will we be clubbed to death, it's His will. But what's not His will is that we should let a man die on our doorstep because we were afraid. Why should he give me his gun, besides, if he meant ill to us? So now I'll give him his bite of supper, for he's clemmed with cold and hunger, and then lock him into the kitchen. Meantime you take the money from the cupboard and hide it between your mattresses or mine. Why that's the finish to our dreaming already if you do that, for by the dream it should be from the cupboard in the parlour that he took it.'

Indeed, she needed heartening herself, so strangely had their dream found fulfilment, but taking a hold on her courage, she walked into the kitchen, while Rebecca went upstairs. But she could not bear to remain solitary there, and she came back and helped her sister to get a bite of supper for the man.

The food and the warmth revived him, and presently, leaving

him stretched on two chairs in front of the drowsy fire, they
turned the key of the kitchen door on him and went to their
room.

Neither of them undressed, but with locked doors and light
burning they lay on their beds to pass the vigil till day. The
wind had fallen by midnight, the driven snow no longer pattered
on the panes, and the stillness sang in their ears. Ellen's bed was
nearest to the window, and presently she sat up to listen more
intently, without alarming her sister, to a noise that ever so faintly
overscored the silence. There it was again; someone was rattling
at the window immediately below, the window of the passage
along the front of the house which led to the kitchen. Rebecca
heard also, and like a ghost she slid across to her sister's bed.

'There's someone outside,' she whispered. 'That's his fellow,
Ellen; there are two of them now, one within and the other
outside. He'll go round to the kitchen presently, and the man
we left there will let him in. Sister, why did you suffer him to
come in? We're done for now; ah, we're done for, and naught
can save us!'

Ellen's heart sank. The interpretation seemed only too terribly
probable. She drew her sister towards her and kissed her.

'You must try to forgive me, Rebecca,' she said, 'if I've brought
your death upon you. But God knows I couldn't do different if
I hoped for salvation. It's the money they've come for, and the
dream is true. Ah, where is it? Give it me, and I'll go down to
the fellow in the kitchen and offer it him, and swear to let him
go scot free if he'll only take it and spare our lives. We'll lay no
information to identify him; we'll let it be known we've just
been robbed, and there's the end of it. And yet, why did he give
me his rifle and off with his boots? That was a strange thing for
him to do.'

Rebecca sat huddled on the bed.

'Strange or no,' she said, 'it's all over with us. There's no help
nor succour for us.'

She was half distraught with terror; there was no reasoning
with her, and Ellen, leaving the rifle she had brought upstairs
with her sister, took the wallet containing the notes in her hand
and went forth on her midnight and unconjecturable errand. At
the bottom of the stairs she must pass the window where they
had heard the stir of movement, and now outside there was the

grating and grinding of some tool against the glass, and she guessed that whoever was outside was cutting the pane.

She unlocked the kitchen door and entered. The man she had fed and sheltered was awake and standing on his feet. There she was quite defenceless, with her money in her hand, and yet he did not close with her nor push her to get into touch with his accomplice. Instead he came close to her and whispered:

'There's someone moving outside and round about the house,' he said. 'A while ago he was at the kitchen window here. I couldn't come to you and warn you, for you had locked me in.'

She held out the wallet.

'I know the manner of man you are,' she said. 'You came to rob and murder us, and that's your confederate outside. A strange warning came to us, but out of compassion I didn't heed it. Here, then, is the money; spare our lives, and take it and begone, for that was your plan, and I swear we'll not set the police on you.'

He looked at her narrowly.

'What are you telling of?' he said. 'I'm neither robber nor murderer. But waste no more time, ma'am; there's someone at the window now, and he's after no good. He'd have knocked at the door if he'd been a lost wayfarer like me. Now I'm here to help you, for you took me in, and we'll catch him. Where's my rifle?'

For one moment, at the thought of restoring that to him nightmare clutched her again, and she envisaged Rebecca clubbed to death, with herself to follow. But then some ray of hope gleamed in her, some confidence born of his speech and his mien.

'I'll fetch it for you,' she said.

She went swiftly upstairs and returned with it, and together they stood by the curtained window, while Rebecca nursed a candle on the stairs to give a glimmer of light. He had picked up his belt with the bayonet, and now, as they waited, he fitted it into its catch and drew on his boots. There he was, now armed again, and she defenceless, and in silence they waited.

Presently the scratching at the pane outside ceased, and a current of cold air poured in, making the curtain belly in the draught. It was clear that the burglar had detached a pane of glass and withdrawn it. Then the curtains were thrust aside from without, and a hand entered, feeling for the catch of the window.

At that her companion laid down his rifle, and took a step forward, and seized it by the wrist. But it slipped from him, and snatching up his rifle, he ran to the door, and unbolted and opened it.

'We'll catch him yet though,' he called to her. 'Lock the door after me, and let none in unless you hear my voice,' and he vanished into the snowflecked blackness of the night.

Rebecca came down to her, and together they went into the kitchen to wait for what might come out of the night to them. It was no longer possible to doubt the good faith of their visitor, for there on the table lay the wallet with the money untouched. Presently they heard a knock at the door, and his voice calling to them to open. The snow shrouded him in white, and for the second time the soldier of their dream stood on the threshold.

'There was no finding him,' he said, 'for it's dark as the pit, and the snow is like a solid thing. Once I heard him close, and I called on him to stop else I would run my bayonet through him. Not a word did I get, and I thrust at the noise of his running and there was a squeal as the point pierced something, but he shook free again, and I heard no more of him. I took him in the arm I reckon. Let's see what the steel can tell us.'

The bayonet confirmed this impression; in the scooped sides of it were runnels of melted snow red with the deeper dye of the blood which for not more than an inch covered the point of it. A flesh wound probably had been inflicted, which had not prevented him from making his escape. With that, there was no more to be done that night, and soon the two sisters were back in their room again, and their guest, with the kitchen door locked no longer, lay down to sleep again. Tomorrow, if no more snow fell, they might perhaps trace and identify the fugitive.

All three were early astir next morning. The snow had ceased and a frosty sun gleamed on the whiteness of the fields. While they were at breakfast the servant-girl, returning from her holiday, came running into the kitchen, breathless and wide-eyed with excitement and alarm.

'There's something in the great dyke, mistress,' she said. 'It's like the body of a man caught among the reeds below the footbridge.'

They ran out, and it was easy to follow certain half-obliterated tracks in the frozen snow that led from under the window in the passage to the edge of the dyke. From there, in the deep water by the half-submerged footbridge the body had drifted but a few yards into the shallows by the reed-bed, where, with head downwards, it had been caught and anchored. A couple of long poles soon towed it to the shore, and turning it over, his nieces looked on the face of Alfred Woollard. His coat-sleeve was torn just below the right shoulder, and the ragged edges were stained with blood.

SOURCES

'The Lovers': *The Tatler* (15 November 1922)

'"Complete Rest"': *The Tatler* (10 January 1923)

'The Five Foolish Virgins': *The Tatler* (25 March 1925)

'My Friend the Murderer': *Chapman's Magazine* (October 1895)

'Professor Burnaby's Discovery': *The Storyteller* (June 1926)

'The Exposure of Pamela': *The Storyteller* (August 1924). Reprinted as *The Exposure of Pamela* (Hermitage Books limited edition, 1992)

'Miss Maria's Romance': *The Queen* (25 November 1899)

'The Eavesdropper': *The Tatler* (19 March 1924)

'James Sutherland, Ltd.': *The Monthly Review* (December 1902).

'Bootles': *Black And White* (26 March 1904)

'Julian's Cottage': *The Storyteller* (August 1931)

'Fine Feathers': *Woman At Home* (March 1914)

'The Defeat of Lady Hartridge': *Black And White* (23 April 1904)

'The Jamboree': *The Tatler* (1 December 1922)

'Complementary Souls': *Cassell's Magazine of Fiction* (September 1925)

'Dodo and the Brick': *Home Magazine* (March 1923, as 'The Brick')

'A Comedy of Styles': *Windsor Magazine* (February 1914)

'Noblesse Oblige': *Windsor Magazine* (December 1917)

'An Entire Mistake': *The Onlooker* (16 January 1904)

'Mr Carew's Game of Croquet': *The Tatler* (5 March 1924)

'The Fall of Augusta': *The Tatler* (24 May 1922)

'The Male Impersonator': *The Male Impersonator* (1929). Reprinted in *Miss Mapp* (1970)

'M.O.M.': *Windsor Magazine* (December 1915)

'The Adventure of Hegel Junior': *Illustrated London News* (21 December 1901)

'The Simple Life': *The World And His Wife* (July 1905)

'Mrs Andrews's Control': *Windsor Magazine* (September 1915). Reprinted in *The Countess of Lowndes Square* (1920)

'George's Secret': *The Sketch* (21 November 1894)

'Buntingford Jugs': *Windsor Magazine* (December 1925)

'By the Sluice': *The Tatler* (25 March 1927)

'Atmospherics': *Radio Times* (28 December 1928)

'Boxing Night': *The Tatler* (30 November 1923). Reprinted in *The Technique of the Ghost Story* (Hermitage Books limited edition, 1993)